Puerto Rico under
Colonial Rule

PUERTO RICO UNDER COLONIAL RULE

*Political Persecution and the
Quest for Human Rights*

Edited by

RAMÓN BOSQUE-PÉREZ
AND
JOSÉ JAVIER COLÓN MORERA

STATE UNIVERSITY OF NEW YORK PRESS

The artwork used on the cover is reproduced with permission from the Estate of Puerto Rican graphic artist Carlos Raquel Rivera (1923–1999). The only known surviving copy of this trial print of *Elecciones coloniales* (1959, Linoleum, 13 ^{1}/$_4$″ × 18 ^{1}/$_2$″) is located at the *Museo de Historia, Antropología y Arte* of the University of Puerto Rico (UPR).

Chapters 1, 4, 6, 7, and 8 are revised English versions of essays previously published in Spanish in the book *Las carpetas: persecución política y derechos civiles en Puerto Rico* (ISBN 0965004309). They are used with permission from *Centro para la Investigación y Promoción de los Derechos Civiles* (CIPDC, Inc.), Río Piedras, Puerto Rico.

Chapter 3 is a revised English version of the section "Epílogo" published in the 1998 edition of *La mordaza: Puerto Rico 1948–1957* (ISBN 8459984699). It is used with permission from *Editorial Edil*, Río Piedras, Puerto Rico.

Published by
STATE UNIVERSITY OF NEW YORK PRESS
ALBANY

For information, address
State University of New York Press
194 Washington Avenue, Suite 305, Albany, NY 12210-2384

Production, Laurie Searl and Diane Ganeles
Marketing, Susan Petrie

Library of Congress Cataloging-in-Publication Data

Puerto Rico under colonial rule : political persecution and the quest for human rights / edited by Ramón Bosque-Pérez, José Javier Colón Morera.
    p. cm.
    Includes bibliographical references and index.
    ISBN 0-7914-6417-2 (hardcover : alk. paper) — ISBN 0-7914-6418-0 (pbk. : alk. paper)
    1. Political persecution—Puerto Rico. 2. Human rights—Puerto Rico. 3. Puerto Rico—History—Autonomy and independence movements. 4. Puerto Rico—Politics and government. I. Bosque Pérez, Ramón. II. Colón Morera, José Javier.

JC599.P9P84 2005
325'.373'097295

2004016237

10   9   8   7   6   5   4   3   2   1

To the people of the island of Vieques, Puerto Rico,
and to those in the United States and abroad
who supported their struggle for peace and justice.

Contents

PART I
POLITICAL PERSECUTION IN TWENTIETH-CENTURY PUERTO RICO

Part II
Contemporary Issues

Part III
The Vieques Case

Illustrations

TABLES

FIGURE

Foreword

ONE OF THE CONSTANT and most important congressional agendas that I have pursued in my long tenure in the U.S. Congress has been protecting human and civil rights. As a Puerto Rican, I know very well that political dissidents and minorities often suffer the most from political repression and institutional racial discrimination.

In the U.S. Congress, I defend a political agenda that promotes civil rights in the United States and human rights all over the world. Puerto Rico, a territory conquered by the United States in 1898, has to be part of this democratizing agenda. As a Puerto Rican, serving a large Latino constituency in New York, I have a particular interest in the political history of the island where I was born and, most importantly, in its future and well-being.

I favor the elimination of the current colonial status and actively promote self-determination for Puerto Rico in accordance with applicable international norms. I am convinced that Puerto Rico is fully prepared to achieve a completely democratic and noncolonial relationship with the United States. It is a moral imperative as much as it is a political necessity.

Both Puerto Rico and the United States are ready for change. I see with hope how important sectors of the political leadership in Puerto Rico are actively promoting consensus-based procedural mechanisms, such as the possible convening of a constitutional convention, to ask Congress to make changes to the current political framework. As long as Puerto Rico remains a nonincorporated territory of the United States, the responsibility of Congress is to facilitate a process of full decolonization. I am going to remind my fellow Congress members of this obligation as many times as I can. In the recent past, Puerto Ricans have fought united against democratic deficits, poverty, discrimination, militarism, and environmental degradation, as in the Vieques case, in one of the most effective peace movements in recent history. What more proof do we need of the Puerto Rican determination to achieve a better future?

If Puerto Rico's effort toward self-determination is to succeed, then it is important to inform ourselves with the historical context. In the past decade, I have insisted in Congress on the need to get the historical record straight as it relates to the facts of the often unknown political repression faced by those Puerto Ricans who have opposed colonialism in Puerto Rico and in the United States during the twentieth century. In March 2000, I asked the then director of the Federal Bureau of Investigation (FBI), Louis J. Freeh, to release classified and unclassified documents related to the FBI's persecution of the *independentista* movement of Puerto Rico in the twentieth century. I was pleased by the fact that the FBI understood the need to begin a process to let the hidden historical facts come to light.

More than 140,000 pages of documents have been released since March 2000. A full set of those documents is being delivered to the Center for Puerto Rican Studies (Hunter College, City University of New York). The documents are being prepared at the center to eventually make them available for use by students, researchers, and the general public. Another set is being sent to the Puerto Rico Senate, where it has assisted in the first stage of a legislative inquiry on the involvement of federal agencies in political persecution in Puerto Rico. The Puerto Rico Senate has made available some of the files to the Puerto Rican Athenaeum and to the Luis Muñoz-Marín Foundation. The accessibility of this rich collection of historical documents, simultaneously in San Juan and New York, opens the door to new research and other educational initiatives and contributes to the effort of uncovering the hidden history of state-sponsored political persecution.

The book you are about to read also is part of that effort to rediscover a true and seldom explored history of how the voices of decolonization in Puerto Rico were silenced by agencies of the United States and Puerto Rico through often illegal means. It is a history that the American public is not aware of, but should be. It is a history that is still in the process of being fully discovered. Now that we face new challenges in the protection of basic civil liberties in the aftermath of the terrible September 11, 2001, incidents, it is important to read books like this one. It reminds us that our liberties cannot be taken for granted; they need to be defended and cultivated.

CONGRESSMAN JOSÉ E. SERRANO
(D-NY)

Acknowledgments

THIS BOOK IS THE COMBINED EFFORT of many individuals and organizations that recognized how important it is to promote the full realization of human rights of Puerto Ricans. As this book goes to press, we wish to give testimony of our gratitude to them. We want to express our appreciation to the individual authors who contributed to this volume, generously allowing us to publish the results of their research and reflections. Earlier versions of some of the chapters in this book were included in our book in Spanish, *Las carpetas: Persecución política y derechos civiles en Puerto Rico* (Río Piedras, Puerto Rico: CIPDC, 1997). Our thanks to those authors, Jorge Benítez-Nazario, Alberto L. Márquez, José (Ché) Paralitici, and Jan Susler, and to the authors who contributed to this book, Ivonne Acosta-Lespier, César J. Ayala and Viviana Carro-Figueroa, María E. Estades-Font, José E. Rivera Santana, and Jalil Sued-Badillo.

During the time we conducted research and editorial work for this book, several students performed a variety of duties and donated their time. Of those, Carmen Melinda Eisenmann-Avilés and Elga M. Castro-Ramos deserve special recognition for their enthusiastic support of our work during the last several years. We also appreciate the valuable work by and support from José Ramón Jiménez, Marilyn Rivera, and Bayoán Olguín, among several other students.

In addition, we are grateful to Congressman José E. Serrano (D-NY) and to his chief of staff and counsel, Ellyn M. Toscano, as well as to the rest of his staff. We deeply appreciate not only Mr. Serrano's foreword to this book but also his multiple contributions to the struggle for human rights, in particular, his efforts to promote the release of thousands of formerly secret FBI documents relating to Puerto Rican organizations and individuals.

The Estate of Carlos Raquel Rivera (1923–1999) generously allowed the use of artwork by this distinguished Puerto Rican graphic artist. We thank the family of Carlos Raquel Rivera and particularly his son Edgardo Rivera

Rodríguez. The work used on the cover was a trial print of *Elecciones coloniales* (1959, Linoleum, 13 1/4" x 18 1/2") that displayed the full eagle. The version of the work finally printed and circulated by the artist only showed the lower part of the eagle (1959, Linoleum, 8 1/4" x 18 1/4"). The only known surviving copy of the trial version is located at the *Museo de Historia, Antropología y Arte* of the University of Puerto Rico (UPR). Our special thanks to Flavia Marichal Lugo, Associate Director of the *Museo de Historia, Antropología y Arte* at UPR, who facilitated access to the artwork. We also thank UPR photographer Jesús E. Marrero who provided the digital images.

Numerous friends and colleagues also have provided support, advice, and encouragement. Dr. Carlos Severino, dean of the social science faculty at the University of Puerto Rico, Río Piedras, and Dr. Félix V. Matos-Rodríguez, Director of the Center for Puerto Rican Studies at Hunter College, City University of New York, provided many types of support, including their always wise and generous advice. We express our gratitude to Sylvia Solá Fernández for the translation of text originally written in Spanish and to Dr. Carlos Vélez-Ibáñez, University of California at Riverside, for his support. We also are indebted to the staff of the library and archives at the Center for Puerto Rican Studies and to the personnel of *Colección El Mundo* and *Colección Puertorriqueña* at the main library of the University of Puerto Rico, Río Piedras, as well as to the Puerto Rican Institute of Civil Rights.

The Professional Staff Congress and City University of New York provided a two-year research grant through its Research Award Competition, which supported the work of co-editor Ramón Bosque-Pérez (awards #62335-00-31 and #63254-00-32).

We also wish to thank Ana María García Blanco and Ada G. Fuentes-Rivera for their help and encouragement, along with many colleagues and friends, such as Celina Romany, David Noriega Rodríguez, Angel Israel Rivera, Luis F. Coss, José Juan Nazario, Juan Santiago Nieves, and Ivelisse Rosario Natal, who supported our efforts in a variety of ways. Thanks also go to two anonymous reviewers who made valuable recommendations to improve the manuscript. We, of course, assume responsibility for any shortcomings that the book may have.

To all of those mentioned, and to those who have been omitted due to space limitations, our deepest gratitude.

INTRODUCTION

Puerto Rico's Quest
for Human Rights

AS ONE OF THE VERY LAST and most populated colonial territories in the modern world, Puerto Rico occupies a relatively unique position. Like other nonindependent countries in the Caribbean, the island is seeking, with great difficulties, to leave its colonial legacy behind and initiate a new partnership with the United States, with the Caribbean and Latin American region, and with other countries of the world.

After four centuries under Spanish colonial rule and a century under U.S. hegemony, Puerto Rico remains today an "unincorporated territory" that "belongs to" but "is not part of" the United States.[1] During the past three decades, the United Nations Decolonization Committee has repeatedly recognized the right to self-determination of Puerto Ricans and the need to initiate a process conducive to full decolonization. The last century left a mixed balance in diverse areas of the social and economic life of 7 million persons who identify themselves as Puerto Ricans or are of Puerto Rican descent, the 3.7 million that live on the islands,[2] and the 3.4 million residing in the Continental United States.[3]

While Puerto Rico has shown substantial progress in areas such as education, health, and economic infrastructure, surpassing a large number of less-developed countries in a variety of socioeconomic indicators, it continues to present a profile of high unemployment rates and a distressing crime and drug trafficking problem, paired with growing social inequalities. More than a century of interaction with the United States has produced an economy that is largely integrated to the mainland. Still, Puerto Rican society clearly shows its Caribbean and Latin American personality, including the predominance of the Spanish language on the islands and a noticeably strong cultural national identity that extends to Puerto Rican communities in the United States.

1

On another level, the long interaction with the United States, at least in the long run, has resulted in the acquisition of expanded legal rights and relative political stability.[4] Contradictorily, it also has injected strong elements of political intolerance and the denial of basic rights for some political sectors, primarily those that have challenged colonialism.[5] Indeed, the process of construction of U.S. hegemony in Puerto Rico has involved a combination of "carrot and stick"—rewards and punishment—practices.

But neither the coercions nor the rewards have been able to erase unresolved contradictions that afflict the colonial arrangement. Therefore, some key conflicts re-emerge on a cyclical basis. A case in point is Vieques, where the movement to end the use of the island for military exercises by the U.S. Navy intensified in recent years,[6] particularly after the accidental death of David Sanes, a civilian killed during military trainings in April 1999. Since then, a wave of massive civil disobedience interrupted many times the military exercises, attracted the interest of the international public opinion, and sparked a strong community building process inside of Vieques.

During four years of renewed activism, the struggle resulted in the detention of more than 1,000 protestors. Hundreds of persons from all three traditional political tendencies (pro-independence, pro-statehood, and pro-commonwealth) endured several days to several months of incarceration after being accused of "trespassing" by federal authorities. While this type of offense is normally punished with a fine, particularly in cases of civil disobedience, U.S. authorities in Puerto Rico opted for the extremely harsher approach of sending hundreds of protestors to prison. Among the prisoners of conscience were members of the clergy, teachers, students, artists, labor leaders, and even legislators.[7] The Vieques story illustrates how a human rights claim can generate a successful consensus-building coalition that mobilizes the emerging Puerto Rican civil society and sectors of the international community to object to increasing militarization and environmental degradation. At the same time, such a coalition was effectively proposing an alternate model of self-sustained local economic development. It also shows how a community struggle that emphasizes unity beyond party lines and the creation of solidarity bridges can overcome repressive measures.

Indeed, the Vieques struggle was able to achieve a major victory as the U.S. Navy decided to cease the use of the island for storage of ammunition, training, and maneuvers as of May 2003. By that date, the navy transferred most of the lands still under its control—some 14,500 acres—to the U.S. Department of the Interior.[8] In 2001, the navy had transferred another 8,200 acres to the U.S. Department of the Interior (3,050 acres), the Vieques municipal government (4,250 acres), and the Puerto Rico Conservation Trust (800 acres). The navy still retains around 100 acres where two communication facilities exist. At the present time, community efforts concentrate on achieving the full devolution of those lands and the complete cleanup of the areas affected by the U.S. Navy's military practices.

The decades' long Vieques struggle, although characterized by peaceful civil disobedience during the last few years, was not exempt from the violent events of the past decades. During a previous wave of protest, when twenty peaceful protestors were sent to prison in November 1979, one of the activists was found hanging in his cell in the Tallahassee Federal Correctional Institution. Noting that the body of Angel Rodríguez Cristóbal showed signs of violence, several pro-independence organizations labeled this a case of political assassination.[9] Shortly after, the *Macheteros* and two other Puerto Rican clandestine organizations responded with a deadly attack on a navy bus carrying personnel assigned to the Sabana Seca Naval Communications Station. In the attack, two members of the U.S. Navy were killed and several others wounded.[10] The potential for more violence continued to grow as a bomb was planted in front of the Puerto Rico Bar Association building on January 7, 1980, and a U.S. Navy officer, Lieutenant Alex de la Zerda, was linked to the incident and, in fact, subsequently indicted by federal authorities.[11]

Quite frequently the denial of political and civil rights precipitates this type of spiral of violence that can easily grow out of control. The Puerto Rican experience presents an excellent case study of these conflictive dynamics within the United States' jurisdiction. In times when there are strong currents in the direction of strengthening mechanisms for the surveillance and investigation of citizens and hastily drafted laws chip away fundamental civil liberties, it would be wise, especially for democratic sectors, to examine the experiences with file compiling, political policing, and overt and covert political repression on the island.

Coercion and open repression by legal and/or physical means have been distinctively present under U.S. rule. Among others, as the reader would see in this book, this includes the incarceration of journalists and the closing of opposition newspapers by U.S. colonial authorities early in the twentieth century, the imprisonment of the Nationalist Party leadership in the mid-1930s, the killing in 1937 of twenty independence sympathizers in what came to be known as the "Ponce Massacre," the implementation in the 1950s of *la mordaza* (a gag law that sent to prison many independence advocates for making written or verbal expressions against the government), and the decades' long police practice of compiling secret files that affected tens of thousands of independence advocates.

However, at least partially as a result of ideologies promoted by the metropolitan and colonial states, the instances of political repression, both overt and covert, are largely overlooked and left out of most academic works.

While diverse scholarly projects have explored the evolution of the United States–Puerto Rico political interactions, the changes in the island's economy, and the dynamics of migration to the United States, among others,[12] there is limited research and published scholarly work, particularly in English, in the area of human rights and political persecution and intolerance in the Puerto Rican context. The multidisciplinary book presented here tries to begin to fill that gap. The chapters were authored by academics and intellectuals working within and beyond the academy who come from a variety of disciplines, including political science, sociology, history, and law.

This book does not attempt to cover all of the topics that could conceivably fall under the rubric of human rights in the Puerto Rican context, but rather it offers a sampling that intends to provoke thought and expand knowledge in an area largely understudied. The chapters deal with issues of human rights and political persecution during the twentieth century, paying particular attention to a set of historical and contemporary cases and current ones, including the recent Vieques case. Accordingly, the chapters have been grouped in three parts: Political Persecution in Twentieth-Century Puerto Rico, Contemporary Issues, and The Vieques Case.

The decision to devote a full section to the Vieques case responds to the fact that, in many ways, this struggle sums up the vast majority of the human rights issues that this book will cover. In Vieques, issues of colonialism and militarism, the popular struggles that emerge and challenge those structures, and the responses generated by the state as a reaction to them constantly overlap. If the Vieques case illustrates the complexity and prevalence of those issues, then it needs to be examined and understood in the context of the larger Puerto Rican reality. The first two parts of this book provide tools for such a study.

The four chapters included in the first part of the book are intended to give the reader a historical background on the topic of political persecution. The opening chapter, "Political Persecution against Puerto Rican Anti-Colonial Activists in the Twentieth Century," by co-editor Ramón Bosque-Pérez, offers an overview of how metropolitan authorities have shaped repressive institutions in Puerto Rico and the role played by those in curtailing anti-colonial activism. Particular attention is given to the role of the FBI and its influence on local police. The chapter analyzes the *carpetas* police espionage scandal, which erupted in the late 1980s, and traces the FBI's involvement in the design, implementation, and use of the secret files that the island's police maintained for decades. The author suggests that the effects of the "culture of fear" that developed early in the twentieth century have not disappeared, in spite of the steps taken in the aftermath of the scandal.

The exploration of the twentieth century continues in chapter 2, "The Critical Year of 1936 through the Reports of the Military Intelligence Division," by María E. Estades-Font. Estades-Font examines secret reports on "subversive activities" produced by the Military Intelligence Division (MID) of the U.S. Army. The author documents the surveillance conducted by that branch against the leadership and members of the Nationalist Party, particularly during 1936, and the involvement of the MID in political persecution. The year 1936 was critical, because it marked a turning point in the escalation of violence between the *Nacionalistas* and the colonial government.

In chapter 3, "The Smith Act Goes to San Juan: *La Mordaza*, 1948–1957," Ivonne Acosta-Lespier examines and places in historical perspective Law 53 of 1948, a statute that mimicked sections of the Smith Law and was known in Puerto Rico as *la mordaza*, or the "Gag Order." According to Acosta-Lespier, for nearly ten crucial years, the Gag Order managed to mortally wound the Nationalist Party, and through fear it decreased the electoral force of the pro-independence movement, giving way to the electoral rise of the pro status quo and annexation forces. She also proposes that Law 53 was instrumental in providing an adequate political environment for the establishment of the Commonwealth of Puerto Rico.

Part I closes with chapter 4, "Imprisonment and Colonial Domination, 1898–1958," where the author, José (Ché) Paralitici, presents a historical overview of the cases that have involved the incarceration of anti-colonial activists. It covers persecution and imprisonment of journalists early in the twentieth century, those jailed for opposing the draft (compulsory military service) since 1917, and the cases of Nationalists and other anti-colonial fighters from the 1930s to the 1950s.

Part II of this book includes four chapters that deal with contemporary issues. It is intended to contribute to some of the current debates over human rights in Puerto Rican society, including new scenarios of political intolerance. Chapter 5, "Puerto Rico: The Puzzle of Human Rights and Self-Determination," by co-editor José Javier Colón Morera, explores the recent developments in the discussion of the so-called political status and inserts the subject of political persecution as an unavoidable element to be considered when discussing the possible steps that would lead to the island's complete decolonization. The author argues that there are still enormous challenges to the climate conducive to the respect of human rights. Colón Morera argues that the relative intra-elite consensus reflected in the Bill of Rights of the 1952 Commonwealth Constitution has been under attack on various fronts: by some "tough-hand," anti-crime initiatives implemented by the government of Puerto Rico during the 1990s and by the effects of some federal initiatives such as the imposition of the death penalty (which is prohibited by the Constitution of Puerto Rico).

Chapter 6, "The Changing Nature of Intolerance," by Jorge Benítez-Nazario, presents the main findings of research on patterns of prejudice in Puerto Rico based on data from the World Values Survey (WVS). This chapter places the reader in the intersection between human rights and political culture and provides elements that allow reflection on the levels of intolerance in different aspects of daily life. Benítez-Nazario takes a critical view of the generalized belief that Puerto Rican society is characterized by civility and tolerance of ideas and lifestyles different from those of the majority. The author discusses problems of religious, racial, and ethnic prejudice and demonstrates that none of the traditional political sectors are free from the problem of hostility and fear toward "the other."

Chapter 7, "Puerto Rican Political Prisoners in U.S. Prisons," by Jan Susler, discusses the presidential pardons granted by former President Clinton in 1999 to several Puerto Rican pro-independence activists who had been in prison for fifteen to twenty years. She argues that, although a step in the right direction, the action taken by former President Clinton left various issues unresolved. Susler discusses the political and social background that led to the imprisonment of previous and present activists, as well as their prison conditions. The author also discusses the campaign for the release of these political prisoners and closes with an analysis of how the September 11, 2001, aftermath affected their treatment, prison conditions, and overall climate.

Chapter 8, "Puerto Rican *Independentistas*: Subversives or Subverted?," by Alberto Márquez, reflects on the role played by the process of political intelligence as a means to repress or advance social struggles in a colonial context. The author suggests that pro-independence organizations have been more *subverted* than *subversives* and argues that they must develop a greater capacity to understand and act upon the intelligence process as a way to promote their own agendas.

Part III of this book is devoted fully to Vieques as a case that captures the diversity and complexity of issues involved in human rights struggles in contemporary Puerto Rico. Chapter 9, "Vieques: To Be or Not to Be," by Jalil Sued-Badillo, provides an overview of the role played by this island as a conflictive frontier since the times of the Spanish colonization. Sued-Badillo traces this history, emphasizing how a strong, cultural Puerto Rican identity was formed in Vieques early on during that period. Sued-Badillo advances the notion that Vieques was a crucial part of the Puerto Rican process of national identity building.

Chapter 10, "Expropriation and Displacement of Civilians in Vieques, 1940–1950," by César J. Ayala and Viviana Carro-Figueroa, examines the expropriation of civilian lands in the periods 1942–1943 and 1947–1950 by combining archival data from the *Archivo General de Puerto Rico* with data from fifty-three interviews of residents of Vieques who were displaced. This integration of data allows the researchers to thoroughly describe the process of displacement.

Part III closes with chapter 11, "New Dimensions in Civil Society Mobilization: The Struggle for Peace in Vieques," by co-editor José Javier Colón Morera and José E. Rivera Santana. This chapter explores the ways in which this movement for peace has been able to overcome political persecution and develop strategies that create more active, regular, and public manifestations of political protest. The chapter contains a specific and detailed description of the detrimental ecological impact of the military trainings. The authors contend that this case is only one example, an extreme one, of the need to give a voice to the communities in the development of their collective future.

As a whole, the chapters in this book present compelling historical evidence of a pattern of state-sponsored political persecution on the island during the twentieth century. Those practices should not be overlooked or underestimated while assessing current conflicts and outcomes or while formulating or refining state policies on Puerto Rico's political future.

It is our hope that this book will serve scholars, students, and policy makers, as well as the general public, in the process of understanding today's Puerto Rican reality.

NOTES

1. The distinction comes from a set of decisions made by the U.S. Supreme Court in the early years after the acquisition of Puerto Rico and other overseas territories. The cases, known collectively as the *Insular Cases*, addressed the constitutional rights of the new territories and their peoples. For a discussion of the cases and their implications, see, for instance, Rivera Ramos 2001.

2. The archipelago of Puerto Rico is located in the eastern part of the Caribbean. It is formed by three inhabited islands—Puerto Rico, Vieques, and Culebra—plus a number of smaller noninhabited islands and islets.

3. The most recent U.S. Census shows that Puerto Ricans continue to be the second largest Latino group in the United States (U.S. Census Bureau 2001).

4. For detailed explorations of that arduous evolution during the twentieth century, see, for instance, Cabán 1999; Fernández 1996; Rivera Ramos 2001; Trías Monge 1997.

5. See, for instance, Bosque-Pérez and Colón Morera 1997; Comisión de Derechos Civiles 1989.

6. Vieques activism has been more visible in recent years but is hardly a new phenomenon. For background information and an analysis of the Vieques movement, see, for instance, Barreto 2002; McCaffrey 2002; Murillo 2001.

7. For instance, Norma Burgos, a pro-statehood leader and member of the Puerto Rico Senate, and Lolita Lebrón, a pro-independence activist and former political prisoner, were both sentenced to sixty days in prison. Also, numerous persons from the Continental United States who participated in acts of civil disobedience assumed a share of the prison sentences, among others, Jacqueline Jackson (the wife of Reverend Jesse Jackson); U.S. Congressman Luis Gutiérrez; labor leader Dennis Rivera; environmental lawyer Robert F. Kennedy Jr.; the Reverend Al Sharpton; actor Edward James Olmos; New York Democratic Party leader Roberto Ramírez; New York State legislator José Rivera; and New York City Council member Adolfo Carrión (more recently Bronx borough president).

8. U.S. Department of Defense, "Department of Navy Transfers Vieques Property," News Release No. 291-03, April 30, 2003, http://www.defenselink.mil/news/Apr2003/b04302003_bt291-03.html (accessed December 26, 2003).

9. See "Puerto Ricans Vow to Avenge Death in U.S. Prison," *New York Times*, November 18, 1979, p. 33.

10. The organizations *Ejército Popular Boricua—Macheteros* (Popular Boricua Army), *Organización de Voluntarios por la Revolución Puertorriqueña* (Organization of Volunteers for the Puerto Rican Revolution), and *Fuerzas Armadas de Resistencia Popular* (Armed Forces of Popular Resistance) claimed responsibility for the armed action. See "2 Sailors Dead, 8 Wounded in Independentista Ambush," *San Juan Star*, December 4, 1979, pp. 1, 20. Also see "Navy Men Slain Near San Juan in Terrorist Ambush; Terrorists Kill 2 U.S. Sailors Near San Juan," *Washington Post*, December 4, 1979, p. A1.

11. On January 25, 1980, federal authorities indicted Lieutenant Alex de la Zerda, at the time the spokesperson for the U.S. Navy at the Roosevelt Road Naval Base, and another two men. They were charged with bombing the Puerto Rico Bar Association building and conspiring to bomb an airplane. See the *New York Times*, "Navy Officer and 2 Others Held in San Juan Bombing" (January 26, 1980, p. 8) and "3 Arrested in Bomb Plot Linked to Protest on Puerto Rico Island" (January 27, 1980, p. 18).

12. See, for instance, Acosta-Belén 1986; Bonilla and Campos 1986; Cabán 1999; Dietz 1986; Fernández 1996; History Task Force 1979; Pérez y González 2000; Rodríguez 1989; Sánchez Korrol 1994; Trías Monge 1997; Weisskoff 1985.

WORKS CITED

Acosta-Belén, Edna, ed. 1986. *The Puerto Rican Woman: Perspectives on Culture, History, and Society*. 2d ed. Westport, Conn.: Praeger.

Barreto, Amílcar Antonio. 2002. *Vieques, the Navy, and Puerto Rican Politics*. Gainesville, Fla.: University Press of Florida.

Bonilla, Frank, and Ricardo Campos. 1986. *Industry and Idleness*. New York: Centro de Estudios Puertorriqueños.

Bosque-Pérez, Ramón, and José Javier Colón Morera. 1997. *Las carpetas: Persecución política y derechos civiles en Puerto Rico (ensayos y documentos)*. Río Piedras, Puerto Rico: Centro para la Investigación y Promoción de los Derechos Civiles.

Cabán, Pedro A. 1999. *Constructing a Colonial People: Puerto Rico and the United States, 1898–1932*. Boulder, Colo.: Westview Press.

Comisión de Derechos Civiles. 1989. *Informe sobre discrimen y persecución por razones políticas: la práctica gubernamental de mantener listas, ficheros y expedientes de ciudadanos por razón de su ideología política*. 1989-CDC-028. San Juan: Comisión de Derechos Civiles.

Dietz, James L. 1986. *Economic History of Puerto Rico: Institutional Change and Capitalist Development*. Princeton: Princeton University Press.

Fernández, Ronald. 1996. *The Disenchanted Island: Puerto Rico and the United States in the Twentieth Century*. 2d ed. Westport, Conn.: Praeger.

History Task Force (*Centro de Estudios Puertorriqueños*). 1979. *Labor Migration under Capitalism: The Puerto Rican Experience*. New York and London: Monthly Review Press.

McCaffrey, Katherine T. 2002. *Military Power and Popular Protest: The U.S. Navy in Vieques, Puerto Rico*. New Brunswick, N.J.: Rutgers University Press.

Murillo, Mario. 2001. *Islands of Resistance: Puerto Rico, Vieques, and U.S. Policy*. New York: Seven Stories Press.

New York Times, November 28, 1991, "Officials in Puerto Rico Aimed to Kill, Panel Hears," p. A21.

Pérez y González, María E. 2000. *Puerto Ricans in the United States*. Westport, Conn.: Greenwood Press.

Ramos, Aarón G., and Angel I. Rivera Ortiz. 2001. *Islands at the Crossroads: Politics in the Non-Independent Caribbean*. Boulder, Colo.: Lynne Rienner.

Rivera Ramos, Efrén. 2001. *The Legal Construction of Identity: The Judicial and Social Legacy of American Colonialism in Puerto Rico*. Washington, D.C.: American Psychological Association.

Rodríguez, Clara E. 1989. *Puerto Ricans: Born in the U.S.A.* Boston: Unwin Hyman.

Sánchez Korrol, Virginia E. 1994. *From Colonia to Community: The History of Puerto Ricans in New York*. Berkeley: University of California Press.

Trías Monge, José. 1997. *Puerto Rico: The Trials of the Oldest Colony of the World*. New Haven, Conn., and London: Yale University Press.

U.S. Census Bureau. 2001. "The Hispanic Population: Census 2000 Brief." Washington, D.C.: U.S. Department of Commerce.

Weisskoff, Richard. 1985. *Factories and Food Stamps: The Puerto Rico Model of Development*. Baltimore and London: Johns Hopkins University Press.

PART I

Political Persecution in
Twentieth-Century Puerto Rico

ONE

Political Persecution against Puerto Rican Anti-Colonial Activists in the Twentieth Century

Ramón Bosque-Pérez

[Intelligence work] does not always show in arrests . . . but it does show in a remarkable collection of facts, available for future use . . . and it shows also in the knowledge that it imparts to these persons of revolutionary design that the government is watching.
  —A. Mitchel Palmer, U.S. Attorney General, 1920 Annual Report[1]

We have to investigate in such a way that neither the interviewed persons nor those under investigation learn about our work. [. . .] This is so, because our investigations deal with individuals who hold pro-independence ideals and when they learn that we are investigating they argue that we are engaging in persecution and repression because of their political beliefs and, as we all know, this is prohibited by our constitution.
  —Intelligence Division, Police of Puerto Rico,
from a confidential *Investigations Handbook*, discovered in 1987.[2]

DURING THE SUMMER of 1987, Puerto Ricans were hit by the "revelation" that the Police of Puerto Rico had been compiling secret files and lists of alleged "subversives," and that tens of thousands of individuals of all ages and social sectors were listed. The scandal was big news in the local media and was even covered by some periodicals in the United States.[3] Within weeks, the Puerto Rico Civil Rights Commission opened an investigation. As the local legislature approved a resolution asking for explanations from the police, the governor and the secretary of justice labeled the practice "unconstitutional." Meanwhile, several victims of the practice brought legal actions against the police and the government of Puerto Rico (Bosque-Pérez and Colón Morera 1997; Comisión de Derechos Civiles 1989).

After five years of legal battles, the Puerto Rico Supreme Court finally decided the case and ordered the return to the victims of all of the documents compiled during decades of illegal surveillance. The court decision went even farther by not allowing the police to delete or otherwise conceal the identity of hundreds of infiltrated agents or informers.[4]

The inquiry conducted by the Civil Rights Commission, as well as the legal actions, produced a body of documentation never available before on the topic of political persecution in Puerto Rico and opened the door for further explorations. The documentation demonstrated that, for many decades, the police of Puerto Rico had compiled dossiers with information on the legal political activities of thousands of individuals and organizations, mostly advocates of independence for Puerto Rico (i.e., *independentistas*). The police unit in charge of the political spying enterprise, the *División de Inteligencia* (Intelligence Division), would conduct investigations and surveillance of individuals and organizations. The unit relied on infiltrated agents and paid informers to compile information on every pro-independence activity that took place. The reports, which were reproduced and added to the dossier of each participant and organization, kept accumulating to produce dossiers that in many cases were thousands of pages long. Within the Intelligence Division of the Police of Puerto Rico, the dossiers were discreetly known as *carpetas*.[5]

When the scandal erupted in 1987, no less than 75,000 persons had active files that ranged from a few index cards to full dossiers.[6] Not only Puerto Ricans residing on the island were listed. A presumably large number of Puerto Ricans residing permanently in the Continental United States and even some U.S. nationals also were victims of the practice as well as some Dominicans and Cubans residing in Puerto Rico.[7]

The collapse in 1987 of this vast repressive enterprise was to no small extent due to another scandal that took place almost ten years earlier: the Cerro Maravilla case. The case takes the name of a mountain in the south-central part of Puerto Rico, where two *independentista* youths were victims of a police entrapment. Instigated by an infiltrated agent, the two went to Cerro Maravilla to perform a revolutionary action but were instead ambushed, detained, brutalized, and subsequently murdered by members of the police. The infiltrated agent, as well as several of the police officers involved in the incident, worked for the Intelligence Division of the Police of Puerto Rico. Although *independentista* organizations claimed from the start that Cerro Maravilla was a case of political assassination, the details of the incident remained in the dark for several years until a series of investigations led by the Puerto Rico Senate uncovered the large-scale cover-up (Senado de Puerto Rico 1984, 1992; Suárez 1987; Aponte Pérez 1995). During the investigations, it became clear that for the police leadership and higher government circles, the executions were intended as a way to teach "a hard lesson" to so-called Puerto Rican subversives, or *independentistas*.[8] The exposure of the involvement of the Intelligence Division in the Cerro Maravilla killings left that police unit in extremely bad shape and helped give credence to *independentista* claims of political persecution by the police.[9]

Ironically, one of the former members of the Intelligence Division who went to prison because of his involvement in the Cerro Maravilla case[10] contributed to the exposure of the *carpetas* affair by accusing the local chief of police and several other government officials of being *independentista* sympathizers and therefore "subversives." As "proof," he argued that those individuals were included in a "list of subversives" kept by the police. Referring to Carlos López Feliciano, the then police superintendent, the agent said that "the Intelligence Division opened a dossier" on him "for being a sympathizer of *independentistas*," and that later on, "those documents disappeared."[11]

In this chapter, I discuss the historical roots of these and other instances of political persecution and violence and the massive violation of human rights against Puerto Rican political activists. I argue that these are just two modalities among many others that are part of a pattern of a long-lasting, state-sponsored denial of basic political rights to sectors, organizations, and individuals that have presented opposition to U.S. presence in Puerto Rico. I use a variety of documentary sources that have become available during the last few decades (including documents from numerous *carpetas* belonging to individuals and organizations), as well as secondary sources and scholarly work. In order to provide historical context, examples of similar processes in the United States also are discussed.

POLICE BODIES AND UNITED STATES HEGEMONY IN PUERTO RICO

When the United States arrived in Puerto Rico in 1898, there already existed some police and security bodies that had been previously created by the Spanish colonial authorities. In 1850, for instance, Spanish Lieutenant General Pezuela had sponsored a project for the creation of a police and security corp for the city of San Juan. During the last decades of the century, there was a *Guardia de Orden Público* for the urban areas and a *Guardia Civil* for the rural areas. However, since very early in the nineteenth century, coinciding with the independence wars in Latin America, the Spanish colonial regime (under the governorship of Brigadier Salvador Meléndez) had already created a sophisticated apparatus of political espionage. That body was reorganized in 1824 by Governor Miguel de la Torre, who effectively used it for the detection of pro-independence activity and for facilitating arrests and deportations (Delgado Pasapera 1984; Cruz Monclova 1979).

Immediately after U.S. military occupation of Puerto Rico in 1898, the colonial authorities began taking steps toward the full control of the island, its resources, and its people. Consistent with this, any movements or actions that were perceived as a challenge to the stability or consolidation of U.S. hegemony on the island prompted responses from the colonial authorities. The consolidation of U.S. hegemony in Puerto Rico has been a gradual process influenced by the complex combination of objective conditions that existed on the island at the time of the U.S. military intervention, measures taken by colonial authorities within the next few decades, and the responses generated by different social sectors (Mattos Cintrón 1988; Cabán 1999).[12]

But it was not until after the U.S. invasion of 1898, under the military government of Major Guy V. Henry, that the creation of a modern sort of police body was initiated. The reorganization of the repressive apparatus was one of the earliest projects undertaken by the military regime established in Puerto Rico after the 1898 invasion. Police forces in Puerto Rico acquired and carried distinct traits as a result of this. Although military rule in Puerto Rico lasted for less than two years, military control over the police lasted for at least fifty years. In fact, up to 1956, the body was directed by members of the U.S. military with the rank of colonel. In its origins, an officer of the U.S. Army served as police inspector while guns were supplied by the U.S. military. During the first ten years of existence of the body, its members even used U.S. military uniforms. The rank system was adopted from the U.S. Navy and denoted by insignia adopted from the U.S. Army. At the end of the two-year service period, the member of the Insular Police received the customary military discharge and could rejoin for another period (Martínez Valentín 1995). The level of military control is further exemplified by the fact that, during certain periods, the officer in charge of the Insular Police was at the same time the chief of U.S. Army Military Intelligence for the District of Puerto Rico[13] or an officer with extensive experience in military intelligence matters.[14]

As early as 1899, the recently created police force was using infiltrated agents to assess the extent of anti-American sentiments in the central region of the island. A handwritten report by covert agent Leopoldo García Miguens states that in the towns of Ciales and Utuado, "a very sharp and active propaganda was being made against the United States and its Government." The agent enumerates several residents of those towns as "enemies" of the United States and identifies some that are allegedly hiding "fire arms and ammunitions."[15] In the years ahead, the U.S. colonial government in Puerto Rico continued to use the local police for political spying. According to one author,

> [. . .] circular letters show that since 1904 information on political meetings was being compiled. The District Chiefs of Police had no choice but to be

alert to all kinds of political statements and comments and relay them to
their superiors. Otherwise, they were under the threat of being fired from
the police.[16] (Martínez Valentín 1995)

Other documentation confirms that the Insular Police played a key role
in the intelligence network developed by the U.S. Armed Forces in Puerto
Rico since the very first decades of the century. For instance, a confidential
memorandum from the Office of the Intelligence Officer in San Juan, Puerto
Rico, dated 1918, mentions as part of the "counter-espionage organization in
Porto Rico [sic]" the military intelligence officer and his assistants, the naval
intelligence officer and his assistants, the marshal and deputy marshals in the
federal court, and one special agent in the Department of Justice. Also listed
are the commissioner of immigration and his assistants, the collector of customs and his assistants, and the steamship and railway ticket offices. The
memorandum adds as another key part of the U.S. intelligence network in
Puerto Rico

[. . .] the local or district chiefs of the Insular Police assisted by such members of their respective commands as are specially adapted for surveillance
and investigative work. In this way the federal authorities at San Juan are
enabled, through the Chief of Insular Police, to keep their fingers on the
pulse of the entire island [. . .] the police have thus proved of constant and
invaluable assistance to federal heads of departments.[17]

It is important to notice that in addition to the local police, other bodies created in the first decades of the century were key parts of the repressive
apparatus and also played an important role in surveillance activities and in
the dissemination of ideologies supportive of the colonial regime. For
instance, in the 1920s, the U.S. War Department financed the establishment
of a program called the "Citizens Military Training Camps" (CMTC). An
author who has researched U.S. military practices in Puerto Rico states the
following:

The CMTC originated in the United States as a private initiative of conservative officers and civilians concerned about growing "bolchevistic tendencies" among working class youths in the context of the "red scare." It
eventually obtained official government support. The program in Puerto
Rico was financed by the War Department. In the summer camps held at
Camp Buchanan, about 500 youths were provided with military instruction
and infused with patriotism every year.[18] (Rodríguez Beruff 1994)

The American Legion was established in Puerto Rico in late 1919 in an
effort to mobilize island veterans, and it expanded rapidly after the 1930s.[19]
In 1919, the Puerto Rico National Guard also was established following
requests from colonial Governor Yager to the Bureau of Insular Affairs in

response to concerns about increased social tensions and unrest (Carrión 1987).[20] In addition, in 1920, what had been known so far as the "Porto Rico Regiment of Infantry" was officially renamed the 65th Infantry Regiment of the U.S. Army (Negroni c1993, 370). Intelligence documents released in recent years hint at how active that regiment was in the surveillance activities on the island (CDC 1989).

During those first decades of the century, surveillance and political espionage were not limited to the island. Some Puerto Ricans also were the object of surveillance while traveling abroad. That was the case of nationalist leader Pedro Albizu Campos, even before he assumed the presidency of that organization. During a trip in the late 1920s to promote solidarity with the independence cause, U.S. military intelligence was receiving reports from different parts of Latin America with details about Albizu Campos's activities (Rosado 1992).

POLITICAL PERSECUTION AND LISTS
OF SUBVERSIVES IN THE UNITED STATES

Although U.S. society is commonly seen as being highly tolerant of dissent, a closer look at the historical record shows otherwise. As documented by numerous historical works, there is a long history of exclusion, intolerance, political persecution, and even brutal violence against dissenters.[21] In the United States, as well as in Puerto Rico, the first and second decades of the century consisted of years of expanded labor activity. In the United States, with the increased activism of organizations such as the Industrial Workers of the World (IWW), the political persecution of dissenters also intensified dramatically. In Puerto Rico, as the working conditions deteriorated and the level of exploitation increased, workers' struggles and militancy also expanded.[22] As the number, intensity, and effectiveness of workers' strikes increased dramatically, workers' political organizations emerged and made impressive headway.[23] Those decades also saw violent repression against Puerto Rican workers.

With the approval in the United States of the Espionage Act of 1917 and the Sedition Act of 1918, new mechanisms for the political persecution of "radicals" were added (Goldstein 1978a, 550). In spite of the name, the laws were not intended to deal with "espionage" and specifically criminalized the making of "statements that might cause 'insubordination' or 'disloyalty' in the armed services or statements that could 'obstruct' enlistment into the armed services" (Kohn 1994). According to Kohn (1994, 8), the analysis of congressional debates shows that the laws were to a great extent directed against workers and socialist organizations.

In all, over 2,000 citizens were prosecuted under the provisions of these laws, including the leader of the American Socialist Party, Eugene V. Debs;

the general secretary of the IWW, William D. Haywood; anarchist leader Emma Goldman; Mexican anarchists Ricardo and Enrique Flores Magón; as well as many other members of the above-mentioned organizations and other individuals.

Although little known, some residents of Puerto Rico went to prison for alleged violations of these laws based on their public expressions against the war. In these cases, forced exile further augmented the harshness of the sentences since prison terms (ranging from four to eight years) were served in prisons in the Continental United States, including the Atlanta Penitentiary (Kohn 1994; Paralitici 1994, 1990).

However, political persecution in the United States would not end with the incarceration of those hundreds of dissidents. In 1919, the Justice Department created the General Intelligence Division (GID) with the goal of watching "radical" and "subversive" activity (Donner 1980, 33). Within months, the "Radical Division," as the GID was known, compiled lists and dossiers of thousands of dissidents and "radicals" (Ungar 1975, 43) that were used to conduct massive detentions and deportations as part of the infamous Palmer Raids.[24]

It should not be a surprise that a key feature in the compilation of the lists and dossiers was the use of informers planted in diverse organizations. Those who dared question the legality of the actions, including lawyers and private citizens, were accused of being "radicals" and "subversives" and were subsequently investigated (ibid., 38ff.). A key figure in the organization of the system of dossiers in the GID was J. Edgar Hoover. When the GID was eliminated in 1924, in part due to its scandalous illegal activities, Hoover assumed the directorship of the Bureau of Investigation, which in 1935 became the Federal Bureau of Investigation, or FBI (ibid., 55). When the GID was disbanded, U.S. Attorney General Stone announced that the Bureau of Investigation would limit its scope to the investigation of illegal activities and would not be concerned with the political opinions and activities of citizens. But in spite of this publicly stated commitment, the practice of compiling lists and dossiers not only continued but even expanded. The dossiers previously compiled by the GID went to the files of the Bureau (Goldstein 1978, 553; Theoharis and Cox 1988, 92–94).

The 1930s was a period of expansion of surveillance activities and political persecution in the United States.[25] On September 5, 1936, FBI Director J. Edgar Hoover transmitted the following directive to his subalterns:

> The Bureau desires to obtain from all possible sources information concerning *subversive activities* conducted in the United States by Communists, Fascisti, *and representatives or advocates of other organizations or groups advocating the overthrow or replacement of the Government of the United States.*[26]

This "anti-subversive" effort included the organization of a vast program of informers with daily reports to the Bureau. The number of "subversives" expanded rapidly, of course, as well as the collection of dossiers and printed materials produced by the organizations under surveillance (Donner 1980, 55). In a 1938 memorandum to President Roosevelt, Hoover described in general terms the operation: the data on "radicals" were stored on index cards and filed by topic and name of the individual (Goldstein 1978, 553). The detailed index permitted searching by geographic area, organization, type of activity, or industry. One of the ultimate purposes of these lists was to facilitate the mass detention of dissenters.

Late in 1939, in a memorandum to the agents in charge of field offices, Hoover referred to the purpose of the lists being collected: the citizens listed were candidates for "preventive detention" in case of a "national emergency." In fact, the program was referred to as "custodial detention." In the memorandum, the FBI director stated that the Bureau was

> [. . .] preparing a list of individuals, both aliens and citizens of the United
> States, on whom there is information available to indicate their presence at
> liberty in this country in time of war or national emergency would be danger-
> ous to the public peace and safety of the United States. (Goldstein 1978, 554)

In 1943, U.S. Attorney General Francis Biddle ordered the practice of maintaining such lists to cease, arguing that there was no legal base or practical need for it. However, as has been documented by historians, the FBI ignored such an order by a subterfuge commonly used by Hoover: the name of the detention program was simply changed from "custodial detention" to "security index" (Theoharis 1978b, 1014–15; Goldstein 1978b, 556–57).

Later, in 1949, the FBI worked a refined version of the preventive detention lists and specified the criteria for inclusion of someone in the "security index." According to Hoover: "[. . .] basic qualification required for inclusion of an individual . . . is that such an individual is potentially dangerous or would be dangerous in the event of an emergency to the internal security of the country" (Goldstein 1978, 560). One may ask, how would dangerousness be determined? Hoover listed as first "membership, affiliation or activity indicating sympathy with" either "the Communist Party or similar ideological groups" or "the Nationalist Party of Puerto Rico."[27]

SURVEILLANCE IN THE COLONY

The interest in the Nationalist Party of Puerto Rico was not new to the FBI. A February 1936 FBI document, for instance, contains a detailed list (with names, occupations, and other information) of officers of the Nationalist Party *Juntas Locales* (municipal branches).[28] It is precisely in February 1936 that information circulates in Puerto Rico about the presence of federal agents investigating the activities of the Nationalist Party. On February 20, 1936, the front page of *El Imparcial*, a daily newspaper, announced "G-men

Investigate Nationalists" and "Federal G-men sent to Puerto Rico." The news piece added: "They secretly investigate the activities of the Nationalist Party. Agents brought with them 'Thompson' submachine guns and tear gas bombs."[29]

It was indeed true that federal agents were investigating the Nationalist Party, as FBI documents have eventually shown. But the news report gives the impression that a full battalion of FBI (G-men) went to Puerto Rico and were scattered all over the island armed with Thompson submachine guns (popularized by the gangsters of the period). What was scattered all over the island was a network of informers that started in the local police force itself. The team of two G-men sent from the United States included agents Edgar K. Thompson, from the Bureau's central office, and Dante DiLillo, from the Pittsburgh office.

In their February 1936 report, FBI special agents Thompson and DiLillo included a list of officers of the Nationalist Party. The report, dated February 10–20, 1936, also contains a review of the contents of issues 2–18 of the Nationalist newspaper, La Palabra, including long excerpts translated into English.[30] The report contains numerous references to the chiefs of the Puerto Rico Insular Police at the local level and the information they provided regarding the number of active nacionalistas, their activities, supporters, and so on. Such close contact between the FBI and the Puerto Rico Insular Police would further develop. Members of the Insular Police started graduating from the FBI National Academy just one year after it was inaugurated in 1935. FBI-trained members of the Insular Police would eventually occupy key positions, including chief of the body (Superintendente) and chief of the notorious Internal Security Squad, the predecessor of the Intelligence Division.[31]

In addition to the FBI, the army and navy intelligence offices were quite busy engaging in political surveillance of Puerto Ricans since very early in the century.[32] Documents reproduced by the Puerto Rico Civil Rights Commission provide useful insights into the matter (CDC 1989, vol. 2). Among the documents are several samples of memoranda with the following subject: "Weekly Summary of Subversive Activities—Puerto Rico Area." These memoranda, dated in the 1930s and 1940s, were submitted by the commanding officers of the 65th Infantry Regiment to the area commanding officer in New York.

The "Weekly Summary of Subversive Activities" that corresponds to the period of July 10–18, 1936 (timely submitted on the 18th), among other things contains details about the trial that was taking place at the moment against Pedro Albizu Campos and the leadership of the Nationalist Party. The following quote is taken from that report:

> The personnel of the Intelligence Section of this headquarters is operating during the trial in civilian clothes, as follows: one man in the courtroom

covering the case; one man mingling with the witnesses, policemen and officials on the second floor (location of the Courtroom); two men on the first floor (location of the Post Office); two men on the outside of the building mingling with the crowd and covering contiguous area; one man at each of the principal plazas in San Juan, which are gathering places.

Periodic reports are received by (G-2) from these operators. The Intelligence officer (G-2) is in close liaison with the U.S. Marshal and the Chief of the Insular Police. Information is freely exchanged.[33]

This particular document suggests, among other things, how Puerto Rican members of the military were used to spy on political and other activities, some of the techniques used in those endeavors, the intervention (at least to gather information) in the legal procedures against the *nacionalistas*, and the close communication between military intelligence and the local police.

The *nacionalistas* were not the only targets, nor did the military intelligence services limit their role to surveillance. They also infiltrated agents and used paid informers. In a document dated October 15, 1940, the U.S. Army intelligence office in San Juan reports to the Military Intelligence Division in Washington, D.C., that on September 13, 1940, "the Communist Party of Puerto Rico started giving classes on Communism," and that "Mr. Cesar Andreu, a well-known local Communist, was in charge of the classes." Regarding attendance of the meeting, the report stated:

Attendance: first Friday, 14 persons; second Friday, 7 persons; third Friday, 4 persons; and fourth Friday, 3 persons. All individuals attending the classes, except the intelligence agent from this headquarters, are active members of the Communist Party in Puerto Rico. Due to lack of interest and attendance, the classes were discontinued after October 4.[34]

From the content of the document itself it is not possible to determine to what extent it is true that the classes were "discontinued," since it is always possible that the Puerto Rican reds detected the informer and regrouped elsewhere. A note at the bottom of the report shows that copies of it were sent to the Office of Naval Intelligence (ONI) and to the FBI.

Other documents show how even members of the colonial executive and legislative bodies were carefully scrutinized by army and navy intelligence branches established in Puerto Rico. For instance, a confidential document, originated in the Intelligence Division of the U.S. Navy, reports on a speech delivered at the University of Puerto Rico on December 8, 1942, by a member of the Puerto Rico Senate and Popular Democratic Party leader Vicente Géigel Polanco.[35]

At the time, the ONI in Puerto Rico developed an interest in the curriculum at the University of Puerto Rico. Another 1942 confidential "Intelligence Report" from the "District Intelligence Officer" in Puerto Rico is introduced

with the following bullet: "Political leader giving course on radical social legislation at the University of Puerto Rico, said to be communistic."[36] The course,
"Social Legislation," was taught by Senator Vicente Géigel Polanco, who
apparently was a constant source of concern for navy intelligence.

The report also contained information, provided by an informer who was
a member of the University Administrative Board, that other "radical teachers" were to be "imported" and that there were plans "to eliminate English
language and all cultural relations with the United States from the University." The allegations were a gross exaggeration. However, information like
this, provided by supposedly "reliable sources," was uncritically incorporated
into intelligence reports and presumably had an impact in colonial policy
making. The same report claims that another evidence of "communistic lean-
ings" at the University of Puerto Rico was "the effort of the Chancellor, Jaime
Benítez, to bring Vicente Herrero, a noted Spanish Communist refugee, to
the University as Professor of Political Science."

A couple of years later, Chancellor Benítez was still a concern, but this
time the tone is more of a progress report. A document containing a "recent
intelligence report" on the chancellor, dated October 4, 1944, and transmitted in secret code, discusses how Benítez had been changing his political
views and "is no longer in favor of Puerto Rican independence."[37]

Not even the members of the Insular Police escaped from suspicion and
surveillance. A confidential "Intelligence Report" from the "District Intelligence Officer" in San Juan, dated March 1, 1943, explains the internal organization of the Insular Police and provides a list of members of the Police
Commission and the chiefs of the nine districts into which the body was
divided. The report records the political affiliation of each person as a "member of the Popular Party," or "no political affiliation known." One case is singled out as a "member of the Popular Party; reported by a confidential informant as being very anti-American."[38]

Even the top leadership of the Popular Democratic Party was under suspicion, including its founder and main leader, Luis Muñoz Marín. In 1943, this
is how Hoover's FBI characterized Muñoz Marín, then president of the Puerto
Rico Senate, based on reports from what they called "reliable informants":

Jose Luis Muñoz Marín, president of [the] Puerto Rico Senate, alleged to
have used Communist Party principles and leaders to gain political power
during elections of 1940, [and] since then, for practical reasons, has not
aligned himself with Communists. Described by reliable informants to be
intellectual with [a] bad case of "Puerto Rican inferiority complex," which
results in anti-American tendencies. He is not considered dangerous to [the]
point of acts against [the] United States. Is known to be personally completely irresponsible; reported by reliable informants to be [a] heavy drinker
and narcotics addict.[39]

In the section of the document where "character of case" is recorded, the case of Muñoz Marín is labeled "Internal Security—C" (i.e., Communist) and "Custodial Detention." In other words, even the president of the Puerto Rico Senate and founder of the *Partido Popular Democrático* was at the moment a candidate for preventive detention in case of a "national emergency." After the 1950s, however, FBI documents on Muñoz Marín show more concern with the security of the governor of Puerto Rico than with his subversive potential.

DOSSIERS AND LISTS OF SUBVERSIVES IN PUERTO RICO

The police practice of listing persons based on their political beliefs and affiliations uncovered in 1987 was of a large magnitude and had existed for decades. Even though pro-independence and student organizations and their members were the main targets, the practice eventually reached labor unions and other cultural, religious, feminist, and environmentalist organizations. In their dossier-compiling activities, the Police of Puerto Rico and its Intelligence Division relied on infiltrated agents and paid informers who reported on the activities of groups and individuals.[40] When a person had been mentioned more than four times, a full record was started by (1) assigning a *carpeta* number, and (2) producing a detailed personal profile through a full investigation of the individual. By their own admission, the members of the Intelligence Division were aware of the illegal character of such investigations based on political beliefs and associations.

> [. . .] our investigations deal with individuals who hold pro-independence
> ideals, and when they learn that we are investigating they argue that we are
> engaging in persecution and repression because of their political beliefs and,
> as we all know, this is prohibited by our constitution.[41]

According to the final report produced by the director of the Office for the Disposition of Confidential Documents, over 150,000 cards were recovered (Fraticelli Torres 1993).[42] The same source also reports that over 25,000 *carpetas* were found, close to 16,000 of them of individuals.[43] Information from the same report and other sources will allow one to estimate the number of persons included in the index (in 1987) at around 75,000.[44] It is important to notice that the number refers to the surviving dossiers of individuals at the moment when the scandal erupted rather than the total number of victims historically. An unknown number of *carpetas* and cards are unaccounted for and were presumably destroyed by the police[45] or removed from police headquarters by federal agents.[46] Also, it was a normal practice to destroy the files of deceased persons and afterward to even reassign that *carpeta* number to another individual.

Contrary to what some people think, the existence of lists of subversives was not something new in Puerto Rico. In a report produced by the Puerto

Rico Civil Rights Committee in 1959, David M. Helfeld (1964) documented their existence during the 1950s and the role they played in the massive detentions that followed the 1950 *nacionalista* uprising.[47] The Committee concluded that the massive arrests were "[. . .] illegal, without due process required by the law, and based on an arbitrary list. [. . .]"[48] In a letter to Helfeld and the committee, a former attorney general of Puerto Rico, Vicente Géigel Polanco, affirmed that the practice of compiling those lists was initiated during the administration of Governor Blanton Winship in the 1930s.[49] In his letter, Géigel Polanco explained that when in 1950 Governor Muñoz Marín ordered to carry out mass arrests of *nacionalistas*, the chief of the Insular Police brought some "old lists" from police headquarters. According to Géigel Polanco, the lists were cleaned because they included some people that had never been, or no longer were, *nacionalistas* or sympathizers, including some key figures in the Popular Party, such as José Trías Monge, Jaime Benítez, Víctor Gutiérrez Franqui, and others. In an interview some years later, Géigel Polanco would add that even he was on the list, along with several other key members of the ruling Popular Democratic Party with past histories of *independentista* ideas.

> On those lists of "suspicious persons," I was listed, Jaime Benítez was listed, even Muñoz's wife, Inés; Judge Pérez Pimentel, Senator Gutiérrez Franqui, and even Trias Monge. I told Muñoz that those lists were no good. Orders were given to extract names. The Mayors of towns were consulted. They, and other popular party leaders, took advantage of the opportunity to get some political enemies arrested. I personally ordered that no attorneys be arrested. But some were . . .[50]

While testifying before the Civil Rights Committee in 1958, officers of the Police of Puerto Rico recognized the existence of the "lists of subversives" and admitted that by the mid-1950s, they contained 4,257 names of "Nationalists, Communists, and subversives" (Helfeld 1964, 47, 185).

There were other occasions after the 1950s when the lists of subversives came to the public's attention. A few years later, another Civil Rights Commission report discusses the matter. The report stated:

> It has been shown that repressive authorities in Puerto Rico have compiled lists of persons and groups, and ample details about their activities, understanding that they intend to subvert the established order by forceful means and violence. They have lists of persons, details about their activities and their connections to diverse organizations in Puerto Rico and abroad, of the Communist Party of Puerto Rico, the Pro-Independence Movement, the Federation of Pro-Independence University Students, the supposed Puerto Rican Revolutionary Movement, organized and lead by Dr. Ana Livia Cordero Garcés, and the Nationalist Party of Puerto Rico.[51]

The Civil Rights Commission report concluded that "preparation and maintenance of lists of persons or groups based on their political affiliation or ideological beliefs contravenes existing constitutional norms."[52] But in spite of the denunciations by individuals, organizations, and even governmental bodies, the practice not only continued but expanded through the 1970s and 1980s.

Puerto Rico was not the only place within U.S. jurisdiction that was actively involved in dossier compiling and had a specialized intelligence unit for that purpose within its police department. That also was the case in many places throughout the United States, particularly in large urban areas (Donner 1990).

In the 1960s and 1970s, police intelligence operations in the United States received increased attention. Law enforcement journals and publications discussed the advantages of having such a unit and provided guidelines for its operation (Skousen 1966a). A nationwide network of intelligence units was even created under the auspices of the FBI. The network, called the Law Enforcement Intelligence Unit (LEIU), among other things, intended to "promote the exchange of confidential information not obtainable through regular police channels" and to establish a "central clearinghouse for this information" (Skousen 1966b).

Along with the intensification of intelligence operations at the local level, federal agencies, particularly the FBI, escalated their role and engaged in more aggressive tactics. That was the case of the FBI's Counter-Intelligence Programs (COINTELPRO), which took place from 1956 to 1971.[53] The series of counter-intelligence operations was initially introduced in 1956, directed against the Communist Party of the United States (CPUSA), eventually reaching other groups and movements, including several Puerto Rican organizations (1960–1971), the Socialist Workers Party (1961–1971), several African-American organizations (1967–1971), and organizations of the New Left (1968–1971), among others. The documentation available shows that among Puerto Rican *independentista* organizations, the main targets were the *Movimiento Pro Independencia* (MPI) and the *Federación de Universitarios Pro Independencia* (FUPI).[54]

It is precisely during the mid-to-late 1960s that the local police in Puerto Rico underwent a reorganization to "modernize" it. The Police of Puerto Rico was one of the first governmental agencies in Puerto Rico to be equipped with computers.[55] Details about the reorganization were made public through the press and internal police publications.[56] Early in the 1970s, the local intelligence unit also was reorganized and assigned additional resources. A local newspaper registered the event under the title "New Body Created to Fight Subversives; Gets $1,235,055."[57] The news piece says in part:

A new police intelligence body, trained by FBI and U.S. Navy and Army officers in the most modern techniques and use of electronic espionage equipment, will start operating in Puerto Rico with the purpose of fighting any leftist and subversive movement operating in the country.[58]

Of course, an agency that intends to keep a particular activity in complete secrecy would hardly make use of press releases with this kind of detail.
However, a little publicity would surely discourage some sectors of the population from engaging in certain political activities. The coercive potential of
public statements such as the one quoted should not be underestimated.

THE SUBVERSIVE DIASPORA

Puerto Ricans have had a continuous presence in the Continental United
States since the late nineteenth century and have participated in political
activities and organizations in many different contexts.[59] Precedents go back
at least to the formation in New York City of the *Sección de Puerto Rico* as part
of the *Partido Revolucionario Cubano* in the 1890s.[60] The growth in the presence of Puerto Ricans in the United States has entailed the projection of the
independentista activity into the Continental United States. It also has meant
the extension of repressive policies to Puerto Ricans in the United States.

When in 1958 officers of the Police of Puerto Rico attended hearings of
the government-appointed Civil Rights Committee, they recognized the
existence of the "list of subversives" and admitted that by 1950 it contained
4,257 names of "Nationalists, Communists, and subversives." As of 1958, the
police reported that while 218 were still "members of the Nationalist Party,"
2,505 of those listed were "registered voters" politically active in parties other
than the Nationalist Party of Puerto Rico. In addition, 225 had died, 97 were
"in prison in Puerto Rico or the United States," and 179 were "not active in
political organizations." The Police Internal Security Division reported that
it was "unable to locate" 240 of those listed, and that 215 were yet "to be
investigated" for the update. It is interesting to note that 561 (13.2 percent
of those listed in 1950) were now "residing in the United States." It would be
fair to assume that some of those not yet located (5.6 percent of the total) or
pending investigation (another 5.1 percent) also were residing in the United
States.[61] To what extent did they remain active as *independentistas* is an issue
for further exploration as additional documentation becomes available.
Other questions arise, such as, how much coordination existed between the
Insular Police and the New York or Chicago police departments and how successful were the FBI and other agencies in following the tracks of this *subversive diaspora* before and after this census?

Signs of collaboration, information exchange, and coordination
between police bodies in Puerto Rico, New York, Chicago, and other areas
are present in numerous documents and in other sources. Some interesting
details emerge from a memorandum from a deputy to the attorney general of
Puerto Rico, Vicente Géigel Polanco.[62] In the memo, Carlos J. Faure reports
the results of a meeting with the Internal Security agent, Astol Calero
Toledo and the special agent in charge of the FBI in San Juan, Alvin C.

Schlenker. As a result of those meetings, he proposes several ideas for planting informers in the Puerto Rican Communist Party. A key concern was
obtaining information about the activities of Puerto Rican Communists in
New York City, therefore, one of the recommendations presented was stated
in the following terms:

> Agent Calero suggested the convenience of having a "liaison" between the
> Puerto Rico Internal Security Squad and the New York metropolitan area
> Detective, by sending security agents from Puerto Rico to New York to get
> familiarized with the Puerto Rican zone and by posing as a social worker
> from the Puerto Rico employment office in New York could gather infor-
> mation in the Puerto Rican zone."[63]

The reference to the Office of Puerto Rico in New York suggests that, as
it happened with other Puerto Rico governmental agencies, the New York
office was used in intelligence-gathering and political persecution activities.
    Information on the subversive diaspora was indeed being collected. Early
in April 1954, the Internal Security Bureau of the Police of Puerto Rico produced a confidential report on "the activities in Puerto Rico of members of
the Nationalist Party residents of New York and Chicago."[64]
    The report, perhaps prompted by the *nacionalista* shooting at the U.S.
House of Representatives,[65] was compiled by agent Astol Calero in response
to a request submitted by special prosecutor José C. Aponte. It appears that
the special prosecutor requested information on specific persons who at some
point were residing in the United States, because the report includes a list
with the names of thirty-five persons for whom no records were found. It also
includes other lists of persons (most identified as *nacionalistas*, but also some
Communists), many of whom were listed with addresses in New York City or
Chicago. The entries include the full name and a short description of the
"subversive" activities of the individual being investigated. Most of the
entries make reference to the *carpeta* number assigned by the Police of Puerto
Rico to that person.
    Another section of the same report contains the names of sixteen
nationalists, residents of Chicago. One of those listed is Gonzalo Lebrón
Sotomayor, identified as the president of the Chicago branch of the *Partido
Nacionalista de Puerto Rico*.[66] Although it seems that Gonzalo Lebrón had previously been a legitimate member of the Nationalist Party, after 1954, he
emerged as a witness in cases against fellow members of the party in New
York, including his own sister, Lolita Lebrón.[67] From that point on, he would
provide detailed information on the Nationalists to the police. In a "confidential" memorandum, Sergeant Víctor B. Rodríguez reports to the chief of
the Internal Security Bureau a conversation sustained with Lebrón
Sotomayor on January 3, 1955:

[. . .] Lebrón suggested keeping an eye on Nationalist Ruth Reynolds, since he is certain that her visits to Puerto Rico are connected to Nationalist activities. [. . .] He has personal knowledge that she is used by the Nationalist Party leadership to carry secret messages that she hides in her brassiere. That when he was a leader of the movement in Chicago, she visited him on three occasions, and each time she carried messages sent from New York by Pinto Gandía.[68]

Political espionage was directed not only against activists or suspected members of the Nationalist Party. A Spanish exile, Jesús de Galíndez, who for many years was a very active figure in Basque and Latino organizations, also was a prolific FBI informer. He not only infiltrated the *Comité Pro Conmutación de Sentencia de Muerte de Oscar Collazo* in the early 1950s but also provided information on the Puerto Rican Independence Party and its leader, Gilberto Concepción de Gracia, as well as organizations such as the *Mutualista Obrera Mexicana, Club Obrero Español, Club Cultural Chileno,* and the American Labor Party.[69] Galíndez also helped in the identification of U.S. nationals who sympathized with the Puerto Rican Nationalist movement, Dominican activists in New York who were fighting the Trujillo dictatorship, and Cubans who were organizing against the Batista dictatorship.[70]

Even Puerto Rican activists who attempted to expand their participation in mainstream organizations in the United States were victims of surveillance. In December 1954, FBI informer Jesús de Galíndez gave J. Edgar Hoover "the best possible Christmas gift," as one author put it,

[. . .] a detailed report containing the names of all Hispanics, particularly Puerto Ricans, that were "infiltrating" the Hispanic sections of the Democratic and Republican parties in New York.[71]

The FBI was clearly aware of the "subversive" potential of the Puerto Rican Diaspora. Therefore, it is not strange that, from the very beginning, FBI's COINTELPRO operations were directed against Puerto Rican organizations and individuals on the island and various cities across the United States, particularly New York and Chicago. In fact, the August 4, 1960,[72] memorandum authorizing the first COINTELPRO operations against Puerto Ricans stated: "San Juan and New York should give this matter studied consideration and thereafter furnish the Bureau observations, suggestions and recommendations." A copy of this memorandum was sent to the Chicago office and another to the Washington field office.

In another memorandum later that year, Hoover insisted:

Because of the large number of Puerto Ricans residing in New York, and the fact that a number of Puerto Rican independence organizations are active in New York, New York and San Juan should exchange ideas relative to tactics and techniques which may be effective in your divisions.[73]

THE FEDERAL CONNECTION

In December 1999, the governor of Puerto Rico at the time presented a public "solemn and sincere apology" to the thousands of Puerto Ricans who had
been the victims of political spying during the previous decades and
announced the creation of a special fund to compensate them.[74] Although
the apology represented a moral victory for the thousands of victims, many
issues remained unresolved, particularly to what extent the FBI and other
federal agencies were responsible for the decades' long campaign of political
persecution against *independentistas*.

The claim that the FBI was involved in activities of political persecution
of Puerto Rican *independentistas* is not new. Advocates of Puerto Rican independence have been denouncing FBI persecution from the 1930s to the present time. However, the FBI has almost consistently denied that allegation.
Only a few weeks after the governor's apology, the special agent in charge of
the FBI field office in San Juan, Marlene Hunter, insisted that the Bureau had
no connection with the *carpetas* scandal or with the political persecution of
Puerto Ricans.[75]

The examination of documentary evidence that I have conducted clearly
shows otherwise. The evidence found in the police *carpetas* in Puerto Rico
showed that the FBI not only received and supplied information for the
police files but also had physical access to those files. Furthermore, there is
evidence that the FBI trained and directed the police agents involved and
was even responsible for the design of the system (Bosque-Pérez 2001).

The persistent claim for answers, coming from concerned citizens, human
rights advocates, academics, and journalists, led the Puerto Rico Senate to
approve a resolution in March 2000 to investigate the involvement of federal
agencies in the persecution of Puerto Rican *independentistas*.[76] Only a few days
later, U.S. Representative José E. Serrano (D-NY) raised the issue with FBI
Director Louis J. Freeh during the FBI's budget hearing before a subcommittee
of the House Appropriations Committee. Surprising many observers, the FBI
director not only admitted the agency's involvement in previous abuses but
also offered to conduct a thorough search of FBI files.[77] Director Freeh subsequently appointed a task force that has identified a large number of documents
(up to 1.8 million pages, according to some estimates) related to Puerto
Ricans.[78] Boxes with thousands of documents began arriving to Congressman
Serrano's office by mid-May 2000.[79] The first few glimpses of the documents
begin to confirm what some have anticipated in the debates of recent years:
the hidden history of political persecution against Puerto Rican independence
activists could be one of the most shameful infringements of political and
human rights under U.S. jurisdiction during the twentieth century.

While the involvement of the FBI in the political persecution of Puerto
Ricans is now difficult to deny, the scope, duration, and consequences of

those activities are matters that would take years to research. Clearly, sectors, organizations, and individuals that have presented some degree of opposition to U.S. presence in Puerto Rico have faced a long-lasting pattern of state-sponsored denial of basic political rights. That pattern of political persecution is characterized among others by the following:

- U.S.-sponsored political persecution against Puerto Rican *independentistas* is as old as the U.S. military intervention of the island. The organization of the colonial repressive apparatuses started only weeks after the invasion of July 25, 1898.
- In one way or another, political persecution has reached large sectors of the Puerto Rican population, not only by repression or persecution of anti-colonial activists but also by attempts to prevent other sectors from becoming *independentistas*.
- Throughout the twentieth century, the United States implemented a policy of criminalization of the pro-independence movement and its followers; it propagated the ideology that being *independentista* was a criminal activity.
- At different points, U.S. federal agencies have made preparations for massive "preventive" arrests of Puerto Ricans. As part of those plans, for decades the FBI has compiled lists of thousands of Puerto Ricans.
- Puerto Rico has experienced cases of political assassination ranging from massive, such as the 1937 Ponce Massacre, where twenty unarmed civilians were killed, to more selective. The most prominent among the latter are the 1978 Cerro Maravilla killings and the still-unresolved politically motivated murders of Santiago Mari Pesquera (March 24, 1976), Juan Rafael Caballero (October 13, 1977), Carlos Muñiz Varela (April 28, 1979), and Angel Rodríguez Cristóbal (November 11, 1979).[80]
- In many of the actions against Puerto Rican *independentistas*, the FBI and other federal agencies have violated Puerto Rican and U.S. laws and have violated the basic constitutional and human rights of thousands of Puerto Ricans.
- While the U.S. government publicly proclaimed its respect for the right to self-determination of the Puerto Rican people, the FBI secretly interfered with electoral processes, including the 1967 referendum, and it tried to sabotage *independentista* participation in those processes (see Fernandez 1996).
- Participating in the political persecution against Puerto Rican *independentistas* were state and city police bodies from places such as New York and Chicago, as well as federal agencies such as the FBI and the intelligence branches of the armed forces.
- As the presence of Puerto Ricans in the United States expanded throughout the twentieth century, the political persecution of Puerto Rican activists in the mainland also has increased.

• Since 1898, hundreds of Puerto Ricans have suffered terms of imprisonment as a result of being prosecuted for actions connected to their militancy in the struggle for independence. In many cases, the disproportionate prison terms imposed—when contrasted to violations charged—clearly
illustrate the political nature of the trials (see the chapters by Paralitici and
Susler in this book).

A CULTURE OF FEAR

The activities involved in compiling *carpetas* (*carpeteo*, as it is called in
Puerto Rico) were much more than a system of political espionage. Spying
on law-abiding citizens based on their political beliefs and associations was
only a fraction of it. Through the extensive use of paid informers to infiltrate organizations, visits by intelligence agents to neighborhoods, schools,
or work centers, and even occasional acts of harassment or physical aggression, the *carpeteo* contributed to the generation of a culture of fear among
large sectors of the population. Furthermore, the system helped in the
implementation of other extraordinary repressive measures, such as the
mass arrests that took place in Puerto Rico early in November 1950 (immediately after the *Nacionalista* uprising), as well as the court cases and incarcerations of 1950 and 1954 under the Puerto Rican version of the Smith
Act, known as *La Mordaza* (Acosta 1987).[81] The extent of state involvement in other cases of violence against political dissidents, such as several
unresolved cases of political assassination that took place during the 1970s,
has yet to be determined.

The practice of *carpeteo*, in which the Police of Puerto Rico engaged for
so many decades, rather than being an anomaly must be understood as one
of the key features of a larger system by which colonial domination was
established and sustained in Puerto Rico. To the extent that it combines a
variety of coercive and ideological factors, it presents an excellent opportunity for the examination of important features in the process of formation
and reproduction of U.S. hegemony in Puerto Rico. Still, cases of political
violence, persecution, and violation of human rights in the twentieth century have received relatively limited attention in Puerto Rican historiography. The two recent scandals, Cerro Maravilla and the *carpetas* cases, have
helped call attention to these matters, both in terms of media coverage and
academic research.

Attempts to analyze the process of consolidation of U.S. hegemony in
Puerto Rico should carefully consider the role played by the mechanisms
described here. When taken as a whole, it is clear that the diversity of repressive practices implemented since 1898 against Puerto Rican anti-colonial
activists has attempted to eradicate dissent and promote acquiescence and
has tended to generate a culture of fear. With deep, one-century-old roots,

that culture of fear still survives. Its full eradication would require a strong determination of the Puerto Rican people to affirm and defend key political, civil, and human rights as well as the will of the U.S. government to respect those rights. Nothing less would be able to protect all involved sectors from the ghosts of political violence and conflict that so easily can degenerate into painful and costly terrorism.

NOTES

The author wishes to express gratitude to many colleagues, students, and friends who provided encouragement and critical comments regarding several versions of this chapter. Special thanks to Ada G. Fuentes-Rivera.

1. U.S. Attorney General Annual Report, 1920, 180. As quoted in Donner 1980.

2. My translation. The full text was reproduced in Bosque-Pérez and Colón Morera 1997.

3. For news coverage by U.S.-based media, see, for instance, "Puerto Rico Finds Police Kept Track of Private Citizens," *Miami Herald*, August 21, 1987; "Island of Repression," *The Progressive*, September 1989, p. 35; "The Bureau Goes to San Juan," *The Nation*, November 7, 1988, pp. 456–60; *"Los que fueron fichados pueden solicitar sus carpetas,"* *El Diario-La Prensa*, July 25, 1989, p. 11; "Big Brother Kept Tabs on Activists in Puerto Rico," *Miami Herald*, July 19, 1992, p. 1A; "Secret Puerto Rico Spy Files Released," *Miami Herald*, August 8, 1992, p. 6A. See also Cornell 1987.

4. See *Noriega Rodríguez et al. v. Hernández Colón*, 122 DPR 650 (November 21, 1988); 130 DPR 919 (June 30, 1992).

5. In Puerto Rico, before 1987 the term *carpeta*, translated as "folder," was not commonly used to refer to a file. It is possible that the police deliberately used the uncommon term in order to protect the secrecy of the files, or that the term was copied through contact and exchange with other repressive bodies in Latin America, where it was indeed used to refer to files. For some instances where the term *carpeta* is used to refer to police files, see the works on the disappeared in Argentina (Comisión Nacional sobre la Desaparición de Personas 1986 and Mellibovsky 1990).

6. Around 16,000 individuals had detailed *carpetas*, ranging from a few pages to several thousand.

7. For instance, there was a *carpeta* for Ruth M. Reynolds, a U.S. pacifist who sustained a long-term association with the Puerto Rican Nationalist Party, and another for Conrad Lynn, an African-American lawyer who provided legal representation to several *nacionalistas*.

8. According to some sources, at a meeting in *La Fortaleza* (the governor's mansion) between then Governor Carlos Romero Barceló and top police officials, someone said, "We can't let Puerto Rico become another Northern Ireland. We have to give these people a hard lesson" (Suárez 1987; Comisión de Derechos Civiles 1989, 87 ff.).

9. Several members of the police department went to prison after being convicted of perjury and other charges in local and federal courts. Some of them also pleaded guilty to reduced charges of second-degree murder. See "5 Ex-Puerto Rican Officers Sentenced in 1978 Slayings," *New York Times*, June 20, 1987, p. 34.

10. William Colón Berríos pleaded guilty to conspiracy and perjury charges related to the Cerro Maravilla case.

11. *"Ex-Agente de Inteligencia Denuncia: 'Hay Subversivos en el Gobierno de Puerto Rico,'"* *Crónica Gráfica* 10:137 (June 1987). My translation.

12. Mattos Cintrón (1988) has elaborated on the main elements that contributed to the consolidation of U.S. hegemony in Puerto Rico. In addition to the military invasion (a first act that permits the others) and the formation of a repressive apparatus, he mentions: (1) the formation and consolidation of an economic base; (2) the development of political hegemony (through the expansion of civil rights and control of the electoral process); (3) control over the cultural spaces (in particular, the educational apparatus and religious institutions); (4) the gradual expansion of women's rights (through expanded access to education and work).

13. This was the case of Colonel George Shanton, who was chief of the Insular Police from 1909 to 1922, and Colonel G. W. Lewis, from 1923 to 1930. See Martínez Valentín 1995, 70–71.

14. For instance, Colonel E. Francis Riggs, who was chief of the Insular Police from 1933 to 1936, had performed important intelligence and military duties in Russia (1916–1920) and in the Philippines (1913–1914). See Rosado 1992; Bidwell 1986; Francis 1970.

15. A facsimile of the report was made available to the Civil Rights Commission investigation of 1987 (Comisión de Derechos Civiles 1989, hereafter quoted as CDC 1989), vol. 2, 132–35, document 11, February 24, 1900.

16. My translation.

17. May 11, 1918, confidential memorandum from Lieutenant Colonel Orval P. Townshend to the Chief of Military Intelligence Branch, CDC 1989.

18. See also Negroni c1993, 400.

19. After the extension of U.S. citizenship to Puerto Ricans in 1917, compulsory military service also was extended to Puerto Rican males. By 1919, there were Puerto Rican veterans of World War I. See Rodríguez Beruff 1988; Estades Font 1988; Paralitici 1998.

20. The Puerto Rico National Guard has been used in a few occasions to repress political or social "unrest" (1950, 1973, and 1974). However, it receives constant training in "riot control" techniques and therefore serves as a "reserve." During the mid-1930s, it was partially mobilized to deal with student protests on the island.

21. Particularly helpful in understanding the dynamics of political repression in the United States are works such as Amnesty International 1981; Churchill and Wall 1990a, 1990b; Davis 1992, 1997; Donner 1980, 1990; Goldstein 1978a, 1978b; Kohn 1994, 1986; Preston 1994; Talbert 1991; Theoharis 1978a, 1978b, 1976–1977.

22. For background on the social conditions during the first decades of the century, see Scarano 1993 (chapters 20–21).

23. Increased activism is reflected by the fact that, starting in 1914, the Governor's Annual Report included a section devoted to labor strike activity (see García and Quintero Rivera 1986). In 1917, the recently created Socialist Party obtained 14 percent of the vote and won six municipalities. In 1920, it increased to 23.7 percent of the vote and eight municipalities. For an overview of workers' activism during the period, see García and Quintero Rivera 1986.

24. The raids came to be known by the name of Mitchell Palmer, then the U.S. attorney general. On January 2, 1920, alone, between 5,000 and 10,000 persons were arrested, including aliens and citizens (Donner 1980, 36).

25. Although J. Edgar Hoover's files in the FBI refer to a secret 1936 presidential directive to expand the surveillance activities of so-called "subversives," there has been some debate as to what extent President Roosevelt was behind such a directive. Compare, for instance, Theoharis 1976–1977 and Croog 1992.

26. As quoted by Theoharis 1976–1977, 655; emphasis in original.

27. Sections of this memorandum are quoted in different works, for instance, Goldstein 1978a, 560, and Theoharis 1978b, 1020. The latter, however, omits the reference to the Nationalist Party.

28. CDC 1989, vol. 2, 1–17, document 1, February 27, 1936.

29. *El Imparcial*, February 20, 1936, pp. 1–3. My translation.

30. CDC 1989, vol. 2, p. 11, Document 1. Regarding the first issue of the newspaper, the agents reported that "no copy of it could be found."

31. That was the case of Astol Calero Toledo, who graduated from the academy in 1946 and was chief of the *Escuadrón de Seguridad Interna* and later the *Superintendente*. Other FBI academy-trained *Superintendentes* were: Salvador T. Roig (class of 1946), Luis Maldonado Trinidad (1961), Jorge L. Collazo (1965), and Desiderio Cartagena Ortiz (1968). See U.S. Government Printing Office 1990, 212.

32. See the chapter by Estades-Font in this book.

33. CDC 1989, vol. 2, document 21, July 16, 1936.

34. Ibid., document 31, October 15, 1940.

35. Ibid., document 19, December 24, 1942.

36. Ibid., document 34, December 22, 1942.

37. Ibid., document 18, February 8, 1945.

38. Ibid., document 36, March 1, 1943.

39. Federal Bureau of Investigation, File # 100-5745, April 1, 1943.

40. Following the model used by the FBI, such information was indexed using 4″ by 6″ cards.

41. From a confidential *Investigations Handbook* of the Intelligence Division (Police of Puerto Rico), discovered in 1987. See the full text in Bosque-Pérez and Colón Morera 1997.

42. According to this report, 151,541 cards were recovered: 135,188 were found in the central headquarters of the Police of Puerto Rico, 11,353 in the *Comandancias de Distrito* (district headquarters), and another 5,000 in the *Negociado de Investigaciones Especiales* (NIE), a division of the Puerto Rico Justice Department.

43. A total of 25,165 *carpetas* were found: 16,657 in the central headquarters of the Police of Puerto Rico and 8,608 in the district headquarters. Since most of the latter were duplicates, the final count of persons with *carpetas* was 15,589. Individual *carpetas* vary in size, from a few dozen to several thousand pages.

44. There were also over 60,000 cards of organizations, vehicles, and so on. One person could have several cards: for each organization to which he or she belonged, for each vehicle registered under his or her name, and so on.

45. According to news reports in 1992, the *carpetas* of César Andreu Iglesias and Santiago "Chagui" Mari (the assassinated son of *independentista* leader Juan Mari Brás) had disappeared and were presumably destroyed. See *"Desaparecida la carpeta de 'Chagui,'"* *Claridad* (San Juan, Puerto Rico), July 10–16, 1992, p. 5; *"Ex Rector UPR: Jaime Benítez también recogió una carpeta,"* *Claridad* (San Juan, Puerto Rico), July 17–23, 1992, p. 3; *"Destruída la carpeta de César Andreu Iglesias,"* *Claridad* (San Juan, Puerto Rico), July 17–23, 1992, p. 5; *"Investigan intervención del gobierno en destrucción de carpetas,"* *Claridad* (San Juan, Puerto Rico), July 10–16, 1992, p. 7.). For awhile, the voluminous *carpeta* of Pedro Albizu Campos was presumed "lost," but it was eventually found.

46. News reports indicated that during an expedition to police headquarters, a group of FBI agents removed *carpetas* and documents. See *"Federales se apropian de expedientes y carpetas,"* *Claridad* (San Juan, Puerto Rico), July 10–16, 1992, p. 3.

47. The *Comité del Gobernador para el Estudio de los Derechos Civiles* was created in 1956 by Governor Luis Muñoz Marín and produced several reports on civil rights issues in Puerto Rico. One of those reports was written by Helfeld (1964).

48. Comisión de Derechos Civiles 1973, 91 (my translation).

49. General Blanton Winship was the governor of Puerto Rico from February 1934 to 1939. For some details on his practices, see Rosado 1992. Also see Ferrao 1990, 150ff.

50. My translation. This interview with César Andreu Iglesias and Samuel A. Aponte, published in April 1972 in *La Hora*, was reproduced in Bothwell González 1979, vol. 4, 497–504. In a testimony before the Civil Rights Commission, José Trías Monge, former chief justice of the Puerto Rico Supreme Court, confirmed some of these names (see CDC 1989, 49). Jaime Benítez, former chancellor of the University of Puerto Rico, was among the citizens who received a *carpeta* when they were returned in 1992. *"Ex Rector UPR: Jaime Benítez también recogió una carpeta,"* *Claridad* (San Juan, Puerto Rico), July 17–23, 1992, p. 3.

51. Comisión de Derechos Civiles 1970, 24. Annotations omitted; my translation.

52. Ibid., 58.

53. For a brief, yet an excellent, discussion of COINTELPRO operations see Chomsky 1975. For more detailed accounts, see Davis 1992; Churchill and Wall 1990b.

54. For more specific details on COINTELPRO against Puerto Ricans, see the excellent work of Merrill-Ramírez 1990. See also Gautier Mayoral and Blanco Stahl 1997 [1979].

55. *"En Torno al Centro de Máquinas,"* El Retén, Vocero Informativo de la Policía de Puerto Rico 1:3 (August 15, 1967): 12.

56. See, for instance, *"Comienza la reorganización de la Policía,"* El Retén, Vocero Informativo de la Policía de Puerto Rico 1:4 (September 15, 1967): 1–2, and *"Reorganización total en cuerpo Policía: Rodríguez Aponte anuncia serán reorganizados todos los cuerpos,"* El Imparcial, July 31, 1967, p. A3.

57. *"Crean nuevo cuerpo combatirá subversivos: Le asignan $1,235,055,"* El Imparcial (San Juan, Puerto Rico), January 11, 1972.

58. Ibid. My translation.

59. Although the body of work that deals with the political participation and political activism of Puerto Ricans in the United States is growing, there is still much to study in terms of Puerto Ricans and their participation in progressive and revolutionary organizations.

60. See Bernardo Vega's (1984) memoirs, particularly chapters 7 to 10, for a vivid description of the activities of Puerto Rican and Cuban political exiles in New York City during the last decades of the nineteenth century.

61. The figures are taken from the 1958 Internal Security Division inventory reproduced in Helfeld 1964.

62. CDC 1989, document 10, December 19, 1950.

63. Ibid. My translation.

64. CDC 1989, document 7, April 8, 1954.

65. The shooting took place on March 1, 1954. See Medina Ramírez 1970; Rosado 1992.

66. That particular entry reads:

Gonzalo Lebrón Sotomayor—Resides at 2110 West Jackson Boulevard, Chicago, Illinois. Brother of Lolita Lebrón, Nationalist that shot four Congressmen in the United States. President of the Nationalist Party in Chicago. Considered a dangerous Nationalist. Has been seen in meetings and rallies with Nationalist leaders in Lares [from where] it is said has come in special mission for the Party. (see note 68, below)

67. Gonzalo was part of a group of seventeen *nacionalistas* accused in 1954 in New York of "conspiring to overthrow the U.S. government." With another three of the accused, Gonzalo testified in exchange for a suspended sentence. For details, see, for instance, Medina Ramírez 1970.

68. Ruth Reynolds Papers, *Carpeta #1340, División de Inteligencia, Policía de Puerto Rico* (000203–000204). My translation.

69. See Unanue 1999 for an account of Galíndez and his activities.

70. I have partially examined the massive file on Galíndez released by the FBI under the Freedom of Information Act.

71. Unanue 1999, 56. My translation.

72. J. Edgar Hoover, FBI Director, Memorandum to Special Agent in Charge, San Juan Field Office, August 4, 1960.

73. CDC 1989, document 39, November 14, 1960.

74. Executive Order OE-1999–62, December 14, 1999. The Executive Order signed by Governor Rosselló provided for compensations ranging from $6,000, for those who had already sued the government, to $3,000, for those who could prove that they intended to do so. Only persons with *carpetas* longer than 30 pages and those willing to sign a document releasing the government and third parties from any further legal action qualified for the compensation. After the June 12, 2000, deadline established by the government, not all of those who qualified finally accepted the compensation. Many of the victims announced that they would not accept the symbolic compensation offered by Governor Rosselló and would pursue legal action. Before the Executive Order was issued, there were over 1,300 *carpetas*-related lawsuits pending in Puerto Rican courts, seeking more than $1 billion in damages. Several cases have been resolved so far, the first one through a settlement in which José Caraballo López received a compensation of $45,000 from the government. In the fall of 2003, the court granted compensations of up to $75,000 per person to other plaintiffs. See *El Nuevo Día, "Testimonio de la persecución política,"* June 4, 2003, and *"Justicia negociará sobre carpetas,"* June 6, 2003, p. 46.

75. See Laura Candelas, *"FBI tiene expedientes, no carpetas," Primera Hora,* January 17, 2000, p. 4A.

76. Puerto Rican Senate, Resolution No. 3063, March 14, 2000. Copies of this and other documents mentioned in this section are posted on http://www.cipdc.org.

77. "Serrano Questions FBI Director Freeh about Independentistas," Congressman Serrano's Office, Press Release, March 16, 2000.

78. See "FBI Chief Turns over Agency's Files of P.R.," *San Juan Star,* May 18, 2000, cover, p. 6.

79. See Bosque-Pérez 2000; also see "Feds' Files Reveal Dirty War," *Daily News,* May 23, 2000, p. 14.

80. On January 11, 1975, Angel Luis Charbonier and another Puerto Rican worker were killed (and more than a dozen were hurt) by a bomb that exploded in a restaurant in Mayagüez just minutes before a public rally. On March 24, 1976, Santiago Mari Pesquera, the eldest son of one of the main leaders of the independence movement in Puerto Rico (Juan Mari Brás), was mysteriously assassinated (see Mari Brás 1993; also see "Mari Bras' Son Murdered; Slaying Termed Execution," *San Juan Star,* March 26, 1976, p. 1). On or around October 13, 1977, labor organizer Juan Rafael Caballero was kidnapped, tortured, and assassinated by elements of a death squad operating inside of the Puerto Rican Police. On July 25, 1978, Carlos Soto Arriví and Arnaldo Darío Rosado were led by an infiltrated agent to an ambush in Cerro Maravilla, where they were brutalized and killed in cold blood, as was eventually established by an investigation of the Puerto Rican Senate (see Suárez 1987). On

April 28, 1979, Carlos Muñiz Varela, a member of the Cuban community in Puerto Rico who promoted dialogue with Cuba, was assassinated (see Villablanca 1979b). On November 11, 1979, Angel Rodríguez Cristóbal, who had been arrested for his participation in the campaign against the presence of the U.S. Navy in Vieques, was found dead in his cell under mysterious circumstances.

81. See also the chapter by Acosta in this book.

WORKS CITED

Acosta, Ivonne. 1987. *La Mordaza: Puerto Rico 1948–1957*. Río Piedras, Puerto Rico: Editorial Edil.

———. 1992. "*Hacia una historia de la persecución política en Puerto Rico.*" *Homines* 15:2–16:1:142–51.

———. 1993. *La palabra como delito. Los discursos por los que condenaron a Pedro Albizu Campos, 1948–1950*. San Juan: Editorial Cultural.

———. 1995. "De Winship a las Carpetas." Pp. 91–102 in *Controversias Históricas*, ed. I. Acosta. San Juan: Librería Editorial Ateneo.

Acosta-Belén, Edna, and Virginia Sánchez Korrol. 1993. "The World of Jesús Colón." Pp. 13–30 in *The Way It Was and Other Writings: Jesús Colón*, ed. E. Acosta-Belén and V. Sánchez Korrol. Houston: Arte Público Press.

Amnesty International. 1981. *Proposal for a Commission of Inquiry into the effect of Domestic Intelligence Activities on Criminal Trials in the United States of America*. Nottingham, England: Russell Press.

Aponte Pérez, Francisco. 1995. *Las Víctimas del Cerro Maravilla*. San Juan: Centro de Estudios Legales y Sociales (CELS).

Bennett, William R. 1923. "El Departamento de Policía." Pp. 272–78 in *El libro de Puerto Rico*, ed. Eugenio Fernández García et al. San Juan: El Libro Azul.

Bidwell, Bruce W. 1986. *History of the Military Intelligence Division, Department of the Army General Staff: 1775–1941*. Frederick, Md.: University Publications of America.

Blackstock, Nelson. 1988. *COINTELPRO: The FBI's Secret War on Political Freedom*. New York: Pathfinder.

Boccia Paz, Alfredo, and Myrian Angélica González y Rosa Palau Aguilar. 1994. *Es mi informe.—Los archivos secretos de la Policía de Stroessner*. 2d ed. Asunción, Paraguay: Centro de Documentación y Estudios.

Bosque-Pérez, Ramón. 1997a. "A diez años del caso de las carpetas: Una reflexión necesaria." *Diálogo* (August 1997): 27.

———. 1997b. "Carpetas y persecución política en Puerto Rico: la dimensión federal." Pp. 37–90 in *Las carpetas: Persecución política y derechos civiles en Puerto Rico (ensayos y documentos)*, ed. Bosque-Pérez and Colón Morera. Río Piedras, Puerto Rico: Centro para la Investigación y Promoción de los Derechos Civiles.

40 RAMÓN BOSQUE-PÉREZ

————. 2000. "Puerto Ricans and the *Carpetas* Case: Public Apology Unable to Close the Old Wounds of Political Persecution." *The NPRC Report* 19:1 (Summer 2000): 4–5, 11.

————. 2001. "Los federales y el carpeteo en Puerto Rico." Presentation at a forum sponsored by the Puerto Rico Journalists Association and the Puerto Rico Bar Association, March 9, 2001, San Juan, Puerto Rico.

Bosque-Pérez, Ramón, and José Javier Colón Morera, eds. 1997. *Las carpetas: Persecución política y derechos civiles en Puerto Rico (ensayos y documentos)*. Río Piedras, Puerto Rico: Centro para la Investigación y Promoción de los Derechos Civiles.

Bothwell González, Reece B. 1979. *Puerto Rico: Cien años de lucha política*. Volume 4. Río Piedras, Puerto Rico: Editorial Universitaria.

Browning, Frank. 1970. "From Rumble to Revolution: The Young Lords." Pp. 231–45 in *The Puerto Rican Experience: A Sociological Sourcebook*, ed. Francesco Cordasco and Eugene Bucchioni. Totowa, N.J.: Rowman & Littlefield.

Cabán, Pedro A. 1999. *Constructing a Colonial People: Puerto Rico and the United States, 1898–1932*. Boulder, Colo.: Westview Press.

Calloni, Stella. 1994. "The Horror Archives of Operation Condor." *CovertAction Quarterly* 50 (Fall 1994): 7–13, 57–61.

Carnoy, Martin. 1984. *The State and Political Theory*. Princeton: Princeton University Press.

Carrión, Juan Manuel. 1987. "*Centinelas de la democracia: La Guardia Nacional de Puerto Rico (Crítica a un aspecto de la ideología dominante).*" *El Caribe Contemporáneo* 14 (June 1987): 67–91.

Carson, Clayborne. 1991. *Malcolm X: The FBI File*. New York: Carroll and Graf.

Chomsky, Noam. 1975. "Introduction." Pp. 9–38 in *COINTELPRO: The FBI's Secret War on Political Freedom*, ed. Nelson Blackstock. New York: Pathfinder.

Churchill, Ward, and Jim Vander Wall. 1990a. *Agents of Repression: The FBI's Secret Wars against the Black Panther Party and the American Indian Movement*. Boston: South End Press.

————. 1990b. *The COINTELPRO Papers: Documents from the FBI's Secret Wars against Domestic Dissent*. Boston: South End Press.

Colangelo, Philip. 1995. "The Secret FISA Court: Rubber Stamping on Rights." *CovertAction Quarterly* 53 (Summer): 43–49.

Colón, Jesús. 1982. *A Puerto Rican in New York and Other Sketches*. New York: International Publishers.

————. 1993. *The Way It Was and Other Writings*. Houston: Arte Público Press.

Colón-Morera, José Javier. 1997. "Consenso, represión y descolonización," in *Las carpetas: persecución política y derechos civiles en Puerto Rico (ensayos y documentos)*, R. Bosque-Pérez and J.J. Colón-Morera (editors). Río Piedras, Puerto Rico: Centro para la Investigación y Promoción de los Derechos Civiles.

———. 1997. "Consenso, represión y descolonización." Pp. 3–35 in *Las carpetas: Persecución política y derechos civiles en Puerto Rico (ensayos y documentos)*, eds. Ramón Bosque-Pérez, and José Javier Colón Morera. Río Piedras, Puerto Rico: Centro para la Investigación y Promoción de los Derechos Civiles (CIPDC).

Comisión de Derechos Civiles (CDC). 1970. *La vigilancia e investigación policíaca y los derechos civiles*. San Juan: Comisión de Derechos Civiles.

———. 1973. *Informes de la Comisión de Derechos Civiles del Estado Libre Asociado de Puerto Rico, Tomo 1*. Orford, N.H.: Equity.

———. 1989. *Informe sobre discrimen y persecución por razones políticas: la práctica gubernamental de mantener listas, ficheros y expedientes de ciudadanos por razón de su ideología política*. 1989-CDC-028. San Juan: Comisión de Derechos Civiles.

Comisión Nacional sobre la Desaparición de Personas. 1986. *Nunca más*. Buenos Aires: Editorial Universitaria de Buenos Aires (EUDEBA).

Cornell, Barbara. 1987. "An Island Full of Subversives." *Columbia Journalism Review* 26:4: 9–10.

Cowan, Paul, Nick Egleson, and Nat Hentoff. 1974. *State Secrets: Police Surveillance in America*. New York: Holt, Rinehart, and Winston.

Croog, Charles F. 1992. "FBI Political Surveillance and the Isolationist-Interventionist Debate, 1939–1941." *The Historian* 54:3: 441–58.

Cruz Monclova, Lidio. 1979. *Historia de Puerto Rico (siglo XIX)*. Río Piedras, Puerto Rico: Editorial Universitaria.

Curry, Richard O., ed. 1988. *Freedom at Risk, Secrecy, Censorship, and Repression in the 1980s*. Philadelphia: Temple University Press.

Davidson, Osha. 1989. "Keeping Track of a Colony: U.S. Intelligence in Puerto Rico." *CovertAction Information Bulletin* 31 (Winter 1989): 40–41.

Davis, Darién J. 1996. *"The Arquivos Das Policias Politicais of the State of Rio de Janeiro."* *Latin American Research Review* 31:1: 99–104.

Davis, James K. 1992. *Spying on America: The FBI's Domestic Counter-Intelligence Program*. New York: Praeger.

———. 1997. *Assault on the Left: The FBI and the Sixties Antiwar Movement*. Westport, Conn.: Praeger.

Delgado Pasapera, Germán. 1984. *Puerto Rico: Sus luchas emancipadoras (1850–1898)*. Río Piedras, Puerto Rico: Editorial Cultural.

Donner, Frank J. 1980. *The Age of Surveillance: The Aims and Methods of America's Political Intelligence System*. New York: Alfred A. Knopf.

———. 1990. *Protectors of Privilege: Red Squads and Police Surveillance in Urban America*. Berkeley: University of California Press.

Elliff, John T. 1979. *The Reform of FBI Intelligence Operations*. Princeton: Princeton University Press.

Estades Font, María E. 1988. *La presencia militar de Estados Unidos en Puerto Rico 1898–1918: Intereses estratégicos y dominación colonial*. Río Piedras, Puerto Rico: Ediciones Huracán.

———. 1996. "Colonialismo y democracia: Los informes de la División de Inteligencia Militar del Ejército de los Estados Unidos sobre las actividades subversivas en Puerto Rico, 1936–1941." *Revista Universidad de América* 8:1–2: 83–90.

Fernandez, Ronald. 1994. *Prisoners of Colonialism: The Struggle for Justice in Puerto Rico*. Monroe, Maine: Common Courage Press.

———. 1996. *The Disenchanted Island: Puerto Rico and the United States in the Twentieth Century*. 2d ed. Westport, Conn.: Praeger.

Ferrao, Luis Angel. 1990. *Pedro Albizu Campus y el nacionalismo puertorriqueño: 1930–1939*. N.p.: Editorial Cultural.

Francis, David R. 1970. *Russia from the American Embassy: 1916–1918*. New York: Arno Press.

Fraticelli Torres, Migdalia. 1993. *Informe final de la Directora Ejecutiva al concluir las gestiones del Centro Para Disponer de Documentos Confidenciales*. San Juan: Tribunal Superior de Puerto Rico.

García, Gervasio L., and Angel G. Quintero Rivera. 1986. *Desafío y solidaridad: Breve historia del movimiento obrero puertorriqueño*. Río Piedras, Puerto Rico: Ediciones Huracán.

Garrow, David J. 1983. *The FBI and Martin Luther King Jr*. New York: Penguin Books.

Gautier Mayoral, Carmen. 1983. "Notes on the Repression Practiced by U.S. Intelligence Agencies in Puerto Rico." *Revista Jurídica de la Universidad de Puerto Rico* 52:3: 431–50.

Gautier Mayoral, Carmen et al. 1979. *Persecution of the Puerto Rican Independence Movements and Their Leaders by the Counterintelligence Program (COINTELPRO) of the United States' Federal Bureau of Investigation (FBI), 1960–1971*. San Juan, Puerto Rico. Mimeograph. Unpublished manuscript.

Gautier Mayoral, Carmen, and Teresa Blanco Stahl. 1997 [1979]. "COINTELPRO en Puerto Rico. Análisis de documentos secretos del FBI, 1960–1971." Pp. 255–97 in *Las carpetas: Persecución política y derechos civiles en Puerto Rico (ensayos y documentos)*, ed. R. Bosque-Pérez and J. J. Colón Morera. Río Piedras, Puerto Rico: Centro para la Investigación y Promoción de los Derechos Civiles.

Gelbspan, Ross. 1991. *Break-ins, Death Threats, and the FBI: The Covert War against the Central America Movement*. Boston: South End Press.

Gentry, Curt. 1992. *J. Edgar Hoover: The Man and the Secrets*. New York: Plume.

Glick, Brian. 1989. *War at Home: Covert Action against U.S. Activists and What We Can Do about It*. Boston: South End Press.

Goldstein, Robert Justin. 1978a. "An American Gulag? Summary Arrest and Emergency Detention of Political Dissidents in the United States." *Columbia Human Rights Law Review* 10: 541–73.

————. 1978b. *Political Repression in Modern America: From 1870 to the Present*. Cambridge, Mass.: Schenkman.

Gutiérrez, José Angel. 1986. "Chicanos and Mexicans Under Surveillance, 1940 to 1980." Pp. 29–58 in *Renato Rosaldo Lecture Series Monograph, vol. 2, series 1984–85* (Spring 1986), ed. Ignacio M. García. Tucson: University of Arizona, Mexican American Studies and Research Center.

Guzmán, Pablo Yoruba. 1980. "Puerto Rican Barrio Politics in the United States." Pp. 121–28 in *The Puerto Rican Struggle: Essays on Survival in the U.S.*, ed. C. E. Rodríguez, V. Sánchez Korrol, and J. O. Alers. Maplewood, N.J.: Waterfront Press.

Haines, Gerald K., and David A. Langbart. 1993. *Unlocking the Files of the FBI: A Guide to Its Records and Classification System*. Wilmington, Del.: Scholarly Resources.

Harring, Sidney L. 1993. "Policing a Class Society: The Expansion of the Urban Police in the Late Nineteenth and Early Twentieth Centuries." Pp. 546–67 in *Crime and Capitalism: Readings in Marxist Criminology*, ed. David F. Greenberg. Philadelphia: Temple University Press.

Helfeld, David M. 1964. "Discrimination for Political Beliefs and Associations." *Revista del Colegio de Abogados de Puerto Rico* 25:1 (November 1964): 5–276.

Huggins, Martha K. 1987. "U.S.-Supported State Terror: A History of Police Training in Latin America." *Crime and Social Justice* 27–28: 149–71.

————. 1998. *Political Policing: The United States and Latin America*. Durham, N.C.: Duke University Press.

Jayko, Margaret, ed. 1988. *FBI on Trial: The Victory in the Socialist Workers Party Suit against Government Spying*. New York: Pathfinder.

Jensen, Joan M. 1991. *Army Surveillance in America, 1775–1980*. New Haven, Conn.: Yale University Press.

Kessler, Ronald. 1993. *The FBI: The World's Most Powerful Law Enforcement Agency*. New York: Pockect Books.

Kohn, Stephen M. 1986. *Jailed for Peace: The History of American Draft Law Violators, 1658–1985*. Westport, Conn.: Greenwood Press.

————. 1994. *American Political Prisoners: Prosecution under the Espionage and Sedition Acts*. Westport, Conn.: Praeger.

Lindorff, Dave. 1988. "Victims of Police Spying Struggle to Discover What's in Their Files." *In These Times* 12:9: 8.

Mari Brás, Juan. 1993. "A quince años de un asesinato político." *Patria y universo: Ideas y sentimientos de un puertorriqueño libre*. Mayagüez, Puerto Rico: Causa Común Independentista.

Martínez-Valentín, José E. 1995. *La presencia de la Policía en la historia de Puerto Rico, 1898–1995*. San Juan: N.p.

Marx, Gary T. 1988. *Undercover: Police Surveillance in America*. Berkeley: University of California Press.

Mattos Cintrón, Wilfredo. 1988. *"La formación de la hegemonía de Estados Unidos en Puerto Rico y el independentismo, los derechos civiles y la cuestión nacional."* El Caribe Contemporáneo 16 (January–June): 21–57.

———. 1993. "The Struggle for Independence: The Long March to the Twenty-First Century." Pp. 201–14 in *Colonial Dilemma: Critical Perspectives on Contemporary Puerto Rico*, ed. E. Meléndez and E. Meléndez. Boston: South End Press.

Medina Ramírez, Ramón. 1970. *El Movimiento Libertador en la historia de Puerto Rico*. San Juan: N.p.

Mellibovsky, Matilde. 1990. *Círculo de amor sobre la muerte*. Buenos Aires: Ediciones del Pensamiento Nacional.

Merrill-Ramírez, Marie A. 1990. *The Other Side of Colonialism: COINTELPRO Activities in Puerto Rico in the 1960s*. Ph.D. dissertation. University of Texas, Austin.

Meyer, Gerald. 1989. *Vito Marcantonio: Radical Politician, 1902–1954*. Albany: State University of New York Press.

———. 1992a. "Marcantonio and El Barrio." *Centro: Journal of the Center for Puerto Rican Studies* 4:2: 66–87.

———. 1992b. "Puerto Ricans." Pp. 614–17 in *Encyclopedia of the American Left*, ed. M. J. Buhle, P. Buhle, and D. Georgakas. Urbana: University of Illinois Press.

Nadelman, Ethan A. 1993. *Cops across Borders: The Internationalization of U.S. Criminal Law Enforcement*. University Park: Pennsylvania State University Press.

Navarro Rivera, Pablo. 2000. *Universidad de Puerto Rico: De control político a crisis permanente, 1903–1952*. Río Piedras, Puerto Rico: Ediciones Huracán.

Negroni, Héctor Andrés. c1993. *Historia Militar de Puerto Rico*. San Juan: Colección Encuentros.

Newton, Huey P. 1980. *War against the Panthers: A Study of Repression in America*. Ph.D. dissertation. University of California, Santa Cruz.

O'Reilly, Kenneth. 1989. *"Racial Matters": The FBI's Secret File on Black America, 1960–1972*. New York: The Free Press.

———. 1994. *Black Americans: The FBI Files*. New York: Carrol and Graf.

Pabón, Milton. 1970. *La cultura política puertorriqueña*. San Juan: Editorial Cultural.

Pabón, Milton, Robert W. Anderson, and Víctor J. Rivera Rodríguez. 1968. *Los derechos y los partidos políticos en la sociedad puertorriqueña*. Río Piedras, Puerto Rico: Ediciones Edil.

Paralitici, José (Ché). 1990. "Oposición al Servicio Militar Obligatorio durante la Primera Guerra Mundial." *Revista Universidad de América* 2:2: 120–23.

———. 1994. "Vicente Balbás Capó: Tenaz Opositor a la ciudadanía y al Servicio Militar Obligatorio estadounidenses en Puerto Rico." *Revista Universidad de América* 6:1: 66–72.

———. 1998. *No quiero mi cuerpo pa' tambor: El servicio militar obligatorio en Puerto Rico*. San Juan: Ediciones Puerto.

Poveda, Tony G. 1990. *Lawlessness and Reform: The FBI in Transition*. Pacific Grove, Calif.: Brooks/Cole.

Powers, Richard G. 1987. *Secrecy and Power: The Life of J. Edgar Hoover*. New York: The Free Press.

Preston, William, Jr. 1994. *Aliens and Dissenters: Federal Supression of Radicals, 1903–1933*. 2d ed. Urbana and Chicago: University of Illinois Press.

Reynolds, Ruth M. 1989. *Campus in Bondage: A 1948 Microcosm of Puerto Rico in Bondage*. Edited by Carlos Rodríguez-Fraticelli, Blanca Vázquez-Erazo, and Antonio Lauria-Pericelli. New York: Center for Puerto Rican Studies.

Rodríguez Beruff, Jorge. 1988. *Política militar y dominación: Puerto Rico en el contexto latinoamericano*. Río Piedras, Puerto Rico: Ediciones Huracán.

———. 1994. "Puerto Rico at the Outset of the Second World War: Strategic Interests, Colonial Policy, and Internal Politics." Paper presented at the Seminar on War and Peace in Historical Perspective, Center for Historical Analysis, Rutgers University.

Rodríguez-Fraticelli, Carlos. 1993. "U.S. Solidarity with Puerto Rico: Rockwell Kent, 1937." Pp. 189–200 in *Colonial Dilemma: Critical Perspectives on Contemporary Puerto Rico*, ed. E. Meléndez and E. Meléndez. Boston: South End Press.

Rodríguez-Fraticelli, Carlos, and Amílcar Tirado. 1989. "Notes Towards a History of Puerto Rican Community Organizations in New York City." *Centro: Journal of the Center for Puerto Rican Studies* 2:6: 35–47.

Rodríguez-Morazzani, Roberto P. 1992. "Puerto Rican Political Generations in New York: Pioneros, Young Turks, and Radicals." *Centro: Journal of the Center for Puerto Rican Studies* 7:1: 97–116.

———. 1995. "Linking a Fractured Past: The World of the Puerto Rican Old Left." *Centro: Journal of the Center for Puerto Rican Studies* 7:1: 20–30.

Rosado, Marisa. 1992. *Las llamas de la aurora: Acercamiento a una biografía de Pedro Albizu Campos*. San Juan: Author.

Rosenfeld, Susan. 1999. "Organization and Day-to-Day Activities." *The FBI: A Comprehensive Reference Guide*. Phoenix: Oryx Press.

Sanabria, Carlos. 1991. "Patriotism and Class Conflict in the Puerto Rican Community in New York during the 1920s." *Latino Studies Journal* 2:2: 3–16.

Sánchez Korrol, Virginia E. 1994. *From Colonia to Community: The History of Puerto Ricans in New York*. Berkeley: University of California Press.

Santiago Nieves, Juan. 1993. "*La lucha por la independencia de Puerto Rico y la justicia social: Un siglo de persecución política.*" Pp. 93–99 in *Ponencias: Segundo Congreso Puertorriqueño Sobre Derechos Civiles*, ed. Oficina de Educación de la Comisión de Derechos Civiles de Puerto Rico. San Juan: Comisión de Derechos Civiles.

Scarano, Francisco A. 1993. *Puerto Rico: Cinco siglos de historia*. Bogotá, Colombia: McGraw-Hill Interamericana.

Seijo Bruno, Miñi. 1989. *La insurrección nacionalista en Puerto Rico, 1950*. Río Piedras, Puerto Rico: Editorial Edil.

Senado de Puerto Rico. 1984. *Informe Final Parcial de la Comisión de lo Jurídico del Senado de Puerto Rico (sobre Cerro Maravilla)*. San Juan: Senado de Puerto Rico.

———. 1992. *Informe Final de la Investigación del Senado de Puerto Rico Sobre los Sucesos del Cerro Maravilla. Estado Libre Asociado de Puerto Rico, 11ª Asamblea Legislativa, 11ª Sesión Extraordinaria. 31 de diciembre de 1992*.

Skousen, W. Cleon. 1966a. "The Intelligence Unit." *Law & Order* (June): 68–72.

———. 1966b. "The National Network of Police Intelligence Units." *Law & Order* (July): 10–14.

Suárez, Manuel. 1987. *Requiem on Cerro Maravilla: The Police Murders in Puerto Rico and the U.S. Government Coverup*. Maplewood, N.J.: Waterfront Press.

Swearingen, M. Wesley. 1995. *FBI Secrets: An Agent's Exposé*. Boston: South End Press.

Talbert, Roy, Jr. 1991. *Negative Intelligence: The Army and the American Left, 1917–1941*. Jackson: University of Mississippi Press.

Theoharis, Athan. 1976–1977. "The FBI's Stretching of Presidential Directives, 1936–1953." *Political Science Quarterly* 91:4: 649–72.

———. 1978a. *Spying on Americans: Political Surveillance from Hoover to the Huston Plan*. Philadelphia: Temple University Press.

———. 1978b. "The Truman Administration and the Decline of Civil Liberties: The FBI's Success in Securing Authorization for a Preventive Detention Program." *Journal of American History* 64 (March 1978): 1010–1030.

———. 1991. *From the Secret Files of J. Edgar Hoover*. Chicago: Ivan R. Dee.

———. 1994. *The FBI: An Annotated Bibliography and Research Guide*. New York and London: Garland.

Theoharris, Athan, ed. 1991. *From the Secret Files of J. Edgar Hoover*. Chicago: Ivan R. Dee.

Theoharis, Athan et al., eds. 1999. *The FBI: A Comprehensive Reference Guide*. Phoenix: Oryx Press.

Theoharis, Athan G., and John Stuart Cox. 1988. *The Boss: J. Edgar Hoover and the Great American Inquisition*. Philadelphia: Temple University Press.

Torres, Andrés, and José E. Velázquez, eds. 1998. *The Puerto Rican Movement: Voices from the Diaspora*. Philadelphia: Temple University Press.

Unanue, Manuel de Dios. 1999. *El caso Galíndez: Los vascos en los servicios de inteligencia de EEUU*. Tafalla: Txalaparta.

Ungar, Sanford J. 1975. *FBI*. Boston and Toronto: Little Brown & Co.

U.S. Government Printing Office. 1990. *Directory of Graduates of the FBI National Academy and Officers of the FBI National Academy Associates*. Washington, D.C.: U.S. Government Printing Office.

Vega, Bernardo. 1984. *Memoirs of Bernardo Vega: A Contribution to the History of the Puerto Rican Community in New York.* Edited by César Andreu Iglesias. New York: Monthly Review Press.

Villablanca, Guillermo. 1979a. *"Confidentes y agentes encubiertos." Pensamiento Crítico* 2:15 (April): 8–10.

———. 1979b. *"El asesinato de Carlos Muñiz Varela." Pensamiento Crítico* 2:16 (November–December): 12–13.

TWO

The Critical Year of 1936 through the Reports of the Military Intelligence Division

María E. Estades-Font

THIS CHAPTER WILL EXAMINE some aspects of an extraordinary series of historical documents, the secret reports rendered by the Military Intelligence Division (MID) of the U.S. Army, on "subversive" activities in Puerto Rico from 1936 to 1941, with particular attention to the critical events of 1936, as reported by the MID.[1]

The Puerto Rican Nationalist Party was the main target of the MID's surveillance during the early years of the 1930s. According to historian Roy Talbert, the MID's activities in Puerto Rico during this period were "full-fledged operations against the Nationalists."[2] Its secret reports demonstrate the attention paid by this intelligence agency to every aspect of Nationalist political activity: its leadership, organization, arrests and trials, and the reaction of different sectors of Puerto Rican society to Nationalist discourse and strategy. These texts also provide a rich source for studying the representation made by the U.S. military of colonial society during a period of profound crisis when the Nationalist Party threatened internal order and colonial control itself.

Other matters of great historical importance also are discussed within these documents: the Communist Party, the labor movement, Puerto Rican newspapers, and the impact of the First World War. These texts reveal the leading roles ascribed by military intelligence to two key political figures: Pedro Albizu Campos, main leader of the Nationalist Party, and Luis Muñoz Marín, an important leader of the pro-independence Liberal Party and founder in 1938 of the Popular Democratic Party.

In order to assess the historical significance of these reports, it is necessary to take into account that from 1898 to the present, the United States has
assigned to Puerto Rico a strategic role of outstanding importance in its plan
to achieve naval supremacy in the Caribbean region.[3] One of the fundamental reasons for establishing and maintaining colonial control over Puerto
Rico was precisely the need to guarantee these strategic interests.

The strategic value assigned to Puerto Rico by the United States has had
a major impact on the island's historical development throughout the twentieth century. Naval and military bases have been established in its territory,
its population has been subjected to forced military recruitment, and U.S.
military officers have played a leading role in the policy-making process and
government of the colony.

In addition, the MID's classified documents reveal the early existence of
espionage activities carried out by the U.S. Army, with Puerto Rican collaboration, in the midst of civil society, both during times of war and peace.[4]
These reports can shed light on the institutional history, sources, and agents
of federal intelligence activities in Puerto Rico.

There is evidence that systematic surveillance activities date back to
1898.[5] Historian Joan M. Jensen describes their origin, right after the 1898
invasion of Puerto Rico by the U.S. Army:

> In Puerto Rico, where the United States planned permanent occupation,
> the army also used civilian spies. The Secret Service sent one man to Puerto
> Rico to investigate counterfeiting and to establish a permanent agency
> there. A record of five civilians hired in Puerto Rico also remains.[6]

Jensen's analysis clearly points out that intelligence activities carried
out by the MID in "overseas colonies" were of a different nature from those
carried out in the metropolitan country. In Hawaii, Puerto Rico, the Philippines, and the Panama Canal Zone, all territories of strategic importance,
the focus of these activities was not only alien enemies but also political
dissenters.

For instance, commenting on the First World War period, Jensen states:

> Surveillance had originated in these overseas colonies and remained more
> pervasive there than in the United States. While these overseas outposts
> guarded non-citizen civilians as part of their regular activities, surveillance
> in these areas shows most clearly what [the] MID could do when unham-
> pered by citizen control and how its focus moved from alien enemy to dis-
> senter. In Hawaii there were only three hundred German enemy aliens, but
> the Hawaiian Department kept the entire population of three hundred
> thousand under surveillance. In Puerto Rico, the intelligence officer for the
> district simply took over the insular police force of eight hundred men. In
> the Panama Canal Zone, the intelligence officer organized a civilian secret

service and police force composed of Americans and Panamanians. . . . In the Philippines, where there were only four hundred Germans, surveillance was extended to all Filipinos and Japanese.[7]

In Puerto Rico, the term *subversive* was evidently defined by the MID in a very loose way, making anyone participating actively in social and political life a potential target of scrutiny. Concerning the critical period of the 1930s and 1940s, the MID's weekly reports reflect an active and a secret interference by the U.S. government in the internal affairs of its Caribbean colony.[8]

On February 23, 1936, Colonel E. Francis Riggs, chief of Puerto Rico's Insular Police, was assassinated by Nationalists Hiram Rosado and Elías Beauchamp.[9] In turn, Rosado and Beauchamp were murdered by police in the San Juan headquarters, while being held for the death of Riggs.[10]

These dramatic events, unprecedented in Puerto Rican history, provoked a strong reaction from the U.S. War Department. In April, Lt. Col. R. L. Eichelberger, secretary of the general staff, instructed the MID to keep the prevailing situation in Puerto Rico under close scrutiny and to keep him informed.[11] As a result, from this point onward, intelligence reports were rendered weekly instead of monthly. They were sent to the War Department by the commander in chief of U.S. troops in Puerto Rico, the 65th Infantry.[12]

At the same time, under instructions from the chief of the MID, two intelligence officers met with Dr. Ernest Gruening, director of the Interior Department's Division of Territories and Insular Possessions, the agency in charge of Puerto Rican affairs since 1934.[13] The purpose of the meeting was to establish a close collaboration between both agencies and also to settle two important legal issues.

In the first place, it was necessary to decide who would occupy the governor's office, in case something should happen to Governor Winship. This implied defining the authority of the commander in chief of U.S. troops in Puerto Rico to take action in case of a crisis and in the absence of the governor. Secondly, in the event that martial law was declared, the relationship between the Puerto Rico National Guard and the commander in chief had to be established.

On April 27, 1936, a legal opinion on both matters was issued by the judge advocate general of the War Department.[14] According to this opinion, both the president of the United States and the governor of Puerto Rico had the legal authority to mobilize the militia (including the National Guard) and army troops in order to enforce U.S. laws. In case an emergency occurred during the governor's absence, the commander in chief of the army should call on regular troops to protect U.S. interests. The commander in chief's jurisdiction over the Puerto Rico National Guard was legally valid only if this body was put under his direct command.

According to Gruening, "anything could happen at anytime" in Puerto Rico.[15] The two weeks following the filing of charges against Nationalists leaders would be crucial to the stability of the Puerto Rican government. In his opinion, if the courts did not convict those accused of murder or seditious acts against the governments of the United States or Puerto Rico, then martial law should be imposed to ensure due respect to federal authority. Threats received by juries and other members of the judicial branch could result in acquittals. Gruening also took very seriously the death threats made against Governor Winship and other government officials. The situation was such that the U.S. Justice Department had recently concluded an investigation into subversive activities taking place in Puerto Rico.

In Gruening's opinion, the 65th Infantry seemed loyal and capable of handling any difficult situation. He suggested to the War Department that "native" soldiers, with adequate instructions from their superiors, could have a great influence on Puerto Ricans, explaining properly the good intentions behind the actions of the U.S. government.[16]

The information found in these documents reveals that both civil and military authorities perceived the Nationalist movement as a real threat to the stability of the colonial government and the safety of its representatives in Puerto Rico. This perception led federal officials to take several actions to preserve internal order. These measures included increasing the level of surveillance over the civilian population, establishing a close collaboration among federal agencies in charge of Puerto Rican affairs, and considering the use of martial law and the mobilization of regular and "native" troops. This last measure was considered in spite of doubts expressed by MID agents regarding the loyalty of "native" soldiers; eventually, they too would become targets of surveillance.

Remarks made by Col. O. R. Cole, commander in chief of the 65th Infantry, also indicate the way Puerto Rican nationalism was perceived by the U.S. military:

> The Nationalist Party movement is spread throughout the island, but only a comparatively small number of Puerto Ricans are affiliated with it and are sympathetic to its methods. The party, however, is growing and is becoming more and more emboldened, because it has been unchecked. Its chief danger, it seems to me, is its attractiveness to Latin youths of romantic nature to whom the elements of self-sacrifice, insular patriotism, intrigue, and desire to emulate the deeds of past Latin American heroes undoubtedly makes a tremendous appeal. Practically all of its adherents are this type of young men. The assassins of Colonel Riggs were of this type.
>
> It is my fixed opinion that if this party movement is unchecked there will be other assassinations attempted.
>
> It is not believed that there is any danger of a general uprising in Puerto Rico against the authority of the United States, but there is the danger that at anytime these young men and their organized companies, encouraged and abetted by their leader, Campos, may attempt just such a

coup against the police and National Guard armories as was reported to Captain Andino. The party is publicly dedicated to the proposition of expelling the authority of the United States from the island by force.[17]

Even though it was seen as a minority movement, Cole believed that the Nationalist Party had the potential to grow and carry out other political assassinations and acts of violence if it went unstopped. The strength of the Nationalist movement was due to the "Latin" character and apparently had nothing to do with the critical conditions under which the Puerto Ricans were living; the military officer was unable to consider that Puerto Rican Nationalists could have legitimate demands arising from the colonial status.

The 1936 political crisis was further complicated by the introduction of the Tydings Bill in the U.S. Senate, designed to grant independence to Puerto Rico.[18] According to the May 7 weekly intelligence report, this bill had caused an upheaval on the island.[19] Col. Cole commented that it had mostly provoked opposition, because the conditions under which independence would be granted were seen as bringing economic ruin to the island. Nevertheless, Cole added,

> . . . it is believed that if the bill is passed by Congress and the plebiscite held, an overwhelming majority of the Puerto Ricans will vote in favor of independence.[20]

Based on "impartial observers," the colonel explained this apparent contradiction by the positions adopted by political parties. Regarding the Nationalist Party, he wrote:

> The Nationalists, having nothing to lose and everything to gain in the change, without any doubt will vote for independence. This group is very small at present, but if independence is granted to Puerto Rico, the ensuing lack of organization of the government during the beginning of its independent life, together with the terroristic methods used by the Nationalists, will give Albizu Campos more than a fair chance of becoming the head of government.[21]

On the other hand, the Liberal Party, the main opposition force in electoral terms, had stated that it would accept independence regardless of the circumstances under which it was granted. Cole ascribed this radical stand to the influence of Luis Muñoz Marín, one of its most important leaders.[22] The Republican Party, "the strongest pro-American party in Puerto Rico," had also favored independence as a means of showing its opposition to some of the decisions taken by the Roosevelt administration toward Puerto Rico. The leaders of the Socialist Party had taken the same position as their traditional allies, the Republicans.[23]

Cole concluded his report in the following manner:

The main topic of comment in the island, both among Americans and
Puerto Ricans, is the Tydings independence bill. Those who are and have
always been pro-Americans feel that the United States have let them down;
that no alternative has been offered, and that the United States only
decides to cast Puerto Rico aside. This has made them resentful and . . . they
will vote for independence. Those who are independentists [sic] have been
offered what they wanted and have been encouraged. . . . Until this emotional reaction has subsided, it is difficult to ascertain the course that will
be taken by the trend of opinion. The action of the . . . Liberal Party in supporting the Nationalists . . . is particularly important.[24]

In view of these remarks, it is evident that in the opinion of this key military officer, the introduction of the Tydings Bill only made worse the critical
situation that prevailed in Puerto Rico. According to Col. Cole, the bill had
created a consensus in favor of independence, despite the harsh economic conditions it imposed. Such a political climate could greatly benefit the Nationalist movement, especially if it joined forces with the Liberals. If independence
was really granted, the Nationalists could rise to power in the new republic.

Cole thought that the political frenzy created by Puerto Rican politicians
in response to the Tydings Bill was responsible for the serious disturbances
that took place in San Juan's Central High School on May 12. In view of
police inaction, Governor Winship mobilized two National Guard units to
crush the students' protests.[25]

A state of military alert was again repeated in July 1936. The MID report
stated that several days before the Fourth of July celebration, Albizu Campos
allegedly told National Guard Colonel Luis Raúl Esteves that some Nationalists were planning to assassinate Governor Winship, and that he, the
Nationalist leader, was unable to prevent it.[26] It was added that this information had been corroborated by FBI Chief J. Edgar Hoover in a radio message
to the governor.

In view of these revelations, the commander in chief of the 65th Infantry
ordered his troops to be heavily armed as they marched in the Fourth of July
parade. According to this officer, the Nationalist plan to disrupt the celebration failed because the subversive elements realized the troops were ready to
fight back if necessary. At the same time, he took steps to improve the gathering and distribution of intelligence information in the headquarters and to
establish a closer collaboration with the chief of the Insular Police; further
steps would be taken to make sure that army troops could handle any emergency in Puerto Rico.[27]

The 1936 intelligence reports deal with another important historical
event: the trials held in San Juan Federal Court against several top Nationalist leaders, including Pedro Albizu Campos.[28] No criminal charges were

brought against them in relation to the assassination of the chief of police. Instead, they were accused of a political crime, that of sedition, conspiring to overthrow the U.S. government in Puerto Rico. Most historians agree that the judicial process that followed was carried out under undue political pressures from federal authorities.[29]

The intelligence reports of July and August 1936 describe in great detail the judicial process involving the eight Nationalist leaders, signaling the importance given to this matter by military authorities. The fact that eight municipal assemblies voted to request that the first trial held in San Juan Federal Court be dismissed, a request also made by the presidents of both the Republican and Liberal parties, was seen by MID agents as evidence of the support that nationalism already had among a large number of Puerto Ricans.[30]

The first trial, with a jury composed mainly of Puerto Ricans, ended without a verdict. A second trial was carried out with a jury composed by a majority of U.S. Nationals, who easily arrived at a guilty verdict. The Nationalist leaders were sentenced to serve from two to seven years in Atlanta's federal penitentiary.

Sentencing some of nationalism's top leaders to exile in a U.S. prison undoubtedly dealt a heavy blow against the political potential of the movement. It represented a forceful reaction by the metropolitan state against what was perceived as a serious threat to its colonial control over Puerto Rico. The valuable information supplied by the MID's surveillance activities must have played a decisive role in the formulation of U.S. policy to meet this crisis.

The covert actions taken by the agents of military intelligence in the midst of Puerto Rican civil society constitute an important historical example of the active interference by federal authorities in the island's political process, bringing into question the existence of a democratic order and constitutional rights within the framework of a colonial regime.

NOTES

1. These documents belong to Record Group 165, Records of War Department General and Special Staffs, found at the National Archives in Washington, D.C. The letters, memos, and reports by the MID of the Army General Staff total almost 2,000 single-spaced, typed pages. Although documents exist from 1918, 1920, and 1935, most cover the period 1936–1941. In 1941, the responsibility for this intelligence activity was transferred to the FBI. Some of these documents were published in Comisión de Derechos Civiles 1989.

2. Talbert 1991, 249.

3. See Estades-Font 1988; Rodríguez Beruff 1988; Yerxa c1991.

4. For a comprehensive history of the activities of U.S. military intelligence, see Jensen 1991.

5. According to Talbert (1991, 3), a military office specifically in charge of intelligence activities was created in 1885, while the Office of Naval Intelligence was founded in 1882. Jensen (1991, 51) points out that from 1890 on, the focus of the MID shifted from Canada to the Caribbean region and to those places that could supply the carbon needs of an expanding navy.

6. Jensen 1991, 74.

7. Jensen 1991, 172–73.

8. García Muñiz (1988, 65–72) offers evidence of the role played by the United States in persecuting Nationalist and Communist leaders in the British Antilles during this period.

9. For details on the military career of Col. Riggs, see Ferrao 1990, 151.

10. For further details on these events, see Rosado 1992, 128–35.

11. Lt. Col. R. L. Eichelberger, Secretary, General Staff, Memorandum for the A.C. of S., G-2, April 3, 1936, Doc. 741/NA/165, Archives of *Proyecto Caribeño de Justicia y Paz* (hereafter PCJP).

12. For a history of this regiment, see Negroni 1992.

13. Col. F. H. Lincoln, Assistant Chief of Staff, G-2, Memorandum for the Chief of Staff, April 13, 1936, Doc. 744/NA/165, PCJP.

14. Major General A. W. Brow, the Judge Advocate General, Memorandum for the Assistant Chief of Staff, April 27, 1936, Doc. 752/NA/165, PCJP.

15. Doc. 744/NA/165, PCJP.

16. Ibid.

17. Col. O. R. Cole, 65th Infantry, Commanding, Monthly Summary of Subversive Activities-Puerto Rico Area, to Commanding General, Second Corps Area, Governors Island, New York, February 25, 1936. This report dealt with the assassination of Col. Riggs and was sent by Major Joe N. Dalton, Assistant Chief of Staff, G-2, to Lt. Col. Charles K. Nulsen, Office of Assistant Chief of Staff, on March 6, with the following note: "The nature of this summary indicates that it should be made the subject of a special report" (Doc. 735/NA/165, PCJP).

18. The introduction of the Tydings Bill has been interpreted as an act of vengeance by this influential senator, a personal friend of Col. Riggs. See Bhana 1975, 18–33.

19. Col. O. R. Cole, 65th Infantry, Commanding, Weekly Summary of Subversive Activities—Puerto Rico Area, to Commanding General, Second Corps Area, May 7, 1936, Doc. 750/NA/165, PCJP.

20. Ibid.

21. Ibid.

22. There is an extensive bibliography on the historical role played by Luis Muñoz Marín and the Popular Democratic Party. See, for example, seminal works such as Quintero Rivera 1985.

23. Ibid.

24. Ibid.

25. Col. O. R. Cole, 65th Infantry, Commanding, Weekly Summary of Subversive Activities-Puerto Rico Area, to Commanding General, Second Corps Area, May 14, 1936, Doc. 753/NA/165, PCJP.

26. Col. F. H. Lincoln, Assistant Chief of Staff, G-2, Memorandum for the Chief of Staff, July 31, 1936, Doc. 780/NA/165, PCJP.

27. Ibid.

28. Also Juan Antonio Corretjer, Juan Gallardo Santiago, Luis F. Velázquez, Erasmo Velázquez, Julio H. Velázquez, Clemente Soto Vélez, Rafael Ortiz Pacheco, and Pablo Rosado Ortiz (Ferrao 1990, 144).

29. On this matter, see Rodríguez Reyes 1993, 215–26.

30. Doc. 780/NA/165, PCJP.

WORKS CITED

Bhana, Surendra. 1975. *The United States and the Development of the Puerto Rican Status Question, 1936–1968.* Lawrence: University Press of Kansas.

Comisión de Derechos Civiles. 1989. *Informe sobre discrimen y persecución por razones políticas: La práctica gubernamental de mantener listas, ficheros y expedientes de ciudadanos por razón de su ideología política.* 1989-CDC-028. San Juan: Comisión de Derechos Civiles.

Estades-Font, María E. 1988. *La presencia militar de Estados Unidos en Puerto Rico 1898–1918. Intereses estratégicos y dominación colonial.* Río Piedras, Puerto Rico: Ediciones Huracán.

Ferrao, Luis Angel. 1990. *Pedro Albizu Campos y el nacionalismo puertorriqueño.* San Juan: Editorial Cultural.

García Muñiz, Humberto. 1988. *La estrategia de Estados Unidos y la militarización del Caribe.* Río Piedras, Puerto Rico: Instituto de Estudios del Caribe.

Jensen, Joan M. 1991. *Army Surveillance in America, 1775–1980.* New Haven and London: Yale University Press.

Negroni, Héctor Andrés. 1992. *Historia militar de Puerto Rico.* Madrid: Ediciones Siruela.

Quintero Rivera, Angel G. 1985. "*La base social de la transformación ideológica del Partido Popular en la década del 40.*" Pp. 35–119 in *Cambio y desarrollo en Puerto Rico: La transformación ideológica del Partido Popular Democrático,* ed. Gerardo Navas Dávila. San Juan: Editorial de la Universidad de Puerto Rico.

Rodríguez Beruff, Jorge. 1988. *Política militar y dominación: Puerto Rico en el contexto latinoamericano.* Río Piedras, Puerto Rico: Ediciones Huracán.

Rodríguez Reyes, Harry. 1993. "*Los procesos judiciales incoados contra Pedro Albizu Campos.*" Pp. 215–26 in *La nación puertorriqueña: Ensayos en torno a Pedro Albizu*

Campos, ed. Juan Manuel Carrión, Teresa C. Gracia Ruiz, and Carlos Rodríguez Fraticelli. San Juan: Editorial de la Universidad de Puerto Rico.

Rosado, Marisa. 1992. *Las llamas de la aurora: Acercamiento a una biografía de Pedro Albizu Campos.* San Juan: N.p.

Talbert Jr., Roy. 1991. *Negative Intelligence: The Army and the American Left, 1917–1941.* Jackson and London: University Press of Mississippi.

Yerxa, Donald A. c1991. *Admirals and Empire: The United States Navy and the Caribbean, 1898–1945.* Columbia: University of South Carolina Press.

THREE

The Smith Act Goes to San Juan

La Mordaza, 1948–1957

Ivonne Acosta-Lespier

THE SCANDAL REGARDING the list of subversives that broke out in Puerto Rico in the summer of 1987[1] should remind us of a time in our history that, whether painful or shameful, we have opted to hide behind a veil of oblivion. When we do remember, we do so with a partial and deformed view of the facts. Those were the years when Law 53 was in force, an "anti-sedition" statute known by the name given to it by Puerto Rico Senator Leopoldo Figueroa the very same night it was passed: "the Gag Order." For nearly ten crucial years, the Gag Order managed to mortally wound nationalism, and through fear it decreased the electoral force of the pro-independence movement, giving way to the electoral rise of the annexation forces. Law 53 was also instrumental to the establishment of the Commonwealth of Puerto Rico. It is thus indispensable for the Gag Order to be placed in its proper historical perspective to understand what is happening at present.[2]

Law 53 (approved as Bill 24 in May 1948) made it a felony "to encourage, defend, counsel, or preach, voluntarily or knowingly, the need, desirability, or convenience of overturning, destroying, or paralyzing the Insular Government, or any of its political subdivisions, by way of force or violence; and to publish, edit, circulate, sell, distribute, or publicly exhibit with the intention to overturn . . . (etc.), as well as to organize or help organize any society, group, or assembly of persons who encourage, defend, counsel, or preach any such thing, or for other ends." Law 53 was a copy, a direct translation of Section 2 of Title 1, of a statute known as the "Smith Law," still current in the United States.[3]

The Gag Order was defended at the time of its approval, especially by the then-president of the senate, Luis Muñoz Marín, as protection against the danger of violence that the Nationalist Party posed. Said party had gained in popularity since the return of Pedro Albizu Campos to the country in late 1947.[4] The rationalization by Muñoz prevails today, fostered by collective amnesia and by sheer ignorance of the facts.

Even though Law 53 was approved in 1948, it is said that it was the result of the 1950 Nationalist revolt.[5] It is thus deduced, incorrectly and in defiance of the truth, that the repression following the revolt was reasonable, as any government has the right to protect itself from attempts of being overturned by force or violence. The most elemental logic should lead us to ask: why, if Law 53 was approved in 1948 to prevent violence, was it unsuccessful?

The Gag Order was the result of an attempt to coordinate U.S. security, related to its plans for the hemisphere after the Second World War. The coordination started with the creation in 1947 of the now-famous National Security Council (NSC).[6] Postwar policy, expressed in the Truman Doctrine, was in effect. The famous doctrine strove to contain the spread of communism in Latin America by promoting economic development dependent on the United States. This development of North American industrial capitalism needed a stable political base, and to achieve it (1) North American military presence was reinforced in the Caribbean; (2) organizations to promote solidarity in the hemisphere were created; and (3) it was decided that "internal subversion" groups would be eliminated.

The plans the United States had for the hemisphere were hindered by the campaign in the United Nations of Puerto Rican Nationalists and independence advocates who portrayed the United States as a colonial power. In its eagerness not to be discredited in this aspect, and to beat the Soviet Union in the cold war, the United States was forced to concede reforms to the colonial regime in Puerto Rico. But the reforms depended on the 1948 elections (when Puerto Ricans would vote for a governor for the first time), which were in turn threatened by the rise and popularity of the newly created Independence Party. The return of Albizu Campos was the catalyst that led the U.S. government to take steps.

In April and May 1948, some events took place in Puerto Rico that gave the United States the excuse it needed to activate its security organisms. The events were Albizu Campos's followers' call against Puerto Ricans joining the U.S. Army and the presence of the U.S. Navy on Puerto Rican soil, and the strike held by the students at the University of Puerto Rico. The United States assigned these events emergency status in terms of internal security because they occurred at a moment when the U.S. government was organizing efforts of "hemisphere solidarity" organizations, such as the Organization of American States (OAS) and the Caribbean Commission.[7] The student strike at the University of Puerto Rico (associated with Nationalist violence) began shortly after a violent popular uprising in Bogotá—known in Spanish as the *bogotazo*—during the meeting of what would later become the OAS.[8] The U.S. security organisms made a connection between the two events and feared a repetition of the *bogotazo* in Puerto Rico during the May meeting, for the first time on "North American soil"—as it was then announced—of the Caribbean Commission. Things had to be taken care of before that happened, so the Smith Law was "imported," translated into Spanish, and made into the Gag Order by the colonial legislature that May.

Historians should take note of the importance of Admiral William D. Leahy, who had been governor of Puerto Rico between 1930 and 1940, and in 1948 was President Truman's chief of staff in charge of national security and "secret" international matters. Leahy also was one of the chief promoters of the cold war against the Soviet Union. The role played by Leahy in the enforcement of the Gag Order in Puerto Rico has not been overlooked either in the United States (by U.S. Representative Vito Marcantonio) or on the island.

It should be remembered that there was strong civic opposition to the Gag Order bills, from the principal sectors of the country and all of the press.[9] Despite this, Governor Jesús T. Piñero made it into law in June 1948, regardless of citizen protest. After all, this was about serving the interests of the United States.

In its first stage (1948–1950), the Gag Order achieved three main objectives: (1) to begin an "era of silence" in the University of Puerto Rico, which would last almost two decades; (2) to decrease the votes received by the Independence Party in the 1948 elections and give Muñoz the opportunity to demonstrate to the U.S. Congress that the objections of the independence advocates to the constitutional project could be dismissed because there were so few of them; and (3) through vigilance and harassment, to provoke the Nationalists to resort to violence rather than meekly be led to jail for the mere violation of Law 53. This law, rather than preventing Nationalist violence, provoked it.

The Nationalist insurrection of October 1950 led to the rigorous enforcement of the Gag Order in court. The hysteria it provoked in the Popular Democratic Party also led the Insular Legislature (called by Muñoz) to amend the original Law 53 and make it even more restrictive. Now it would be a crime to merely be a "member" of "subversive" parties. This is the origin of the mentality that is today made evident by the "subversives lists" scandal. Ironically, the application of Law 53 (named "the little Smith Law" in the United States) was so plagued by irregularities that none other than J. Edgar Hoover, FBI director, wrote about his apprehension that the cases might not "make it" in court, and that it would then be very difficult to imprison the Nationalist leaders.

When studying the history of the Gag Order, we find that the whole process of elaborating the Puerto Rican Constitution and establishing the

Commonwealth between 1950 and 1952 was politically vitiated by the persecution against independence advocates and many others who had not
taken part in violent acts during the insurrection. Inscription of new voters
for the referendum of Law 600 was held in an atmosphere in which over
1,000 independence advocates were jailed, an undeclared martial law atmosphere (Helfeld 1964). The November 1950 "preventive" arrests, as they were
called (and which today still cause uproar), of people on the famous lists originated in the (1930s) Winship era were disregarded as soon as the inscription
of new voters was finished. With this repressive mechanism, the majority
party made sure that the votes against Law 600—the votes against the Commonwealth, as it exists today—were eliminated beforehand.

The "official" history conceals the fact that the campaign for the Constitution was based almost exclusively on accusing anybody who dared vote
against it of being a "subversive" and, above all, a Communist. It also hides
the fact that the referendum on the Constitution was held when all of the
Nationalist leaders were in prison for violation of Law 53 (for attending
meetings, clapping in rallies, talking about their ideals, etc.). And it also
hides the fact that the atmosphere of harassment and persecution against
independence advocates led the Puerto Rican Independence Party (PIP) not
to participate in the elections to choose delegates to the Constitutional
Convention, despite the fact that it was already the second party in the
country (as would be demonstrated in the 1952 elections, Gag Order and all
notwithstanding).

"Official" stories never mention that the elections to choose delegates to
the Constitutional Convention were held after the trial against Albizu Campos, who was the first person convicted under Law 53 (and who was sentenced to almost fifty-four years for having given twelve speeches).[10] Amnesia conceals the fact that simultaneously with the Constitutional
Convention, trials were being held against poet Francisco Matos Paoli, José
Enamorado Cuesta, Ramón Medina Ramírez, Deusdedit Marrero, Paulino
Castro, and others for terrible "crimes" such as quoting Betances in speeches
or publications or simply for talking about their ideals. It is best forgotten, or
such is the pretension, that the repressive atmosphere was such that the very
delegates of the pro-statehood opposition demanded amnesty for the prisoners under Law 53. It was then that Muñoz pronounced the famous phrase—
often quoted but seldom in context—that in Puerto Rico there were no political prisoners, only imprisoned politicians. The trials were interrupted only
for the assembly to approve the Constitution and for the people to vote on
said document.

The steps taken to legitimize the Commonwealth to the United Nations
and other organizations were linked to the final and definitive stage of the
implementation of the Gag Order. When going to the United Nations to
sanctify an electoral process held during a time of repression of opposing

ideas, amnesty was given to Pedro Albizu Campos, but not without declaring him a "mental patient" first.

The Nationalist attack on the U.S. Congress was a response to Puerto Rico having been declared a non-colonial state and to the impending OAS meeting in Caracas in March 1954. A new wave of arrests under the amended Law 53 began, and Albizu Campos's amnesty was revoked for having described the attack as a "journey of sublime heroism."[11] The very same government imprisoning him for declaring those words chose not to remember that not long before it had declared him a mental patient in order to provide amnesty.

The second stage of repression (1954) under the Gag Order was so severe that it helped decrease the electoral force of independence between 1954 and 1956, when the PIP lost nearly 80,000 votes. None of the accused under Law 53 could be convicted of violent acts, not even of giving or hearing a violent speech. The "crimes" consisted of acts such as collecting money for the cause, having and distributing printed materials, and even attending mass held in memory of dead Nationalists. The government thus incurred open violation of the recently approved rights of the 1952 Constitution.

The flagrant violation of civil rights in Puerto Rico had been condemned since 1951 by North Americans who had come to witness the process against pacifist Ruth Reynolds, sentenced to prison for taking the oath in a Nationalist assembly. Her lawyer, Conrad Lynn, had strongly denounced the situation of Puerto Rico to the American Civil Liberties Union (ACLU). The only thing he had achieved was for the ACLU to be let in as *amicus curiae* in the appeal of the Ruth Reynolds case and for Santos P. Amadeo to be designated as its representative in that process. In late 1954, the Supreme Court of Puerto Rico acquitted Ruth Reynolds; according to Lynn, this was the second case in the same year in which a statute similar to the Smith Law was attacked (the first had been decided in Pennsylvania in favor of Steve Nelson). In the midst of said judicial victory, Santos P. Amadeo made public his intention to form a civil liberties association in Puerto Rico.

Yet surprisingly, in the beginning of 1956, Roger Baldwin (who besides having presided over the ACLU was now chairman of the board of the United Nations International League of Human Rights) announced that the Commonwealth had requested a study of civil rights in Puerto Rico in keeping with the UN Resolution of December 1955. Muñoz then named a committee to those ends, whose advisor was Baldwin himself. The committee included among its members, nevertheless, aside from other jurists,[12] one of the main defenders of the Gag Order, José Trías Monge.

A short time after the committee was formed, the news of the federal court ruling, *Pennsylvania v. Nelson*, invalidating the laws against subversion in all states, became public. This was the case that mortally wounded Law 53 in Puerto Rico. That was the interpretation of the majority of the jurists at the moment, except for Trías Monge, who insisted that the Gag Order was still current. Baldwin, meanwhile, asked the ACLU to study the effect of said decision on Law 53.

The effect of *Pennsylvania v. Nelson* was felt immediately. It gave Ramón H. Vargas, Pablo García Rodríguez, and Luis Garrastegui, lawyers of Deusdedit Marrero, the necessary argument to obtain absolution of the only Communist jailed under Law 53. In October 1956, Deusdedit Marrero was set free, although by then he was mentally affected. In 1987, his name still appeared in the list of "subversives"!

Also resorting to the famous case, Santos P. Amadeo would make the decisive challenge to Law 53 by demanding the release of Leonides Díaz Díaz, a sixty-year-old woman jailed for the crime of being the wife and mother of convicted Nationalists in 1951.

The day after Leonides Díaz Díaz got parole, in July 1957, Muñoz Marín announced that he would ask the legislature for the derogation of Law 53, and that he would pardon thirteen Nationalists convicted for violating said statute. The newspaper revealed on July 20 that the governor's action followed the recommendations of the Committee of Civil Rights (then presided over by Juan Fernández Badillo). The governor stated that the committee's recommendations had reached him "five days prior to the expiration date for approval of legislative projects, and that he had not had enough time to study them and make the pertinent recommendations to the Legislature."[13] Yet months before, Baldwin had made known that the first committee report recommended the derogation of Law 53 as a first and an urgent matter.

The Gag Order era was officially over on August 5, 1957, when the legislature unanimously voted to derogate Law 53. Yet it was never decided—as Santos P. Amadeo had publicly demanded—if in the future the legislature could again approve a law similar to the Gag Order. Even today, thirty years after its derogation, the constitutionality of the repression established by the Popular Democratic Party government for nearly a decade under the Gag Order has not been examined.

Today, when the mass media have stridently handled one of the effects of the Gag Order—the already famous list of "subversives"—it would be well to finally cure ourselves of the collective amnesia to examine the causes and effects of the Gag Order. Only then will we be in a position to avoid the repetition of that era.

NOTES

1. For more on the 1987 *carpetas* scandal, see Comisión de Derechos Civiles 1989; Bosque-Pérez and Colón Morera 1997.

2. For a detailed analysis of the Gag Order, see Acosta 1998.

3. The Smith Law is the common name for Public Law 678 of June 28, 1940, known as the "Alien Registration Act," because it was originally presented by Representative Howard W. Smith. Title I of the law was the Federal Sedition Act, which was used as a model for Law 53 in Puerto Rico.

4. See Rosado 1992 for a biography of the Puerto Rican Nationalist leader.

5. For a study of the 1950 Nationalist insurrection, see Seijo Bruno 1989.

6. The National Security Council was created by the National Security Act of 1947. Its function was to ". . . advise the President with respect to the integration of domestic, foreign, and military policies relating to the national security so as to enable the military services and the other departments and agencies of the government to cooperate more effectively in matters involving the national security."

7. The Caribbean Commission was created in 1948 ". . . to encourage and strengthen international cooperation in promoting the economic and social welfare and advancement of the non-self-governing territories in the Caribbean area, whose economic and social development is of vital interest to the security of the United States, in accordance with the principles set forth in Chapter XI of the Charter of the United Nations." 22 US Code (Ch. 7, VIII-Caribbean Commission, Section 280h).

8. The day on which Colombian popular leader Jorge Gaitán was killed on the streets of Bogotá, April 9, 1948, marked the beginning of a violent period for the country, which included student riots. For a graphic description of *el bogotazo*, see Mendoza 1984, 246–50.

9. For details, see Acosta 1998, particularly chapter 3.

10. See Acosta 1993 for more on the speeches for which Albizu Campos was incarcerated.

11. As quoted by Newspaper columnist Teófilo Maldonado, *El Imparcial*, March 3, 1954, pp. 1, 8. Also see Acosta 1998, 202–3.

12. See Helfeld 1964 for one of the reports that emerged from the work of the Committee.

13. Quoted in *El Mundo*, July 20, 1957, pp. 1, 18. Also see Acosta 1998, 235.

WORKS CITED

Acosta, Ivonne. 1998. *La Mordaza: Puerto Rico 1948–1957*. Río Piedras, Puerto Rico: Editorial Edil.

———. 1993. *La palabra como delito: Los discursos por los que condenaron a Pedro Albizu Campos, 1948–1950*. San Juan: Editorial Cultural.

Bosque-Pérez, Ramón, and José Javier Colón Morera. 1997. *Las carpetas: Persecución política y derechos civiles en Puerto Rico (ensayos y documentos)*. Río Piedras, Puerto Rico: Centro para la Investigación y Promoción de los Derechos Civiles (CIPDC).

Comisión de Derechos Civiles. 1989. *Informe sobre discrimen y persecución por razones políticas: La práctica gubernamental de mantener listas, ficheros y expedientes de ciudadanos por razón de su ideología política*. 1989-CDC-028. San Juan: Comisión de Derechos Civiles.

Helfeld, David M. 1964. "Discrimination for Political Beliefs and Associations." *Revista del Colegio de Abogados de Puerto Rico* 25:1: 5–276.

Mendoza, Plinio. 1984. *La llama y el hielo*. Bogotá, Colombia: Planeta Colombiana.

Rosado, Marisa. 1992. *Las llamas de la aurora: Acercamiento a una biografía de Pedro Albizu Campos*. San Juan: N.p.

Seijo Bruno, Miñi. 1989. *La insurrección nacionalista en Puerto Rico, 1950*. Río Piedras, Puerto Rico: Editorial Edil.

FOUR

Imprisonment and Colonial Domination, 1898–1958

José (Ché) Paralitici

AT THE END OF NEARLY a century since the U.S. invasion of Puerto Rico, the history of those sentenced to prison because of their independence ideals has not been thoroughly investigated. This chapter strives to contribute to said history, in a general way, by presenting and discussing the most outstanding cases of the first half of the twentieth century.

Since the United States invaded Puerto Rico in 1898 and established its political and military regime, not a single decade has passed without the incarceration of some independence advocate, with the possible exception of the 1920s. Since 1899, independence strugglers have been accused of violating many laws, thus many have been sentenced to prison terms, both in Puerto Rico and in the United States. Different members of the independence cause have been charged with violating the laws on postage, weapons, explosives, the grand jury, gag laws, and the military draft. They also have been charged with conspiracy, sedition, aggression, contempt, and inciting riots, and for trespassing on U.S. property in Puerto Rico. Aside from the Puerto Ricans living on the island, some of those residing in the United States, as well as people of other nationalities who sympathize with the independence cause, have suffered imprisonment during the first half of the twentieth century.

PERSECUTION AND IMPRISONMENT
OF JOURNALISTS AND STUDENTS

The first to have a taste of the iron hand of the invaders were several journalists who opposed both the invasion and the anti-democratic practices that were being instituted within just weeks of the establishment of military rule, after Spain lost the Spanish-Cuban-American War of 1898.

The end of the nineteenth century witnessed the entrance to Puerto Rican jails of renowned journalists Evaristo Izcoa Díaz, Tomás Carrión Maduro, Manuel Guzmán Rodríguez, and Luis Cabalier. The most known, tragic, and polemical of the cases, as well as the most remarked upon by historians, is that of Izcoa Díaz, who was polemical during Spanish rule also. His controversial articles appearing in the newspaper La Bomba ("The Bomb") sent him to jail on several occasions in the 1890s.

It was in La Bomba, as a matter of fact, that Izcoa Díaz published an article criticizing the vandalism acts of some U.S. soldiers in Ponce as part of the invasion, which caused the closing of the newspaper and his arrest. Afterward, in a new paper with the suggestive name El Combate ("Combat"), he launched another attack reproving the suggestion of a private citizen to the government that corporal punishment be imposed as a practice in the schools. Given that he had made use of the mail to distribute a newspaper with material classified as insulting, he was charged and sentenced to a year and a half of hard labor in jail and paid a $500 fine.

Interventions on his behalf and petitions of commutation persuaded Governor Guy V. Henry to grant him freedom after a few months in the Puerta de Tierra prison in San Juan. Nevertheless, the toll on his already debilitated health was irreversible. In August 1901, the thirty-six-year-old journalist died in Ponce. He was released from jail at the end of November 1899 (Gil de Rubio 1978; Figueroa 1983; Ayoroa Santaliz 1983).

The other journalists mentioned also were victims of a policy that Military Governor Henry had made known in December 1898 through a decree sent to the Council of Secretaries. This document established the limitations to free press, clearly specifying that it would not allow articles critical to the authorities or politically inciting. Violation of these stipulations would result in suppression of the papers and punishment for the journalists (Figueroa 1983, 324).

Luis Cabalier, of the paper La Estrella Solitaria ("The Lone Star"), was sent to jail because he made a call for revenge for the death of some Spaniards in Ciales in August 1898. The paper was closed down (Picó 1987, 145, 190). Different authors mention the incarceration of the other two pro-independence journalists without going into much detail (Corretjer 1977, 39; Medina Ramírez 1950, 77).

Puerto Rican patriot Eugenio María de Hostos was one of those with an aired response to the maltreatment of the Puerto Rican press and journalists. The educator and sociologist not only wrote against what he called an abuse of power but also recruited international personalities to speak on behalf of the Puerto Rican journalists (Delgado 1987, 28–29).

Shortly after the start of the new century and of the new colonial law the Puerto Ricans were experiencing, another independence advocate who used the press to speak out against the system also was incarcerated. He was Julio Medina González, a Hostos disciple, labor leader, painter, journalist, and politician. Medina González founded several newspapers, among them *La Voz del Pueblo* ("Peoples' Voice") and *La Revolución* ("Revolution"). His writings in the first cost him charges and several fines. His journalistic work in *La Revolución* led to thirty-two judicial proceedings and the definitive close of the publication.

In 1905, Medina González was elected to the House of Delegates by the District of Mayagüez as a candidate of the *Partido Unión de Puerto Rico* (Puerto Rico Union Party). While a legislator, he founded the journal *La Independencia* ("Independence") and published a caricature against Governor Beckman Winthrop in one of its issues. For this he was charged and sentenced to seven years in jail. He served a full year and a half of this term, which was commuted by Governor Winthrop himself.[1] According to an article written by José Enrique Ayoroa Santaliz, the governor's action was induced by his daughter, who had met Medina González while visiting the *La Princesa* jail and had been given one of his paintings by him (Ayoroa Santaliz 1994). Apparently the noble gesture of the jailed legislator softened the governor.

Medina González was later one of the founders of the Nationalist Party and in the 1932 elections already an old man, its candidate for resident commissioner in Washington (Rodríguez Cruz 1994).[2] His life was fully dedicated to the independence cause and the workers' struggle. With Hostos, he initiated in Puerto Rico the celebration of the International Workers' Day—on the first of May. He also is known as the Puerto Rican legislator who presented an independence project for Puerto Rico in 1905. His brother Félix, also an independence advocate and a renowned painter, was incarcerated in 1905.[3] The colonial government used the postage laws to charge and sentence both Medina González and Izcoa Díaz. The same laws would later be used to charge other independence fighters.

Between 1910 and 1919, several situations occurred in Puerto Rico that led those who decided to challenge the colonial regime in different ways to jail. The first case to warrant discussion is related to the controversy caused by the compulsory teaching in English in the public school system. This imposition had been denounced by teachers and politicians since the past decade and had resulted in a student strike in the nation's capital. Historian Juan Rodríguez Cruz (1994) states that it caused "the imprisonment of 14-year-old students and life expulsion for many of them. . . ."[4] This event, and possibly other similar ones, occurred during the period 1913–1915.

The expulsion of the students from Central High School led to the foundation of the José de Diego Institute, which would, of course, teach in Spanish. De Diego was one of the lawyers for the ousted students as a result of the aforementioned strike (Negrón de Montilla 1977, 154).

THE 1917 DRAFT: REPRESSION AND RESISTANCE

During the same decade, between 1917 and 1919, those opposing compulsory military recruitment were strongly repressed. This little-known fact of Puerto Rican history resulted in the incarceration of over 200 Puerto Ricans.

In March 1917, U.S. citizenship was collectively imposed on the Puerto Ricans. In May 1917, President Woodrow Wilson signed the draft bill that was effective in Puerto Rico on July 5. Within a few days, the parade of Puerto Ricans into the jails of the different districts commenced. During this period, 5,041 Puerto Ricans were declared delinquent by the Selective Service. Of those, over 330 were arrested, of which 229 were placed behind bars for not inscribing in the military register or for not showing up for the compulsory physical examination.

Sentences for these violations fluctuated from one day to a year in jail, although the greatest number of days actually served was thirty-three. There were four exceptions to this average, when four persons received greater sentences for violating the so-called Espionage Act; three of them suffered jail and exile when sent to jails in Atlanta, Georgia (Paralitici 1994, 1990).

Among those sentenced in 1917 was journalist Vicente Balbás Capó. The controversial journalist, in the same manner as Izcoa Díaz and Medina González, was arrested for violating a section of the Selective Service Bill. When the case was heard in the Federal District Court of the United States in Puerto Rico, he was found guilty and sentenced to eight years in jail. Balbás Capó, though, appealed to the First Circuit Court in Boston and was absolved (Paralitici 1994, 66–72).

It also should be said that this journalist was one of those who decided to reject U.S. citizenship and pledge the Puerto Rican one when the Jones Bill was approved in 1917. Likewise, he used his paper, *El Heraldo de las Antillas* ("The Antilles Herald"), to oppose the imposition of U.S. citizenship, the draft, and Americanization (Paralitici 1994).

Among those imprisoned in the period of the First World War, labor leader Florencio Romero must be mentioned. He was one of the three persons sent to jail in Atlanta, Georgia, as was already related.[5] The Caguas cigar maker was accused for pronouncing several speeches urging workers not to submit to the laws of compulsory military recruitment and against the imposition of U.S. citizenship. Later on, he was one of the founders of the Puerto Rican Nationalist Party (Corretjer 1966: 12).

In 1921, nefarious Governor Emmet Montgomery Reily began his short term (1921–1923). He was furiously anti-independence and anti-Puerto Rican, and he is considered one of the least liked and accepted governors of that turbulent era. The people mockingly referred to him as "Moncho Reyes" in a play of words with the way his name sounds in Spanish.

The practice of closing down newspapers also was continued in the beginning of that decade, for example, *Bandera Roja* (Red Flag). Paradoxically, despite "Moncho Reyes" and his anti-independence, we have not yet been able to detect cases of imprisoned independence advocates.

THE WAR AGAINST NATIONALISM

Precisely during this period the Nationalist Party was founded. Beginning in the next decade, its main leaders would be imprisoned. The imprisonment of members of the Nationalist movement would last until the 1970s, when those Nationalists still serving the sentences imposed in the 1950s were freed. Nationalists were in the jails on the island and in the United States for over forty years.

Under the leadership of Pedro Albizu Campos, the Nationalist movement broke away from its traditional method of moderate opposition. At the beginning of the 1930s, recently elected president of the Nationalist Party, Pedro Albizu Campos, started to denounce and challenge colonial politics directly. This strategic change in the independence movement coincided with a rise in the workers' struggle, which Albizu supported as a lawyer and politician. It also coincided with a rise in the independence ideal.

The United States opted to face this situation with the militarization of the Puerto Rican government. With this purpose, Blanton Winship was named governor, Elisha Francis Riggs was appointed chief of police, and Robert A. Cooper was named judge of the U.S. Court in Puerto Rico. All three were directly linked to the U.S. armed forces.

The incarceration of Nationalists began in early 1936, after several confrontations and judicial cases. The first case was that of poet Juan Antonio Corretjer, at the time secretary general of the Nationalist Party and director of the Nationalist paper, *La Palabra* ("The Word"). Corretjer was charged with contempt when he refused to turn over minutes and documents of the Nationalist Party's National Board. A few months prior, the Río Piedras Massacre had taken place, when four nationalists died after entrapment by the police.

Corretjer was sentenced to a year in jail. The one subsequently considered a National Poet was again incarcerated the next year and yet again during the next two decades. He also was imprisoned in 1935 while on a visit to Cuba. There he went to jail for publicly denouncing a threat made by the United States to invade Cuba as a result of a workers' strike, but apparently he was in prison only for a short period of time.[6]

After the Río Piedras Massacre,[7] the Nationalists had vowed revenge for the death of their martyrs. In February 1936, Hiram Rosado and Elías Beauchamp, both members of the Nationalist Party, ambushed and killed

Chief of Police E. Francis Riggs. Their mission accomplished, they were arrested and murdered in the police headquarters at Old San Juan.

From this moment on, leaders and members of different levels alike were persecuted and sentenced to jail. A few days after the death of Riggs, the U.S. District Court in Puerto Rico ordered the arrests of Nationalist leaders Pedro Albizu Campos, Juan Antonio Corretjer, Luis F. Velázquez, Clemente Soto Vélez, Erasmo Velázquez, Julio H.Velázquez, Rafael Ortiz Pacheco, Juan Gallardo Santiago, Juan Juarbe Juarbe, and Pablo Rosado Ortiz. They were accused of conspiracy to overturn by force the U.S. government in Puerto Rico (Rosado 1992, 131–42).

All were sentenced, except Juarbe Juarbe, who was exonerated, and Ortiz Pacheco, who escaped to Santo Domingo. The sentences ranged from six to ten years, to be served in Atlanta, Georgia. It should be mentioned that in this case two trials were celebrated. In the first, the jury could not reach a decision; in the second, composed mainly of North Americans, a verdict of guilty was handed down (Rosado 1992: 144–48).

The period of the mid-1930s was when, according to historian Rodríguez Cruz, "the human rights of the citizenry were trampled with the most impunity than in all of the history of Puerto Rico" (Rodríguez Cruz 1988, 65).[8] The historian from Mayagüez states that after the conviction of Albizu Campos and other pro-independence leaders, Governor Winship resolved to silence all protest and political demonstrations against the regime. Rodríguez Cruz mentions several cases as evidence of his statement. Repression was even worse after a 1938 attempt on Winship's life (Rodríguez Cruz 1988, 72).

Although Puerto Rican historiography has focused mainly on the incarceration of the Nationalist leadership of that particular time, many others were imprisoned. This atmosphere of violation of civil rights served as background for the Ponce Massacre (March 21, 1937), where nineteen persons died and hundreds of other people were injured by police. Among the dead were children, women, and elderly persons. Also among the casualties were two policemen, hit by the cross fire of their own colleagues, as was later established.

Violation of civil rights by the government, as pointed out by Rodríguez Cruz, also was exercised against the committees organized to support the Nationalist prisoners. People were arrested for the mere act of raising funds or collecting money for the defense of the prisoners.[9] The newspaper, *El Nacionalista de Puerto Rico* ("The Puerto Rican Nationalist"), for example, denounces the incarceration of a committee organized for those ends in San Juan and shows a photograph of thirteen persons.[10] Unfortunately, it includes no further information.

In September 1937, seven persons were arrested in Ciales for traffic violations. They were charged with interrupting traffic on the highway by collecting funds for the legal debts and for the families of the prisoners. Among those arrested were José Padrón Mislán, Eugenio Matos, Juan Ortiz Pérez,

Lino Ortiz, José Figueroa Gómez, and Angel Manuel Rodríguez. The latter was president of the Ciales Local Board of the Nationalist Party. Rodríguez expressed, according to El Imparcial, that the reason for the arrest was to boycott the celebration of the Grito de Lares.[11] This was not far from the truth, because that year the Lares mayor banned the celebration of the political acts of the Nationalist Party on September 23.[12]

Of the six charged, only the president of the Nationalist Board in Ciales served time. He was charged with disturbing the peace when, a few days prior in a similar activity, someone tried to run down by car those collecting funds. It was alleged that Rodríguez threatened the driver in front of the police. For this he spent two months in jail.

A group of people was indeed arrested for collecting funds for the Nationalist prisoners in Guánica. Judge Antonio Oliver Frau, of the Yauco Court, declared citizens Alejandro Víctor Sallabery, Agapito del Toro Rivera, Enrique Chacón Izquierdo, Casimiro Alicea Morciglio, Ramón Rivera Pietri, Adrián Víctor Ramos, Ernesto Almodóvar Santiago, Eugenio Santana, Vicente Morciglio Figueroa, and Pedro Almodóvar Figueroa guilty of violating traffic laws. He imposed a fine of five dollars or a day in jail for each unpaid dollar. The sentenced parties rejected the right to appeal and were held prisoner in the Guánica municipal jail.[13]

In the same year of the Ponce Massacre, in June, after Albizu Campos and the other Nationalists had been transferred to Atlanta, it was alleged that some Nationalists had tried to assassinate Judge Robert Cooper of the U.S. court in Puerto Rico. Ten Nationalist leaders were then arrested, including the acting president of the party, Julio Pinto Gandía. The court sentenced them to five years in jail (Medina Ramírez 1950, 140). They went to the Atlanta Federal Penitentiary in January 1938. Of the ten arrested and charged, eight were imprisoned. The other two, cousins Jesús Casellas Torres and Aníbal Arsuaga Casellas, turned "state witnesses."[14]

Others incarcerated besides Pinto Gandía were Manuel Avila, Juan Alamo, Juan Bautista Colón, Raimundo Díaz Pacheco, Julio Monge Hernández, Santiago Nieves Marzán, and Dionisio Vélez Avilés. They started serving their term on the same day they were sentenced, January 10, 1938, and the four months already served would be part of the term. Attorneys J. M. Toro Nazario and Carlos Santana Becerra said the verdict would not be appealed.[15]

According to a report by Prosecutor Cecil Snyder to the attorney general of the United States, Hommer Cummings, the Cooper case was perhaps more important than the Albizu Campos case:

> If Federal judges are shot at with impunity by those offended by their official acts, then we no longer live in a state of law. For being the first case in its class, and due to its importance, we have dedicated most of our scarce time to it since it began. Hopes of success in this case are brilliant.[16]

Cooper and Riggs were not the only targets of the Nationalists. Governor Winship, to whom the deaths of the Ponce Massacre were attributed, also was a target. Winship was bent on celebrating the U.S. invasion of Puerto Rico (July 25) in Ponce. He wanted to do this a year after the massacre and just six months after the second group of Nationalist leaders had been jailed. As the act was beginning, shots were fired from where the public was standing toward where the governor was standing. Angel Esteban Antongiorgi was left standing alone as he fired, but he missed his objective. Puerto Rican Colonel Luis Irizarry died instead. Antongiorgi was executed at the same place by a policeman.

Charges for murder and conspiracy to kill the governor were issued against many Nationalists. Ultimately, five were found guilty and sentenced to life imprisonment: Tomás López de Victoria, Elifaz Escobar, Santiago González Castro, Juan Pietri, and Prudencio Segarra. They served eight years at the Puerto Rico State Penitentiary, after which their sentences were commuted by Governor Rexford Guy Tugwell when acknowledging that the government had committed an injustice (Medina Ramírez 1950, 140).

In 1937, José A. "Nin" Negrón also was jailed for violating the explosives laws.[17] Others also would be charged with the same crime in that active year of 1937. In Ponce, in October, prosecutor Guillermo Pierluissi began raiding countless residences because of supposed information about explosives being entered into the city and other towns in the south.[18] The repressive tactics of Winship's government did not cease during the rest of the decade. Nationalist acts were banned or ways were found to avoid or interrupt them. Nevertheless, and despite having two presidents in jail, the Nationalists continued their work.

Arrests related to the bombing against priest Néstor J. Aguilera and banker Pedro Juan Rosaly began on October 22. The first charged and arrested was Jesús Ruiz Arzola, who entered the district jail in Ponce on October 22 and was released by November 9. Prosecutor Pierluissi ordered his release without any explanation.[19]

In January 1938, another group of Nationalists was sentenced to hard labor at the Ponce district jail. Their names and sentences follow: Antonio Buscaglia, ten years; Alejandro Medina Rodríguez, eight years; Guillermo Hernández, eight years; Candita Collazo, four years. Collazo's husband, Virgilio Torres, also had been charged but was absolved, as well as Ramón Morales. The latter two spent over two months in jail.

It should be mentioned that Candita Collazo was possibly the first pro-independence woman imprisoned in the twentieth century. Others could have spent a few days in jail, as is the case of a group in San Juan arrested for violation of traffic laws while collecting money for the Nationalist prisoners. But Collazo's case stands out for the duration of the sentence and the type of case to which she was linked. Charges against her and the aforementioned group were for possession, storage, use, and transportation of explosives. They also were accused of placing a bomb wrapped in a U.S. flag at the porch of the residence of priest Aguilera, which caused much damage when it exploded. The Catholic priest had been declared "persona non grata" by the Nationalists for his anti-independence stance.[20]

One month later, another group was sentenced to jail for an explosives case. This time the charged Nationalists were from Barrio Obrero, in Santurce, accused of illegal possession of explosives. The judge sentenced Carlos Llauger Díaz, Agustín Pizarro, Guillermo Roque Cortijo, Elí Barreto Pérez, and Pedro Brenes to a year in prison; they entered the San Juan district jail on February 8.

In those last years of the 1930s, many persons were arrested and jailed for destroying U.S. government property. One of the most frequent acts was the damage or destruction of U.S. post office boxes. According to ex-federal Marshall Jorge Bird Arias, in those days two or three arrests were made daily for this cause. Bird Arias attributed those acts to the Nationalists. As he remembers it, the sentence for this type of offense was as long as five years in jail.[21] According to an article published in the *New York Times*, dozens of Puerto Ricans were put in jail for destroying U.S. post office boxes in 1939. Some were sent to jail in Atlanta, while others served time in Puerto Rico.[22]

THE 1940S: NEW WAVE OF IMPRISONMENTS

At the end of the 1930s, many nationalists were charged and sentenced to terms in U.S. prisons for violation of the compulsory military service established prior to the Second World War. Almost 100 persons were incarcerated for this cause, and unlike the war preceding it, the terms ranged from one to five years in prison. In the 1940s, two other directory boards of the Nationalist Party would be imprisoned: one headed by Ramón Medina Ramírez and one by Julio de Santiago.

Violators of the Selective Service Bill were accused of not registering, not attending the physical exam, not complying with the call to register in the draft, and/or not carrying with them the military draft card. Some also were accused, as was the case with Medina Ramírez, for inciting not to register. Arrests started as early as the beginning of the 1940 decade. The first Nationalist arrested was Maricao resident Juan Ramón Martínez. During that year and the next, twenty-three Nationalists were jailed. Martínez was one of the several cases of persons arrested twice for resisting the draft. The second time he was charged with not carrying his Selective Service card.

These first people arrested also were the first Nationalists sent to the Tallahassee, Florida, state prison. A few days after that first group was sent to Tallahassee, a second group was arrested, which included the leaders of the National Board, Medina Ramírez and Rafael López Rosas. One of Medina

Ramírez's sons also was arrested. It should be noted that five of this leader's sons were arrested for refusing the draft.

In 1942, the total of sentenced persons was twenty. Among them were the members of the acting National Board, Julio de Santiago, Paulino Castro, and José Rivera Sotomayor. The year 1943 was one when Nationalists who had already been in jail were again arrested, among other new cases. The total that year reached sixteen, eleven of whom were jailed for the second time. In 1944, six Nationalists were arrested, and the last year of the Second World War, another six.

Nationalists residing in New York also resisted the draft. Four cases have been identified, three of them members of the Nationalist Party Board: Amaury Ruiz, Roberto Acevedo, and César G. Torres Rodríguez. The other person was journalist Rafael López Rosa, who had already been sentenced in Puerto Rico.

From 1941 to 1943, seven protesters were jailed for resisting the draft and for threatening Judge Cooper, the judge who handed down the largest number of guilty verdicts (Paralitici 1993). These persons could not be positively linked to the Nationalist Party, but in some cases they expressed their sympathies with this political movement, or with its leader, Albizu Campos (Paralitici 1993).

Although the practice had been to enforce military registers only in times of war, shortly after the end of the Second World War, in 1948, a new military service law was approved.[23] Six young Nationalists were arrested for violating it: Rafael Cancel Miranda, Ramón Medina Maisonave, Luis M. O'Neill, Reinaldo Trilla, Darío Berríos, and Miguel Angel Ruiz Alicea. They were all cadets of the Nationalist Party (Rodríguez Cruz 1994, 184). Cancel Miranda and Medina Maisonave were both sentenced to two years and a day (Seijo Bruno 1989, 19). The others were sentenced to a year and a day for not registering with the military service.

These six cases were the last of the decade (1940) related to the military draft. The following decade very few arrests related to military service evasion were identified, due mainly to the fact that the Nationalist Party altered its strategy of direct confrontation of the system. Evaders opted to flee, not allowing the authorities to arrest them. Irvin Flores, one of those who in later years would participate in the attack on the U.S. Congress, was one of the evaders who did not permit his arrest.[24]

The last arrests in the 1940s involved the student leaders of the 1948 strike and the subsequent incidents the next year at the University of Puerto Rico. José M. Tejada, Juan Mari Brás, Pelegrín García, Jorge Luis Landing, and José Gil de la Madrid were expelled from the university, charged and sentenced for causing disturbances on the university campus. The cases were seen separately, and all were sentenced to two months in jail.

This was at the time when Albizu returned to the island after ten years in the Atlanta prison. The college students invited him to an act on the Río

Piedras campus, and then-Chancellor Jaime Benítez banned it. This sparked a great deal of student activity. The repression exercised by the police during these student activities was such that several students received injuries that left them hospitalized for months. Ironically, Benítez had been one of the main leaders of a civic group who had pleaded for the release of Albizu Campos and the other Nationalist prisoners in 1937.

NATIONALIST INSURRECTION AND THE GAG LAW

The 1950 decade was witness to several episodes of great repression, particularly those following the Nationalist Insurrection and the enforcement of the Gag Law, as it came to be known. During the Insurrection, over twenty Nationalists died. In the wave of repression that followed, over 1,000 persons were arrested, Nationalists and non-Nationalists alike, including members of other pro-independence and Communist organizations. Of those arrested, 119 were sent to prison (Helfeld 1964). The sentences of the Nationalists linked to the insurrection were extremely harsh, with some people receiving sentences of up to 400 years.

Sixty-seven other persons were declared guilty of violating Law 53, known as the Gag Order.[25] This was a carbon copy of the Smith Bill of the United States, enacted to fight communism in said country during the period known as the McCarthy era. The Gag Order banned pro-independence acts and was responsible for the imprisonment of many a person professing that ideal. Through this anti-democratic law, people were jailed for the mere act of expressing anti-government remarks, whether oral or written, for applauding Nationalist speakers, for requesting signatures for anti-nuclear manifestos, and, unbelievably, for taking flowers to and visiting the gravesite of a Nationalist (Acosta 1987).

In 1950 and 1954, the Nationalists extended their armed actions to the United States. In 1950, they unsuccessfully attempted to assassinate President Harry Truman when he was living at the Blair House, while in 1954 they attacked the U.S. Congress. Nationalist Griselio Torresola died during the attempt on Truman's life, and Oscar Collazo was sentenced to the death penalty, but this was later commuted, and he was given life imprisonment. The act against Congress cost Nationalists Lolita Lebrón, Rafael Cancel Miranda, Irvin Flores, and Andrés Figueroa Cordero sentences of over fifty years each. All five were pardoned in 1979, when they were already the political prisoners imprisoned for the longest terms in the hemisphere. In the 1950s, more arrests were made for evasion of the draft; toward the end of the decade, over seventy persons were still in jail. The last remaining Nationalists in jail in Puerto Rico were released by the then governor in 1970.

As this relation demonstrates, between 1898 and 1958, hundreds of Puerto Ricans were jailed for political reasons. Between 1935 and 1939, for example, over seventy Nationalists were sent to prison. During the Second World War, some eighty Nationalists were jailed in U.S. prisons, with sentences ranging from a year and a half to four years. The 1950s witnessed mass arrests and imprisonment for exercising freedom of speech, which was supposedly guaranteed under the newly enacted Constitution of the Commonwealth of Puerto Rico. In short, the first six decades of the twentieth century saw an average of eight to ten imprisonments each year. At that rate, the end of the century would see almost 1,000 Puerto Rican men and women jailed for their anti-colonial struggle.[26]

NOTES

1. J. Arnaldo Meyners, "*Candidatos a Comisionado Residente de Puerto Rico en Washington,*" *El Mundo*, November 5, 1932, p. 7.

2. See also Delgado (1976, 129–31), for facts on Medina González's life as an artist, and Routte-Gómez 1994.

3. "Indulto J. Medina," *Bandera de Puerto Rico*, June 8, 1905, p. 1.

4. Unfortunately, there are no further details on this incident cited by the historian. It would have been useful that evidence of the source of such important data had been found. Nevertheless, Negrón de Montilla (1977, 147–55) made known the conflict that arose in Santurce Central High School regarding the expulsion of students over language, although she makes no mention that any of them were jailed during the period 1913–1915.

5. The other two were not independence advocates. They were accused for violation of espionage laws. One of them was German.

6. "Juan Antonio Corretjer, 1908–1985: *Breve biografía*," *Claridad*, August 25–31, 1985, pp. 4–5; *Claridad*, January 6–12, 1995, p. 18.

7. In the Río Piedras Massacre, a group of young Nationalists was shot at by the police, and several died. See Medina Ramírez 1950; Rosado 1992.

8. Corretjer states the same thing in *Boletín Nacional* (January 1982): 4–5.

9. See also Ribes Tovar 1971, 79–81.

10. "*Señoritas y caballeros presos por colectar fondos pro-presos en San Juan,*" *El Nacionalista de Puerto Rico* (March 1991): 16.

11. *El Imparcial*, September 18, 1937, p. 5.

12. *El Imparcial*, September 22, 1937, p. 29.

13. *El Imparcial*, September 15, 1937, p. 29 and November 18, 1937, p. 8.

14. Testimony of Manuel Avila when interviewed by Seijo Bruno (1989, 15–16). According to *El Imparcial*, January 11, 1938, pp. 12, 20, 21, Arzuaga Casellas and Torres Casellas declared themselves guilty days before the trial, and the judge sentenced them to two and a half years in prison. The news goes on to say that the lenient sentence was due to the fact that they had declared themselves guilty and "for having cooperated with the state in the discovery and apprehension of the authors of the crime."

15. *El Imparcial*, January 11, 1938, pp. 20–21.

16. Ibid., December 12, 1937, p. 12. The report to Cummings is dated December 6, 1937.

17. Miñi Seijo Bruno, *Claridad-En Rojo* (October 27–November 2, 1978): 2.

18. El Imparcial, October 15, 1937, p. 25; *El Imparcial*, October 17, 1937, p. 1.

19. El Imparcial, October 23, 1937, p. 1; November 1 and 19, 1937, p. 1.

20. El Imparcial, November 13, 1937, p. 2; December 17, 1937, p. 3; January 11, 1938, pp. 1, 10, 21.

21. Interview with Jorge Bird.

22. *New York Times*, August 15, 1939, p. 14.

23. The new draft law operated until 1973.

24. Author's interviews with Irvin Flores Rodríguez and Gil Ramos Cancel.

25. For more information on the Gag Order and nationalism in the 1950s, see the chapter by Acosta in this book; also see Acosta 1987 and Seijo Bruno 1989.

26. For more information on the cases of the current Puerto Rican political prisoners, we refer the reader to Jan Susler's chapter in this book. On the imprisonment of pro-independence advocates in the last decades, see Paralitici 1996.

WORKS CITED

Acosta, Ivonne. 1987. *La Mordaza. Puerto Rico 1948–1957*. Río Piedras, Puerto Rico: Editorial Edil.

Ayoroa Santaliz, José E. 1983. "Evaristo Izcoa Díaz." *Claridad-En Rojo* (May 14–20): 24–25.

———. 1994. "Don Julio Medina González." *Claridad-En Rojo* (April 16–22): 25.

Corretjer, Juan A. 1966. *La sangre en huelga: Notas de la resistencia al Servicio Militar Obligatorio*. Guaynabo, Puerto Rico: N.p.

———. 1977. *La lucha por la independencia de Puerto Rico*. Guaynabo, Puerto Rico: N.p.

Delgado, Juan Manuel. 1987. *"Hostos y los prisioneros de Guerra."* *Claridad-En Rojo* (January 9–15): 28–29.

Delgado, Osiris. 1976. *La Gran Enciclopedia de Puerto Rico*. Vol. 8. Madrid: Ediciones R.C. Corredera.

Figueroa, Loida. 1983. *Breve historia de Puerto Rico: Segunda parte*. Río Piedras, Puerto Rico: Editorial Edil.

Gil de Rubio, Víctor M. 1978. *Periodismo patriótico de Evaristo Izcoa Díaz*. San Juan: Liga de Cooperativas.

Helfeld, David M. 1964. "Discrimination for Political Beliefs and Associations." *Revista del Colegio de Abogados de Puerto Rico* 25:1 (November): 5–276.

Medina Ramírez, Ramón. 1950. *El Movimiento Libertador en la historia de Puerto Rico*. San Juan: Imprenta Nacional.

Negrón de Montilla, Aida. 1977. *La americanización de Puerto Rico y el sistema de instrucción pública, 1900–1930*. Río Piedras, Puerto Rico: Editorial Universitaria.

Paralitici, José (Che). 1990. *"Oposición al Servicio Militar Obligatorio durante la Primera Guerra Mundial," Revista Universidad de América* 2:2: 120–23.

———. 1993. *Imposición, apoyo y oposición al Servicio Militar Obligatorio en Puerto Rico durante la Primera y Segunda Guerra Mundial*. Doctoral dissertation, Universidad de Valladolid, España.

———. 1994. "Vicente Balbás Capó: Tenaz Opositor a la ciudadanía y al Servicio Militar Obligatorio estadounidense en Puerto Rico." *Revista Universidad de América* 6:1: 66–72.

———. 1996. *"100 años de violaciones a los derechos humanos y civiles en Puerto Rico a los luchadores de la independencia." Revista Universidad de América* 8:1–2: 98–107.

———. 1998. *No quiero mi cuerpo pa' tambor: El servicio militar obligatorio en Puerto Rico*. San Juan: Ediciones Puerto.

Picó, Fernando. 1987. *1898: La guerra después de la guerra*. Río Piedras, Puerto Rico: Ediciones Huracán.

Ribes Tovar, Federico. 1971. *Albizu Campos, Puerto Rican Revolutionary*. New York: Plus Ultra.

Rodríguez Cruz, Juan. 1988. *"Violación de los derechos civiles en los años 1937–1938." Islote* (December): 65–76.

———. 1994. *Pedro Albizu Campos (Un asomo a su vida y su época)*. San Juan: N.p.

Rosado, Marisa. 1992. *Las llamas de la aurora: Acercamiento a una biografía de Pedro Albizu Campos*. San Juan: N.p.

Routte-Gómez, Eneid. 1994. "Medina Ramírez Brothers Leave Spiritual Legacy." *San Juan Star-Venue* (February 27): 2.

Seijo Bruno, Miñi. 1989. *La insurrección nacionalista en Puerto Rico, 1950*. Río Piedras, Puerto Rico: Editorial Edil.

PART II

Contemporary Issues

FIVE

Puerto Rico

The Puzzle of Human Rights and Self-Determination

José Javier Colón Morera

BY MANY ACCOUNTS, Puerto Rico is still a colonial dependency of the United States, where significant human rights violations and an intense social crisis, the product of severe income inequality, unfold (Trías Monge 1997; Rivera Ramos 2001; Anderson 1998; Rivera-Batiz and Santiago 1996). This socioeconomic crisis, however, is not producing a rapid or strong push toward self-determination (Rivera Ramos 2001). This chapter elaborates on this paradox presented by Puerto Rico at the beginning of a new century.

I depart from an expansive view of human rights that goes beyond the exercise of traditional liberal individual civil rights (the so-called "first generation rights") of freedom of expression and association, due process, privacy, and freedom of religion, among others (Miller 1997, 222–23). It includes the aim to develop "the human personality to its fullest extent" through a socioeconomic order that encourages such results.[1] It is a vision of human rights that assumes that democracy includes both procedural and substantive requirements, including those socioeconomic rights contained in the United Nations' Declaration of Human Rights (Zinn 1995).

Human rights also are articulated through collective national claims of self-determination that encompass greater control and care of natural resources as well as the need to protect the poor. In the current international context, the protection of human rights is closely connected to the possibility of interdependent economic growth in a regional or global context. There can only exist redistributive social state policies if there is dynamic economic competitiveness and a substantial investment in public infrastructure.

In the Puerto Rican case, human rights are adversely affected by a territorial model that exports profits in astronomical proportions but generates extremely low levels of reinvestment in social capital and in the reproduction of social conditions producing healthy and collaborative social interactions (Daubón 2002).

While this Caribbean island has a liberal constitution with a republican form of government and political autonomy for organizing and administering narrowly defined internal governmental functions, the U.S. Congress retains practically unlimited legislative powers over issues governing external relations, the economy, customs, military powers, and other aspects of governance having to do with U.S. interests (Federal Relations Act, 1 LPRA;[2] Trías Monge 1997). Although Puerto Rican politics unfold in a similar fashion to what happens in Caribbean and Latin American independent countries, as islanders possess their own political party system and a particularly Latin political culture, and although U.S. political parties do not compete in Puerto Rican elections, the U.S. government has regularly interfered with internal political processes, particularly to repress or disrupt the pro-independence movement (see the chapter by Bosque-Pérez in this book; also see Fernández 1992; Gautier Mayoral and Blanco Stahl 1997). Within Puerto Rico, the political class has not been responsive to the growing call from the island's civil society for the establishment of a more democratic, equitable socioeconomic order (Rivera Ortiz 2001).

Presently, the island is showing signs of social crisis and institutional decay. With a chronic real unemployment rate of around 40 percent of its active population and a murder rate of over 18 for every 100,000 inhabitants, the island experiences intense civil conflict that further demonstrates the limitations of the present territorial model. Far from being a model of capitalist expansion, the island manifests the exhaustion of the export-led model that produced rapid modernization in the 1950s and 1960s (Pantojas 1990). As in other territories in the Caribbean, however, the claim for sovereignty continues to be voiced by a minority of voters, although there is some inter-elite consensus in favor of political reform and greater autonomy (Ramos and Rivera Ortiz 2001).

The democratic deficit, which allows the U.S. Congress to decide many of Puerto Rico's internal governmental functions and prevents greater levels of economic self-reliance, is at the root of the island's socioeconomic crisis. Unable to participate in international commercial negotiations and having lost its particular and most salient competitive economic advantages in the U.S. market as a U.S. territory due to the effects of the North American Free Trade Agreement (NAFTA), Caribbean Basin Initiative (CBI), and other accords opening the U.S. market to independent countries in the region, the

Commonwealth of Puerto Rico shows increasing signs of economic stagnation and lack of institutional flexibility (Rivera Ortiz 2001; Catalá Oliveras
N.d.). Under the Commonwealth structure, it has been impossible for Puerto
Rico even to be member of the Association of Caribbean States (ACS) in
order to devise joint regional political, economic, and cultural initiatives.
Economic development is thus handicapped within the boundaries of a territorial framework that fosters continuous dependency on federal governmental funds but encourages few incentives to help Puerto Ricans devise a strategy of interdependent self-reliance. There is no way that Puerto Rico will
improve its human rights record with regard to its significantly poor population in the absence of major institutional changes permitting the island
greater influence over trade and investment agreements.

On the internal political front, the process of activation of the island's
civil society on human rights and political issues, such as the one carried out
on the Vieques issue (see the chapter by Colón Morera and Rivera Santana
in this book), creates a potentially positive environment to initiate a public
discussion of consensus-based proposals to push forward self-determination.
Popular sectors, nevertheless, still resist political change because, among
other reasons, no concrete economic transition plan has been devised to
show, incrementally, how the island would be assuming the new political
responsibilities in a fully non-colonial context. This step would require U.S.
congressional commitment and involvement. Unfortunately, as we will
describe later, congressional involvement is, at the present juncture, totally
lacking. In this context, the equilibrium of electoral power of the two main
political parties, the Popular Democratic Party (PDP) and the New Progressive Party (NPP), which have administered alternatively the internal political process since 1968, legitimizes territorial control (Anderson 1998, 55).

In this chapter I describe some key issues related to the protection of civil
and human rights. I propose that the island's increasingly open social conflict
is contributing to an erosion of the liberal consensus reached in 1952 under its
new constitutional order. I emphasize that some particular areas, such as crime
and drug interdiction policies, are in conflict with the protection of existing
civil rights. I argue that the process of deterioration of the civil rights environment will continue to degenerate unless the territorial issue is addressed
and finally resolved. I also propose that the social crisis, which Puerto Rico
undergoes, has to be closely linked to an effort to remove high levels of authoritarian, sexist, and racist elements in the popular culture. The collective
process of national self-determination, in order to be meaningful for the popular sectors, will have to include a multifaceted approach to the development
of new levels of consciousness about human and civil rights protections.

To place Puerto Rico's quest for political sovereignty and human rights
in its proper historical context, I start with a brief description of the current
political and constitutional arrangement.

THE LIBERAL CONSENSUS

This Caribbean island was made a territorial possession of the United States in 1898 as a result of the Spanish American War. After a process of classic colonialism from 1898 to 1952, in that year the U.S. government granted some autonomy (in the form of a new constitution) to Puerto Rico in order to exclude itself from the list of imperial nations administering dependent territories and, consequently, having to inform the United Nations about the status of their colonies (Trías 1997; Gautier Mayoral and Argüelles 1978).

The creation of the Commonwealth was part of a modernization of the operation of the internal government and a way to rapidly develop an export-led manufacturing economic model for the island (Serrano Geyls 1979; Pantojas 1990). The modernization process, along with a great deal of political repression, decimated the electoral strength of the pro-independence movement. The Puerto Rican Independence Party (PIP), which was the second political party in 1952, was not able to retain its electoral franchise in the 1960, 1964, and 1968 electoral contests and had to register itself again as a political party to compete in subsequent elections.

Repression against all of the sectors that defended the island's political sovereignty during this period was selective but intense (see the chapter by Bosque-Pérez in this book). It was particularly crude while the process of creating a new constitutional order was taking place (see the chapter by Acosta in this book) and selective during 1967 when an effort was made to demonstrate popular support for the colonial regime through a status plebiscite legislated and organized by the Commonwealth government (Gautier Mayoral and Blanco Stahl 1997). Federal direct repression has continued to be a factor every time key U.S. interests in Puerto Rico have been challenged, as the recent 1999–2003 anti-navy Vieques experience shows (see the chapter by Colón Morera and Rivera Santana in this book).

Nevertheless, suppression of the independence movement and other initiatives arising in the island's civil society, especially during the second half of the twentieth century, occurred within a framework of formally liberal politics (Duverger 1984). We know, however, that the official constitutional recognition of legal rights does not necessarily mean they are, or will be, actually implemented. On the contrary, the liberal regime coexists with values, institutions, and practices that are at odds with the constitutional principles purportedly required by the rule of law (Díaz 1973; Burchel, Gordon, and Miller 1991).

Frank Donner (1981) argues that in the context of grave social injustice, this schizophrenic behavior is inherent to the liberal order. From this perspective, the official reluctance to confront the issues of discrimination against the poor is intended to circumvent the clearly evident contradictions between democratic theory, the practices of social control, and growing economic inequality. However, with all of its defects and contradictions, including the registration of voters to participate in the election of delegates amid massive arrests of members of the Nationalist Party and the Puerto Rican Independence Party, the constitutional process that began in 1951 reflected a desire to achieve a modern, liberal, self-governing society within the framework of the rule of law and with full respect for individual and social rights.

The composition of the 1951 Constituent Assembly exerted a certain degree of socialist and populist influence on the resulting constitution of the *Estado Libre Asociado* (ELA). Sections of the constitution outlaw discrimination based on race, social condition, or religious beliefs. The constitution also explicitly upholds the principle of inadmissibility of evidence illegally obtained by the state during a criminal investigation (Constitución . . . 1 LPRA). In addition, the internal constitution clearly protects fundamental social and economic rights, such as the right to collective bargaining and to strike (ibid.), and individual rights, such as the right to privacy (ibid.). Conservatives in the U.S. Congress, however, significantly restrained the scope of this constitution. As a prerequisite for its approval, Congress demanded elimination of Section 20, which defined a broad spectrum of human and social rights, including the inalienable right to be gainfully employed.

The 1952 ELA Constitution is still clearly progressive in its understanding of human rights and the need to protect human dignity from arbitrary attacks by the state. Section 19, as it was approved, left open the possibility for future recognition of civil rights in a continuing process of collective maturation. In some cases, this has in fact occurred. In *Amy v. Secretario* (1985), for example, the Supreme Court of Puerto Rico specifically accepted the right to work, something that had originally been contained in Section 20 of the Bill of Rights.[3]

THE LIBERAL CONSENSUS UNDER ATTACK

Outlawing discrimination and recognizing rights in the constitution does not mean that a country has achieved equality in these areas or enacted those rights or, more importantly, that it is moving in the direction of realizing these constitutional ideals. Let us examine recent data on poverty, since we know that socioeconomic marginality is one of the main factors causing a rapid and general decrease in the quality of life and preventing the achievement of a true modern political context.

According to a study done by the Puerto Rico Bureau of Labor Statistics, "the estimated number of related children ages 5 to 17 in families in poverty in Puerto Rico is 498,937."[4] This number roughly represents one-eighth of the total population of the island! Recent data confirm that more than 59 percent of Puerto Rican residents live under the poverty line drawn by the federal government.

88   JOSÉ JAVIER COLÓN MORERA

Another important aspect of the current crisis of the territorial model is reflected in the island's high crime rate. There is a sense of constant insecurity and fear in social interactions. In the United States, for example, the murder rate per 100,000 inhabitants was 5.5 in 2000, while in Puerto Rico, the rate for the same year was more than three times greater, 18.2 per 100,000.[5] Puerto Rico also has been designated a region of heavy drug abuse and drug trafficking. Most of the offenses committed are not murder, however, but "property damage," a label that is a transparent reference to the structure of social marginality that largely explains the crime wave. Most of those committing these offenses are from housing projects originally built to provide decent homes for the urban poor but that have become centers of despair and want (Santiago Nieves 1994). The young, the poor, and especially young, poor, black men from the projects and barrios often are defined in the public mind as criminals or potential criminals simply on the basis of their skin color and social condition.

If we turn our attention to the traffic and consumption of illegal drugs, the scenario is not any more encouraging. A recent study describes the question quite effectively:

> Drug-related violent crime is common in Puerto Rico. . . . According to law enforcement officials, retail drug distributors in Puerto Rico and the U.S. Virgin Islands are heavily armed and commit violent crimes, including homicide to control lucrative drug markets. The Puerto Rico Police Department reported that 63 percent of the 744 murders on the island in 2001 were related to drug distribution activity. Further, approximately 70 to 80 percent of homicides involving firearms in Puerto Rico are attributed to disputes over drugs and turf. Drug abusers in the territories also commit violent crimes, including robbery, burglary, carjacking, car theft, and home invasion to obtain money to support their drug habits.[6]

On the effects of this high level of drug trafficking in the criminal justice system of the island, the report is equally negative:

> The percentage of federal sentences that were drug-related in Puerto Rico was significantly higher than the national percentage in FY2001. According to [the] U.S. Sentencing Commission (USSC) data, 68.0 percent of federal sentences in Puerto Rico were drug-related in FY2001 compared with 41.2 percent nationwide. Of the drug-related federal sentences in Puerto Rico, 77.7 percent resulted from powdered or crack cocaine offenses, compared with 42.5 percent nationwide.[7]

Finally, the same report establishes the level of economic impact of this illegal enterprise in the territorial economy:

> The financial impact on Puerto Rico's government from substance abuse-related costs is substantial. In 1998, the most recent year for which data are

available, Puerto Rican officials spent nearly $900 million on substance abuse-related programs in areas including justice, education, health, child/family assistance, mental health/developmental disabilities, and public safety. This figure amounted to 6.2 percent of the total expenditures for the commonwealth. When factoring in the cost of lost productivity and nongovernmental expenses by private social services, estimates for total substance abuse-related costs are even higher.[8]

The quality of life of thousands of Puerto Ricans is trapped in a chronic chemical dependence that affects all aspects of human interactions and absolutely departs from the constitutional goal of preserving the "human dignity" of all citizens. Additionally, the result of this crime wave is that wider segments of the poor sectors of the population also have suffered serious intrusions into their private lives. The major focus during the 1990s was in connection with combating crime in barrios and public housing projects. In these communities, also identified as having a high incidence of drug use, police and National Guardsmen have assaulted buildings, entering and searching residences and individuals illegally.

By the beginning of 1997, such operations had been carried out in more than eighty low-income housing projects.[9] Through an expensive publicity campaign, officials actually bragged about their use of violence and their aggressive takeover of a public housing project, exulting in the necessity of using a "heavy hand" in checking crime (Partido Nuevo Progresista 1996). For people living in the projects, the possibility of being subjected without a warrant to unlawful searches in their homes or cars was greater during the 1990s than ever before. The challenges to the 1952 liberal consensus are quite obvious.

Studies of these *toma de caseríos* (invasion of the public housing projects) reveal that in spite of the dubious legality of some of the joint operations by the police force and the National Guard, this practice was initially popular among residents of low-income housing projects. The positive attitude of residents can be explained partially by the sharp increase in crime and the utter neglect to which these communities have been subjected in the past (Albarrán González n.d.). The government of Puerto Rico had essentially given up trying to control certain urban spaces, thereby condemning the residents to their fate.

While this "heavy hand" was applied to poor communities, the island's Justice Department was ignoring the generalized corruption involving government officials and some business sectors closely connected to the 1992–2000 Rosselló administration (Navarro 2002). In a well-received newspaper article, renowned Puerto Rican historian Fernando Picó lucidly described the road down which the Rosselló administration was taking the government:

> The government . . . implemented two seemingly contradictory policies: Economically, greater laissez-faire, the freest hand possible so that economic forces in the private sector can rule the market. In the social arena, in contrast, there [was] the "heavy hand" of state control: occupation and forced closure of residences, stronger jail sentences and little chance for parole, constant searches of motorists, efforts to restrict the right to bail, drug tests in schools and the workplace, publicity in favor of controls over the education of children, neighbors encouraged to spy on each other, and so forth. (Picó 1994, 83)

In his incisive critique, historian Picó charged that the emphasis on the heavy hand of state control in the public housing projects avoided the basic fact that it is the wealthy and powerful who are ultimately responsible for, and are the beneficiaries of, the drug trafficking that generates the crimes against which this policy is unleashed. "Who will bell the cat?" Picó asked ironically. The change in public opinion, coupled with the fact that federal and state money ran out for this massive show of force, led to a decline in the invasion of housing projects (García Muñíz and Rodríguez Beruff 1999), and the practice was drastically reduced in 1996.

With the advent of a new administration of the Popular Democratic Party (PDP) in 2000, new plans were laid out by the Calderón administration in this area. Under the new policy, unveiled by the Police of Puerto Rico in 2002, officials would have to solve a larger proportion of the docket of criminal cases (around 45 percent) under investigation. The pressure to show results could be promoting a tendency to present criminal charges "at any cost." Calls for more interception of private telephone calls and elimination of procedural protections such as the right to bail are again being raised, based on the campaign against terrorism as well as the acute crime rates in public housing.

However, not all challenges to human and civil rights emanate from governmental actions. For instance, Benítez Nazario's chapter in this book shows that there are high levels of intolerance toward gays, lesbians, and Dominicans, among others. Such prejudice, embedded in all classes and within civil society as a whole, lays siege to democratic values.

If we turn our focus to the social environment of women, a prevalent pattern of gender discrimination is detected, for example, in the extremely high levels of domestic violence. According to María Dolores Fernós, director of Women's Affairs, Office of the Commonwealth of Puerto Rico, every fifteen days a woman dies as a result of the so-called "crimes of passion" inflicted by husbands, boyfriends, or partners.[10]

In the case of race, advances in the recognition of civil rights have been particularly slow (Comisión de Derechos Civiles 1998; Muñoz Vázquez and Alegría Ortega 1999). Human rights abuses in this field have occurred too often in job discrimination, police authoritarianism, differential judicial treatment, and limited access to judicial redress. Racism has been publicly aired only in the past few decades, especially through Zenón Cruz's magnificent two-volume treatise *Narciso descubre su trasero*. Self-published in 1974 and 1975 because of publishers' fears, the work received widespread condemnation in the public media but quickly sold out and was never republished. Puerto Ricans reluctantly acknowledge prejudice and racial discrimination without being willing to take real and proactive action on these problems (Nina 2001).

The frustration with the level of day-to-day violence in poor barrios is getting to the point where some sectors of the civil society are demanding increased police presence in those communities to avert the continued murders of mostly young, poor, male and, many times, black youths. The liberal consensus is showing fragility in the middle of a serious social crisis. Pro-independence sectors also are pointing out that the U.S. government is failing to protect Puerto Rico's residents by its negligent supervision of the island's borders from the huge illegal traffic of drugs and firearms.

The social crisis, in this context, is being utilized to try to grant further legitimization to authoritarian anti-crime strategies. The best example of this policy is capital punishment. Recently, the U.S. government has overridden Puerto Rico's active civil society with respect to death penalty, the imposition of which clashes explicitly with the text of the Puerto Rican Constitution. The vast majority of Puerto Ricans continue to firmly oppose it (Sued Badillo 2000; Cámara Fuertes et al., forthcoming). However, in 1996, the U.S. Congress passed legislation imposing this punishment for over sixty different federal crimes and made it applicable to all states and territories, except Native American reservations in the United States.[11] Only three years later, the first death penalty case in many decades was heard in the U.S. Federal District Court of Puerto Rico in mid-1999.

In 2001, a federal district court decided that the imposition of capital punishment violated the Puerto Rican Constitution, but on appeal, other federal courts overturned that decision. The president of the Civil Rights Commission of the Commonwealth at the time stated, "Showing a great deal of lack of sensitivity for the cultural and ethical values of the Puerto Rican people that, since 1929, legislated to prohibit the death penalty, these [Federal Appellate Circuit] judges, with a total disregard of the [Puerto Rican] Constitution approved by the U.S. Congress, overturned Judge Casellas' decision to exclude Puerto Rico from the death penalty" (Fernández Colón 2001, my translation).

In conclusion, three distinct factors continue to act together to undermine the protection of human rights on the island: (1) the increasingly difficult task of defending the protection of civil rights in the face of rising domestic crime (it is expected that Puerto Rico will report around 750 murders in

2003) and Puerto Rico's location at the so-called epicenter of the region's drug traffic; (2) the implementation of legislation and federal jurisprudence that puts at risk achievements of the 1952 Constitution in this area (Rivera Ramos 1995a) (especially after September 11, 2001); and (3) a political culture that continues to exhibit some authoritarian characteristics (see the chapter by Benítez Nazario in this book).

THE ROADBLOCKS TOWARD FULL DECOLONIZATION

There is, as explained before, a close connection between the already described socioeconomic crisis and the territorial context in which it unfolds. The territorial model is based on the fact that Puerto Rico produces enormous benefits for mostly U.S. capital. The vision of an economy developing adequate strategies for an equilibrated development, including progressive policies aimed at improving the quality of life of the poor, is excluded from this territorial model. However, even with such an intensive and extensive social crisis, the process toward self-determination, although advancing, maintains a slow pace. In this section I address some of the obstacles that prevent political development and greater levels of internal democracy.

Even under the most favorable interpretation of the 1952 Constitution, Puerto Rico's level of self-government and freedom from the direct control of the United States is very limited, since the United States has not recognized Puerto Ricans' right of self-determination.[12] By itself, such domination represents a violation of internationally recognized national collective rights (Rivera Ortiz 2001).

To be sure, Puerto Ricans voted in favor of Law 600 in 1950. This law clearly stated that although Puerto Ricans would be empowered to enact their own Commonwealth Constitution, most sovereign powers exerted so far by the United States as determined by the Treaty of Paris of 1898 would remain in effect. Basically, Congress only exerted self-limitation of its sovereign powers over Puerto Rico in terms of the internal structures of the Commonwealth government that were to be determined by the Puerto Rico Constitutional Convention and voted on by the people in a referendum. No longer would the internal government be subject to congressional unilateral organic acts nor would the government be appointed by U.S. authorities. Rather, from then on, this would be determined by Puerto Rican voters in democratic elections. The constitution, however, to enter into effect, first had to be approved by Congress and signed by the president of the United States. Congress also demanded that the Commonwealth Constitution had to possess a republican form of government and include a Bill of Rights, and that it had to be compatible with the U.S. Constitution.

The U.S. government and important sectors within the PDP leadership claim that because in 1950 Puerto Ricans voted favoring Law 600 (enacted in the nature of a compact between Congress and the people of Puerto Rico), in some way, Puerto Ricans did exert some form of self-determination. This, however, has been regarded as essentially fallacious, because Puerto Ricans were not given the opportunity in 1950 to choose freely among different political status alternatives. Rather, they were confronted by a "take it or leave it" offer by the U.S. Congress, including the right to enact a local constitution. In exchange, Puerto Rican voters were forced to legitimize with their votes U.S. sovereign powers and U.S.-Puerto Rico relations as previously determined by Congress through the Jones Act of 1917, a clearly colonial congressional organic statute (Rivera Ortiz 2001).

In economic and social arenas as well, the island experiences extraordinary levels of dependence on the United States, which in turn makes any process of self-determination extremely difficult and complicated. According to economist Catalá Oliveras (N.d.), net federal transfers to Puerto Rico in 1999 amounted to $8.3 billion. Possible termination of such transfers is a source of great anxiety for those citizens receiving federal funds, whether as food stamps or aid to dependent children, Social Security and Medicaid, military retirements, or education assistance, or through the literally hundreds of other programs in dozens of federal agencies, from the administration of national parks to housing.

These federal transfers, however, have to be placed in their proper context. During the 1990–1999 period, the total earnings generated by mostly U.S. multinationals doing business in Puerto Rico were $139.7 billion (Catalá Oliveras N.d.). The federal transfers have been aptly described by some as "compensation for exploitation." Undoubtedly, these economic relationships shape the way Puerto Ricans make their political rational calculations. U.S.-sponsored dependency cements the colonial problem—or the "democratic deficit," as some put it—and its function is to reinforce U.S. territorial control over the Puerto Rican archipelago.

In the past, for each step taken in Puerto Rico in the decolonizing direction, the preservation of U.S. territorial control is reinforced. Bills presented in Congress during the 1990s and congressional reactions to those initiatives show a continuous pattern. Two bills in particular are instructive, since both were to provide for "self-determination": United States-Puerto Rico Political Status Act, H.R. 3024, 1996, and Senate Bill S. 2019, 1996, to provide for referenda to resolve the political status.

Neither made a commitment to decolonization beyond "consulting" with "U.S. citizens residing in Puerto Rico." When these and other legislative bills refer to "Puerto Rican voters," they exclude Puerto Ricans who reside within the Continental United States, Alaska, and Hawaii—that is, individuals (and their descendants) who were forced to emigrate. Consultation is reduced to a rhetorical exercise aimed at delaying and neutralizing tensions created by the island's "political status problem." When Congress tackles the political status issue, it is generally because a great deal of lobbying has been made by the Puerto Rican businessmen and government. Lobbying usually has been complemented with Puerto Rican financial contributions to the reelection campaigns of several Congressmen. This was the case during the Rosselló administration (1992–2000), where a significant flow of money helped in securing approval of pro-statehood legislation in the House of Representatives in 1996.[13]

Nevertheless, neither of these legislative initiatives was seriously examined. Other similar bills considered at the beginning of the 1990s have all been tabled without being thoughtfully debated (Colón Morera 1999). This surely does not look like a serious congressional commitment to honor the inalienable rights of the people of Puerto Rico to national self-determination as recognized by UN resolutions, particularly 1514 (XV) and 1541 (XV) of 1960 (Rivera Ortiz 2001).

Even so, such legislative initiatives generate false expectations on the island, and in the United Nations, that the issue will soon be addressed effectively. In 1998, another Puerto Rican-sponsored referendum was held on the political status question, and again 71 percent of those registered voted (Colón Morera 1999). The vote competition has been between those wishing to reform the present semi-colonial "territorial status" to achieve real autonomy and those wishing statehood; the independence sector has been out voted in every election.

But U.S. politicians also are aware that cultural nationalism and the independence movement as a political force are stronger than what is generally inferred from electoral statistics. This explains, in part, the long tradition of political repression of pro-sovereignty sectors. Accordingly, another roadblock to gain full decolonization is the legacy of long-term official suppression of the independence movement. In the past, this official policy of criminalizing *independentistas* has helped the United States maintain and stabilize current dependence. Bosque-Pérez's chapter in this book addresses social, political, and sometimes violent discrimination at the federal level against pro-independence and anti-colonialist activists and intellectuals; his research emphasizes developments that threaten gains already made in human and civil rights.

The FBI, however, has not taken legal responsibility for its repeated acts of persecution and has reacted very slowly to demands to divulge information about its role in the island-wide repression. Not only does the FBI retain substantial jurisdiction in Puerto Rico, but at least until recently, it remained involved in aggressive intelligence-gathering operations. A partial solution to the historical legacy of federal persecution is needed before, or at least along with, the procedural and substantive proposals for Puerto Rico's political future.

A number of new measures that may reinforce and reintroduce practices of repression have to be taken into account. These include broad anti-terrorism legislation such as the Violent Crime Control and Law Enforcement Act of 1994 (U.S. House of Representatives 1994). Representative José Serrano (D-NY) has spoken out about the dangers of opening the door to the FBI to investigate political and religious groups in the United States and Puerto Rico.[14] Even more recently, activists have been faced with the new anti-terrorist initiatives approved by the U.S. Congress after the September 11, 2001, attacks. These open the door again for the investigation of political ideologies as practiced under the *carpeta* spying system used against *independentistas* and other progressive voices from the democratic civil society (see the chapters by Bosque-Pérez and Márquez in this book).

Under new rules adopted since the September 11 attacks, field office directors of the FBI can initiate criminal investigations in this area "without clearance from headquarters." The international climate supporting the need to protect civil liberties also deteriorated after the September 11 incidents. Even the judicial system has been influenced so gravely that some federal judges in Puerto Rico made references to the September 11 attacks when imposing long jail sentences on those who opposed the navy's presence in Vieques.

CONCLUSION

At the beginning of the twenty-first century, Puerto Rico represents a significant, difficult, and complex puzzle. Intense social conflicts, economic disparities, stagnation, and dissatisfaction with the so-called "democratic deficit" are forcing a new look into the 1952 constitutional and political arrangement. The 1952 ELA model is reaching a point of exhaustion in its political legitimacy and in its socioeconomic results.

There is, on the one hand, recognition that the 1952 Commonwealth Constitution represented a step forward in the process of defining key democratic institutions and values. There is ample consensus on the understanding that the Commonwealth's constitutional order provides the basic framework for the recognition of civil rights in any future political evolution of Puerto Rico outside of the territorial framework. The basic political problem is neither the internal political organization framed by the internal constitution nor the level of internal protection of civil rights that it recognizes.

There is, however, intense pressure on the political system to produce positive results with regard to the problem of the high incidence of violence, in general, and the murder rate, in particular. This popular pressure is utilized, both in Puerto Rico and in the United States, as an excuse to adopt new anti-crime initiatives that limit previously achieved democratic advances. The federal imposition of the death penalty is a good example of such tension. Such legislation, along with the recently enacted "Patriot Act," renders the internal Puerto Rico political system unable to protect civil rights in key areas related to the protection of basic normative values such as life, privacy, and liberty (Ramos 2002). The island, not having full political representation in the U.S. Congress,[15] has to implement federal anti-crime measures by territorial imposition and without internal civic deliberation.

The current political structure is generating, at the very best, slow economic growth. The reasons for such economic deterioration are simple: during the past decade, the U.S. Congress has not been willing to create new special territorial tax incentives to promote investments in Puerto Rico, and the island's relative special advantages in terms of access to the U.S. markets have largely disappeared. The close connection between crime and chronic poverty cannot be addressed in a context where the island lacks the institutional flexibility to implement national economic policies. Puerto Rico cannot engage in international trade agreements nor participate in international organizations without the U.S. Department of State's authorization. In this institutional framework, the particular island's economic needs are seldom recognized, and, in fact, they are generally ignored.

The current territorial extension of federal anti-poverty programs to Puerto Rico has produced mixed results. It has clearly served to address the vital needs of the significantly poor sectors of the island but also has increased levels of public corruption in the hands of the Commonwealth government management and created a dependency mentality that prevents self-sufficiency. In general, federal programs, as implemented on the island by the two principal political parties, are not a way out of poverty but a mechanism fostering permanent dependency and political patronage.

Thus we face the paradox. While there are some inter-elite voices in Puerto Rico seeking major revisions of the constitutional arrangement, including the current political relations between Puerto Rico and the United States, popular sectors remain concerned about immediate, day-to-day socioeconomic pressures. These poor sectors are reluctant to engage in political change in the absence of well-defined political and transitional mechanisms and associate sovereignty with poverty and underdevelopment. Important popular sectors identify the existence of legal rights with the preservation of U.S. citizenship (Rivera Ramos 2001). The legacy of political persecution maintains high levels of distrust toward the pro-independence leadership and fear regarding the possibility of a sovereign scenario in this Caribbean island. Significant popular sectors remain adamant in their commitment to preserve the federal entitlements for the poor, and the security, which they perceive, represents the political integration to the United States.

On the political internal front, however, there is an incipient process of articulating consensus-based initiatives (at least on a procedural level) directed toward the calling for a Puerto Rican special constitutional assembly to propose U.S. Congress modifications to the current territorial scheme. This proposal of a constitutional assembly to be democratically elected by the

Puerto Rican electorate, devoted to promoting and negotiating the terms of a new political relationship with the United States, is gaining acceptance. This could well be an opportunity to break Puerto Rico's current stagnation. The options considered by this assembly would have to be based on internationally recognized decolonization precedents. The committee has favored this mechanism, and Puerto Rico's legislative assembly has adopted it in principle. The United Nations Decolonization Committee has favored in the past both independence and sovereign free association as possible political alternatives to the colonial status quo.

While this complex internal dynamic unfolds, the island is gaining, objectively, new political space that could facilitate a process of full decolonization. The triumphant drive to stop the military presence in Vieques forced the U.S. Navy to close its military installations in Roosevelt Roads, up until then the largest naval base in the United States outside of its Continental borders. The U.S. military, which in the past was a consistent and very powerful actor advocating the continuation of the colonial gradualist arrangement, could become a less significant player in future political status debates.

In the economic area, the island is receiving a great deal of investment in the pharmaceutical and high-technology sectors that do business on the island as "controlled foreign corporations," as though Puerto Rico were an independent jurisdiction. U.S. multinationals stay in Puerto Rico with the implicit understanding that statehood, if at all possible, will not be attained soon, and that consequently, they can operate in Puerto Rico as in any independent republic given the fiscal autonomy granted by Congress to the Commonwealth jurisdiction. This industrial sector, if adequate transitional measures were taken, would not be negatively affected with the emergence of a sovereign Puerto Rico.

Maintaining the current territorial arrangement seems to be, from a strictly economic calculation, in the U.S. government's interest. As explained before, the enormous profits obtained by U.S. multinationals doing business on the island far exceed the transfers that the U.S. federal government distributes in order to prevent radical social mobilization. The U.S. commercial sector doing business in Puerto Rico does generate considerable profits, but it is an oversight of U.S. policy makers to emphasize economic profitability as a reason to maintain the territorial arrangement. Looking at the tree, these policy makers are missing the forest. Puerto Rico is not converging with the United States economically. On the contrary—the economic gap between Puerto Rico and the United States is getting wider. According to the most recent data available, the U.S. GDP per capita income in 2002 was $37,600, while Puerto Rico's was 11,600 (CIA Factbook 2003). The socioeconomic crisis on the island is getting out of control. The federal government of the United States has proven incapable of protecting the island from becoming a major point of transshipment in the lost drug war. Culturally, most Puerto

Ricans remain loyal to their language and cultural symbols of national identity and view their relationship to the United States as a matter of convenience more than as a source of pride or American identity.

Recently, sectors of Puerto Rico's increasingly influential civil society have pushed successfully in some areas to develop more progressive responses from the internal Commonwealth government. They also have tried to exclude Puerto Rico from the application of federal death penalty legislation. Activists have insisted on placing a new emphasis on the need to comply with the rehabilitation policy included in Puerto Rico's constitution. Civil rights advocates have argued strongly for assigning additional resources for the promotion of gender equality, developing a strategy to deal with school violence with less reliance on constant police presence and creating new courses in the area of civil rights. All of these measures have been sponsored by a progressive sector of the island's civil society. Without such measures, Puerto Rico cannot meet the challenges and demands of the twenty-first century and develop greater self-determination in all senses of the word (Rivera Ortiz 1996; Rivera Ramos 1995b).

Could it be possible to convert the objective conditions that favor decolonization into actions to decolonize? The puzzle remains. It is in the mutual interest of Puerto Rico and the United States to solve it sooner rather than later.

NOTES

I am deeply grateful for the comments of friends and colleagues who were kind enough to read this chapter and make suggestions that have helped clarify the issues presented here. They are: Ramón Bosque-Pérez, Ángel Israel Rivera Ortiz, Luis Cámara Fuertes, Idsa Alegría Ortega, Francisco Catalá Oliveras, Carlos Vélez-Ibáñez, and Ana María García Blanco. As always, I take full responsibility for any errors or omissions.

1. United Nations Human Rights Declaration, http://www.un.org/Overview/rights.html (accessed July 2, 2003).

2. LPRA is the acronym for *Leyes de Puerto Rico Anotadas*, which is the collection of public annotated laws of Puerto Rico.

3. Among the issues that the Constituent Assembly left for future resolution is the protection of the rights of homosexuals from the intrusion of the state in their private lives. Despite a public campaign of conservative religious sectors to deny homosexuals any legal protection, political and legal efforts continue to protect those intimate relations.

4. U.S. Census, "Small Area Income and Poverty Estimates, Estimates for 1997 for Puerto Rico," http://www.census.gov/hhes/www/saipe/puertorico/puertall97.html (accessed July 2, 2003).

5. United States' rates come from the U.S. Department of Justice, Federal Bureau of Investigation 2002. Rates for Puerto Rico were calculated using U.S. Census Bureau population estimates and crime data compiled by http://www.tendenci-

aspr.com ("*Delitos de Violencia,*" *Policía de Puerto Rico, Superintendencia Auxiliar en Servicios al Ciudadano, División de Estadísticas*), accessed July 2, 2003. It is shocking to note that the murder rate on Indian reservations in the United States, another social context in which historical human rights violations are abundant, is reported to be five times higher than the national average. A report blames unemployment, broken families and the emergence of gangs in these tribal contexts. See "Crime Rate on Indian Reservations Much Higher than U.S.," *The Associated Press*, October 7, 2003.

6. National Drug Intelligence Center, *Puerto Rico and the U.S. Virgin Islands Drug Threat Assessment*, Publication Date, July 2003, Document ID, 2003-S0381PR-001, http://www.usdoj.gov/ndic/pubs3/3950 (accessed August 4, 2003).

7. Ibid.

8. Ibid.

9. Puerto Rican Police Office of Community Relations, personal communication, January 21, 1997.

10. Personal communication, March 22, 2002.

11. *Antiterrorism and Effective Death Penalty Act* (Public Law 104-132, 104th Congress), signed into law on April 24, 1996.

12. See "The United Nations International Covenant on Civil and Political Rights," http://www.hrweb.org/legal/cpr.html (accessed July 2, 2003).

13. A high-ranking official of the Rosselló administration admitted that public funds were used to secure the approval of the so-called "Young Bill." See Julio Ghigliotty, "*Defiende Morey a los cabilderos,*" *El Nuevo Día*, October 30, 1997, p. 26. According to news reports based on government information, as of January 1998, the lobbying efforts of the Rosselló administration in Washington, D.C., totaled over $22 million (see Leonor Mulero, "*Crece la nómina del cabildeo,*" *El Nuevo Día*, January 21, 1998, p. 30). See also Jeffrey H. Birnbaum, "Ickes, Clinton Insider, and Puerto Rico Advocate Shows Not All Who Lobby Must Wait in the Hall," *Wall Street Journal*, September 21, 1993, p. 24; Thomas J. Fitzgerald, "Puerto Rico's Star Is in His Eye; He's Lobbyist for Statehood," *The Record* (Bergen County, N.J.), April 5, 1998, p. 1.

14. See "Serrano Calls on FBI Director to Avoid Repeat Persecution of Individuals and Groups in Puerto Rico," Press Release, December 6, 2001, http://www.house.gov/apps/list/press/ny16_serrano/pr_011206.FBIpr.html (accessed July 5, 2003).

15. Puerto Rico's formal representation in the U.S. Congress consists of one "Resident Commissioner," a nonvoting member of the U.S. House of Representatives. By constitutional mandate, there is no Puerto Rican representation in the U.S. Senate.

WORKS CITED

Acosta, Ivonne. 1987. *La Mordaza: Puerto Rico 1948–1957*. Río Piedras, Puerto Rico: Editorial EDIL.

Albarrán González, Rafael. N.d. *El rol del estado en la lucha contra el crimen y la droga*. San Juan, Puerto Rico. Unpublished manuscript.

Anderson, Robert. 1995. "Cuentas Claras." *El Nuevo Día, Revista Domingo* (November 26): 4–9.

———. 1998. *Política Electoral de Puerto Rico.* Río Piedras, Puerto Rico: Editorial Plaza Mayor.

Burchel, Graham, Colin Gordon, and Peter Miller. 1991. *The Focault Effect: Studies in Governability.* Chicago: University of Chicago Press.

Cámara Fuertes, Luis Raúl, José Javier Colón Morera, and Héctor Martínez Ramírez. Forthcoming. "The Death Penalty in Puerto Rico: A Multivariate Model of Support and Opposition."

Catalá Oliveras, Francisco A. N.d. *El control económico de los Estados Unidos sobre Puerto Rico.* San Juan, Puerto Rico. Unpublished manuscript.

CIA Factbook. 2003. Http://www.cia.gov/cia/publications/factbook/geos/rq.html#Econ. Accessed August 4, 2003.

Colón Morera, José Javier. 1999. "El repliegue de la estadidad." *Nueva Sociedad* 160 (March–April).

Comisión de Derechos Civiles. 1989. *Informe sobre discrimen y persecución por razones políticas: La práctica gubernamental de mantener listas, ficheros y expedientes de ciudadanos por razón de su ideología política.* 1989-CDC-028 (February). San Juan: Revista del Colegio de Abogados de Puerto Rico 51(4) and 52(1).

———. 1998. *¿Somos racistas?: Cómo podemos combatir el racismo.* San Juan: Comisión de Derechos Civiles.

Daubón, Ramón Enrique. 2002. *Capital social.* San Juan: Editorial Tal Cual.

Díaz, Elías. 1973. *Estado de derecho y sociedad democrática.* Madrid: Editorial Cuadernos para el Diálogo.

Donner, Frank J. 1981. *The Age of Surveillance: The Aims and Methods of America's Political Intelligence System: The Theory and Practice of Domestic Intelligence.* New York: Vintage Books.

Duverger, Maurice. 1984. *Las ideologías de las sociedades liberales: Instituciones Políticas y Derecho Constitucional.* Barcelona: Ediciones Ariel.

Fernández Colón, José. 2001. "Ordena que el Gobierno se una al caso contra la pena de muerte," *El Nuevo Día,* September 13, 2001, p. 8.

Fernández, Ronald. 1992. *The Disenchanted Island: Puerto Rico and the United States in the Twentieth Century.* New York: Praeger.

García Muñiz, Humberto, and Jorge Rodríguez Beruff. 1999. *Fronteras en conflicto: Guerra contra las drogas, militarización y democracia en el Caribe, Puerto Rico y Vieques.* San Juan: Red Caribeña de Geopolítica.

Gautier Mayoral, Carmen, and María del Pilar Argüelles. 1978. *Puerto Rico en la ONU.* Río Piedras: Editoral Edil.

Gautier Mayoral, Carmen, and Teresa Blanco Stahl. 1997. "COINTELPRO en Puerto Rico: Análisis de documentos secretos del FBI, 1960–1971." Pp. 255–97 in *Las carpetas: Persecución política y derechos civiles en Puerto Rico (ensayos y documentos)*, ed. Ramón Bosque-Pérez and José Javier Colón Morera. Río Piedras, Puerto Rico: Centro para la Investigación y Promoción de los Derechos Civiles (CIPDC).

Krigger, Marilyn F. 1994. "The Implications of the 1993 Status Plebiscite in the United States Virgin Islands." Paper presented during the Second National Conference, "Looking to the Future," Washington, D.C.

Mattos Cintrón, Wilfredo. 1988. *"La formación de la hegemonía de Estados Unidos en Puerto Rico y el independentismo, los derechos civiles y la cuestión nacional." El Caribe Contemporáneo* 16 (January–June 1988): 21–57.

Miller, David. 1997. *The Blackwell Encyclopedia of Political Thought*. Oxford: Blackwell.

Muñoz Vázquez, Marya, and Idsa Alegría Ortega. 1999. *Discrimen por razón de raza en los sistemas de seguridad y justicia en Puerto Rico*. San Juan: Comisión de Derechos Civiles de Puerto Rico.

Navarro, Mireya. 2002. "U.S. Says Officials in Puerto Irco Stole for Party and Profit." *New York Times*, January 24, p. 1A.

Nina, Daniel. 2001. *"Fragmentos de nación, modernidad y racismo: Nueva visita al problema de la esclavitud." Revista del Colegio de Abogados de Puerto Rico* 62: 48–65.

Pantojas García, Emilio. 1990. *Development Strategies As Ideology: Puerto Rico's Export-Led Industrialization Experience*. Boulder and London: Lynne Rienner; Río Piedras, Puerto Rico: Editorial UPR.

Partido Nuevo Progresista. 1996. *Programa*. San Juan: Partido Nuevo Progresista.

Picó, Fernando. 1994. *"Los gatos sin cascabel." El Nuevo Día* (August 27): 83.

Ramos, Aarón G., and Angel Israel Rivera Ortíz. 2001. *Islands at the Crossroads: Politics in the Non-Independent Caribbean*. Boulder, Colo.: Lynne Rienner.

Ramos, Josean. 2002. *"Alerta ante la ley patriótica." Diálogo*, March, p. 5.

Rivera-Batiz, Francisco L., and Carlos Santiago. 1996. *Island Paradox: Puerto Rico in the 1990s Crisis and Its Aftermath*. New York: Russell Sage Foundation.

Rivera Ortiz, Ángel Israel. 1996. *Puerto Rico: Ficción y mitología en sus alternativas de status*. San Juan: Ediciones Nueva Aurora.

———. 2001. *Poder social vs. poder electoral en la autodeterminación nacional de Puerto Rico, Tomo I, Los dilemas del tranque*. San Juan: Ediciones Nueva Aurora.

Rivera Ramos, Efrén. 1995a. *"Los derechos civiles: Retos del presente y del porvenir."* Paper presented to the Instituto de Derechos Civiles. Mimeograph.

———. 1995b. "Problems of Self-Determination and Decolonization in the Modern Colonial Welfare States: The Case of Puerto Rico." Pp. 9–20 in *Políticas de descolonización de las potencias en la región caribeña*, ed. C. Gautier Mayoral and I. E. Alegría Ortega. Grupo de Trabajo de Relaciones Internacionales del Caribe and CLACSO. Río Piedras, Puerto Rico: Centro de Investigaciones Sociales.

———. 2001. *The Legal Construction of Identity: The Judicial and Social Legacy of American Colonialism in Puerto Rico*. Washington, D.C.: American Psychological Association.

Santiago Nieves, Juan. 1994. *"Propiedad y castigo."* *Claridad*, June 24, p. 24.

Serrano Geyls, Raúl. 1979. "Executive-Legislative Relationships in the Government of Puerto Rico: 1900–1954." *Revista Jurídica de la Universidad Interamericana* 14 (September–December): 11–52.

Sued Badillo, Jalil. 2000. *La pena de muerte en Puerto Rico: Retrospectiva histórica para una reflexión contemporánea.* Santo Domingo, Dominican Republic: Editora Centenario.

Trías Monge, José. 1997. *Puerto Rico: The Trials of the Oldest Colony of the World.* New Haven, Conn.: Yale University Press.

U.S. Department of Justice. Federal Bureau of Investigation. 2002. *Crime in the United States 2001, Uniform Crime Reports.* Washington, D.C.: U.S. Government Printing Office.

U.S. House of Representatives. 1994. *Violent Crime Control and Law Enforcement Act of 1994.* House Report No. 103-711. Washington, D.C.: U.S. Government Printing Office.

Committee on Resources. 1996. *United States-Puerto Rico Political Status Act, Report to Accompany H.R. 3024,* 104th Cong., 2nd sess., H. Rept. 107-713 Part 1. Washington, D.C.: U.S. Government Printing Office.

U.S. Senate. 1989. "Report of the Energy and Natural Resources Committee on the Puerto Rican Status Referendum Act." Report No. 101-120. Reprinted in *Political Status Referendum, 1989–1991, Vol I.* 1992. J. R. Martínez Ramírez, ed., pp. 209–41. Washington, D.C.: Puerto Rico Federal Affairs Administration.

Zenón Cruz, Isabelo. 1974–1975. *Narciso descubre su trasero: El negro en la cultura puertorriqueña.* Humacao, Puerto Rico: Editorial Furidii.

Zinn, Howard. 1995. "How Democratic Is America?" Pp. 2–13 in *Points of View,* ed. Robert E. Diclerico and Allan S. Hammond. New York: McGraw Hill.

JURISPRUDENCE, LAWS, AND LEGISLATIVE BILLS

Amy v. Secretario, 116 DPR 414 (1985).

Antiterrorism and Effective Death Penalty Act of 1996, 110 Stat.1214, 28 U.S. C. A. §2254(d).Supp. 1997.

Constitución del Estado Libre Asociado de Puerto Rico, 1 LPRA (Leyes de Puerto Rico Anotadas).

Federal Relations Act, 1 LPRA.

H. R. 3024. *United States-Puerto Rico Political Status Act* (104th Congress, 2d Session), 1996.

Programa sobre enseñanza de Gobierno y Derechos Civiles, Law No. 11, January 5, 2002; 18 LPRA Sections 577, 578, 579 (2003).

S. 2019. A bill to provide for referenda to resolve the political status of Puerto Rico, and for other purposes (104th Congress, 2d Session), 1996.

SIX

The Changing Nature
of Intolerance

Jorge Benítez-Nazario

THIS CHAPTER IS THE RESULT of field research conducted by the author and a group of talented students from the Department of Political Science of the University of Puerto Rico. A profile of the political tolerance (or intolerance) of Puerto Ricans in terms of its direction, origin, magnitude, and way of manifesting itself was reached through numerous focal groups and a national public opinion survey. The exercise was completed with the only intention of making a humble contribution to our democratic way of life.

The task was not generated by accident or intellectual whim. The historical and political contour of Puerto Rico in the last twenty years invites us to reflect on the subject of tolerance. From an eminently academic perspective, we propose to do field research on a subject that has not been empirically researched since the 1970s, when Isabelo Zenón Cruz, Milton Pabón, Luis Nieves Falcón, Manuel Maldonado Denis, Robert Anderson, Eduardo Seda Bonilla, and the Commission on Civil Rights undertook the study of the characteristics of intolerance and political and cultural repression in Puerto Rico.[1] Also, from a more political perspective, it is quite interesting to approach the subject within a given historical moment when (at least institutionally) the right to ideological dissidence of previously persecuted groups, such as the pro-independence movement, has been publicly endorsed. This latter development would suppose a greater acceptance of those political minorities and, therefore, a reduction in the levels of intolerance against them. Certainly one of the objectives of this research was to corroborate this supposition, at the same time identifying the patterns of intolerance toward other social groups that have just barely begun to have any real influence in our community and political life.

What follows is a profile of the political intolerance of a country that welcomes the new century committed to the ways of liberal democracy.[2]

INTRODUCTION

The United Nations and the Commission on Civil Rights of Puerto Rico have correctly focused on the subject of political tolerance, understanding that without tolerance, there are no possible ways of democratization. Nevertheless, political science must point out that the concept of tolerance is not central only to the idea of a democratic government. The history of political thought, both Occidental[3] and Oriental,[4] shows that without tolerance there is no civility or social order, that without political tolerance, we cannot conceive of the idea of government. A dramatic example of this point can be found in the anti-democratic and absolutist models of state as defended by Thomas Hobbes in *Leviathan*.[5] Hobbes states that in the absence of prudence, referring to tolerance for freedom of religion, by the ruler and society in general, it would be impossible for any ruler, regardless of fighting capacity, to prevent civil war and to maintain the established social order.

Therefore, when we talk about tolerance, we not only refer to the debate regarding what we generically call "democracy" but also to the very essence of the social contract, in any of its manifestations. The first lesson offered by political science is that to live in a society, whether democratic or not, we must consent to accept our differences. Political science also objects to the concept of tolerance as an eminently democratic quality[6] from another point of view. On the one hand, there is a whole current in the history of political thought that originates in Greek philosophy and is highlighted with German philosophy, especially Spinoza and Karl Marx, which warns that intolerance, whether cultural or political, has its origin in religious monotheism and its frontal attack on freedom and variety of religions.[7] On the other hand, we must consider the allegation on which Herbert Marcuse, Robert Paul Wolff, Barrington Moore, and Norberto Bobbio agree, that although tolerance is certainly a requisite for democratic life, by itself, isolated from other elements it also could become an obstacle for democracy.[8] According to these philosophers, the "negative tolerance" promoted by liberalism, as acceptance of the different or the privileged or those who act unjustly, without recognizing the injustice that certain differences, privileges, and actions validate, supposes the mere preservation of a status quo that tolerates (for lack of another word) inequality and all of the evils associated with it. Therefore, these authors warn us about the insufficiency of a tolerant attitude in the absence of the recognition of the right of many to object to certain differences and consequently to recommend intolerance to injustice as a starting point toward a more democratic society.[9]

Having established these exceptions to the limits and problems inherent to the concept of tolerance, we continue with a brief theoretical discussion about tolerance as an analytical concept in order to evaluate contemporary liberal democracy.

THEORETIC SYNOPSIS OF TOLERANCE
AS A DEMOCRATIZING FACTOR

Inspired by the works of Alexis de Tocqueville in *Democracy in America*,[10] academic studies of diverse ideological orientations, ranging from the conservative stance of Gabriel Almond's and Robert Dahl's liberalism to the champions of new social orders such as Norberto Bobbio and Antonio Negri, political tolerance, at the public opinion level, has been seen as a central element in achieving any type of democratic order.[11] In general terms, the theoretical works developed by this dissimilar group of social scientists agree in favoring that any political order aspiring to democracy should encourage the development of civic spaces and practices that promote respect of the diversity of opinions and allow the free manifestation of minority political groups, whether women, homosexuals and lesbians, political or religious dissidents, or groups of ethnic and racial origins different from those of the majority. In short, academic literature on the subject of political tolerance concurs on accepting that the practice of democracy is much more than an institutional problem. As de Tocqueville stated, the homogenizing intolerance of majorities toward the political positions or lifestyles of minorities, within the context of formal democracy, can be as despotic and dehumanizing in its manifestations and consequences as the intolerance exercised by a tyrant toward the totality of the population governed or repressed.

These normative considerations have generated several empirical studies on the role of tolerance in the political culture of those Occidental societies that have decided to follow the course of some model of formal democracy. It is in this category of studies that much research on the tolerance toward the political practices of blacks, migrant workers, Jews, communists, neofascists, gays, women, Turks, Arabs, Moslems, Vietnamese, and other ethnic groups and national identities of diverse kinds[12] has been generated in the United States, Europe, and Latin America. In light of those same considerations, the Commission on Civil Rights of Puerto Rico sponsored, during its first years, several studies on the violation of civil and political rights of the Puerto Rican pro-independence movement and the intolerance toward them.[13]

We must point out that despite the demographic and social variety of the groups affected by political intolerance in different countries and the diversity of historical contexts that has encouraged such deplorable political practices in terms of public opinion, we can identify a series of tangents in the conclusions of the works examined. At the same time, these concurrences establish the hypothetical framework for our present research. Briefly, these "conclusion hypotheses" are the following:

1. Political intolerance toward the participation and positions of certain groups of political minorities legitimizes the violation of the political and civil rights of those groups.
2. Political intolerance has the effect of discouraging the affected groups from taking part in public life and participating in the formal democratic process (i.e., Puerto Ricans in the United States).
3. Political intolerance bifurcates the notion of political liberty of the affected groups, making them in turn intolerant in their daily spaces of power. In other words, even in societies thought of as democratic, it is a common and an accepted practice to deny certain groups the liberties and rights legally given to most citizens.
4. The group affected by cultural intolerance is associated (factually or fictitiously) with some social or economic problem that bears upon the quality of life of the intolerant subjects.
5. Intolerant subjects harbor an emotional element of disgust or belittlement against those they do not tolerate that makes them perceive the affected group as people who do not deserve to enjoy the virtues (rights) of the system in which they live.
6. Political intolerance is openly manifested only when it is perceived that it is possible for a new group to have access to a sphere of political power that does not want to be shared.
7. Political intolerance varies, in terms of intensity and direction (selected nontolerated group), according to the educational level of the intolerant subjects.
8. The presence and intensity of intolerance vary according to the political climate of the country, a climate whose agenda responds primarily to the commercial interests of mass communication media.
9. Intolerance has its roots in the political socialization processes. That is, the more exposed we are as children to diversity, the more tolerant we tend to be politically as adults.
10. The chance that cultural intolerance will turn to persecution or political repression depends on how focused or vague it is. From this viewpoint, a society with relatively low levels of political intolerance but directed to a specific group will pose a greater risk to democracy than a society with high levels of political intolerance directed to several groups.

In our particular case, the study to which we refer also uses the concept of tolerance in the context of the Puerto Rican political process (and its liberal-democratic order) and from the point of view of a political culture as manifested in the level of public opinion in our country.[14] Therefore, our theoretical and hypothetical starting point transcends the institutional realm and is consistent with the aforementioned ideas.

WHO ARE THE SUBJECTS OF POLITICAL INTOLERANCE IN PUERTO RICO?

Our public opinion survey started with an optional question to the participants, requesting them to identify all of the groups, in a list from A to Z, they would not like to have as neighbors. The aforementioned list had been prepared with the help of the focal groups. This question would help us determine how focused or vague political intolerance was among Puerto Ricans and, thus, how dangerous. The result (Table 6.1) started to illustrate the profile of this aspect of our political culture.

We immediately asked those who chose to answer the previous question to identify, from among the unwanted neighbors, those they disliked most. This was done to identify the presence or absence of an emotional element in the attitude previously expressed (Table 6.2).

Two decades ago, studies placed pro-independence and Communist subjects at the top of the list; today, that place goes to homosexuals and lesbians.[15] In light of the hypotheses mentioned before, we could suggest that the political climate has changed due to events such as the killings at Cerro Maravilla and the subversive files exposure,[16] that Puerto Ricans are convinced of the impossibility of pro-independence advocates sharing

TABLE 6.1
Groups of Disliked Neighbors according to Frequency Obtained

Group	Frequency
Gay or Lesbian	173
Ex-Convict	122
Foreigner (54 Dominicans)	77
Person of Different Social Origin	73
Communist	70
AIDS Patient	57
Political Militant	38
Person with Different Religious Preference	31
Drug Trafficker	25
Police Officer	25

N = 332*

*Interviewees could mention more than one disliked group.

TABLE 6.2
Most Disliked Groups among Disliked Neighbors

Group	Frequency
Gay or Lesbian	92
Ex-Convict	37
Foreigner	29
Communist	21
AIDS Patient	20
Political Militant	9
Person with Different Religious Preference	7
Police Officer	7
Drug Trafficker	5

N = 332

TABLE 6.3
Activities Permissible to Disliked Group (Percentages)

Activities Permitted	Yes	No	Don't Know
Right to Associate Freely	58.5	31.8	7.4
Present Gubernatorial Candidate	37.3	60.1	2.4
Make Public Speeches	47.9	46.1	5.5
Be a Schoolteacher	37.3	58.9	3.3
Organize Protest Rally	30.0	64.7	29.4
Should Be Closely Monitored	65.6	29.4	4.7
Should Have Telephone Tapped	33.7	61.5	3.8
Should Have Dossier Opened	46.7	49.6	3.3

N = 332

political power in the near future, making it unnecessary to be intolerant toward them. On the other hand, taking into account the political persecution that marred our history for several decades, we should be extremely concerned about the existence of a pattern of intolerance concentrated against a group, homosexuals and lesbians, whose defense mechanism (political organization) does not even remotely resemble that of the pro-independence movement when it was openly repressed with the blessings of most of us.

With the purpose of qualifying the intensity of intolerance against the identified groups, we prepared a scale mentioning the political activities in which the nontolerated groups could or could not participate and with the

TABLE 6.4
Age and Disliked Group

Disliked Group	15–30	31–45	46–60	61+
Homosexual	20.5	19.9	23.3	34.1
Ex-Convict	22.8	23.6	14.4	50.0
Foreigner	17.2	20.7	22.4	37.9
Different Social Origin	40.0	5.0	20.0	35.0
Communist	12.2	23.0	21.6	40.5
AIDS Patient	15.4	15.3	23.2	43.1

N = 332

TABLE 6.5
Years of Schooling and Disliked Group

Disliked Group	6 Years	9 Years	12 Years	College
Homosexual	23.3	10.8	31.7	37.2
Ex-Convict	18.1	11.0	29.9	28.9
Foreigner	17.2	18.2	36.3	31.3
Other Social Origin	35.0	10.0	25.5	29.5
Communist	28.4	13.5	25.7	33.4
AIDS Patient	30.8	10.9	35.1	23.3

N = 332

measures the state should take to limit the activities of said groups (Table 6.3). If this table illustrates the levels of intolerance in our society, then it seems that my concern for the well-being of the nontolerated groups is not exaggerated. Among the civil and political rights (some of them constitutional) presented in this table, only one was chosen by over half of the participants as one that should be granted the nontolerated groups. Besides, the percentage that consented to violating the rights of and persecuting these groups was truly alarming.

DEMOGRAPHIC AND SOCIO-EDUCATIONAL ORIGINS OF INTOLERANCE

When we relate the frequency of intolerance to age, educational level, and political status preference of the participants in the aforementioned questionnaire, we can begin to discern the contours of the social origin of political intolerance in Puerto Rico.

TABLE 6.6
Political Status Preference and Disliked Group

Disliked Group	Commonwealth	Independence	Statehood
Homosexual	56.1	5.5	37.8
Ex-Convict	53.8	10.1	35.3
Foreigner	48.2	10.7	39.3
Other Social Origin	52.6	0.0	47.4
Communist	52.1	2.8	60.8
AIDS Patient	55.6	7.9	34.9

N = 332

The patterns of political intolerance in Puerto Rico vary according to the variables of "age," "education," and "political status preference" of all of the groups mentioned here (Tables 6.4, 6.5, and 6.6).

When observing the effect of the "age" variable, the cases of intolerance toward Communists come primarily from people over age sixty, while intolerance of subjects from another social origin comes primarily from young people. Apparently, those who were politically socialized during the years of the cold war feel a greater aversion for Communists. It also is historically sensible that those who have been politicized in the "age of physical separation" (access control) between poor and other social sectors and of the occupation by police forces of public housing projects are more aware of class conflicts than the generation preceding them (even if they do not express it in such terms), having been socialized within the "myth of modernity" and the corresponding social rise of the middle class. The attitude of senior citizens toward ex-convicts evidences their vulnerability to what the mass media have presented as their possible attackers.

In the case of the variable "education," the marked intolerance of the less educated toward gays and AIDS patients is significant. Possibly this tendency is due to the more direct contact that these socio-educational sectors have with an epidemic closely linked to the gay and heroin-addict lifestyle that is more openly exhibited in their living areas. Our evidence also shows that a greater education does not necessarily reduce the level of political intolerance, although the subjects' capacity to redirect or transport their intolerance to groups that in time have a better chance of obtaining the political power held by the more educated ones is augmented. While the less educated are still worried about the Communists, the more educated (who are no less intolerant) are worried about gays.

In the case of the variable "political status preference," the patterns of political intolerance are clearly differentiated. Commonwealth sympathizers are, in general, more intolerant than independence or statehood advocates, possibly showing a more conservative attitude toward any element that might contaminate the status quo. Independence advocates show no political intolerance toward persons of a different social origin, while manifesting a significant political intolerance of foreigners. Both tendencies could be explained in terms of a marked political experience, by campaigns characterized by social justice rhetoric, and from another standpoint, by constant confrontations with the federal government and the Cuban exiles. For their part, statehooders are exaggeratedly intolerant of Communists, evoking the cold war posthumously, possibly responding to their subliminal desire to feel more "American" than the Americans.

THE MECHANISMS OF INTOLERANCE

Before concluding this preliminary analysis of descriptive statistics, we must review the endorsement given by our participants to mechanisms of intolerance, some of them evoking a repressive character. Apparently too many Puerto Ricans are unaware of the close relationship between the extension of civil rights to all citizens of a nation and the possibility of a democratic way of life.

The importance of the following data does not lie in the clear-cut way it is again demonstrated, that the patterns of political intolerance vary according to subject and political status preference. The significance of these facts lies in their illustration of the existing disposition of Puerto Rican political culture to legitimize intolerant acts that are not conceivable within the context of a democratic system. It seems ironic that within the independence advocates, who in our study demonstrate a greater spirit of tolerance, as many as 68 percent answered that the groups they do not tolerate "should be watched closely." Even worse, 39 percent believe that criminal files should be made on the nontolerated groups, even though a great many of them have been victims of such a despotic practice (Table 6.7). This is the irony of a political socialization that results from a negative experience.

THE REGIONAL NATURE OF
INTOLERANCE IN PUERTO RICO

Despite being a relatively small island, which supposes short distances and the existence of relatively high social integration, the results obtained point to the existence of geographically differentiated intolerance. The evidence regarding the levels of intolerance geared to persons of different religion or race or from the Dominican Republic certainly identifies what seem to be differentiated patterns of intolerance in terms of the geographic origins of the intolerant subjects. Intolerance of persons of different religions or races is significantly higher in the highlands as opposed to the coast (17 percent and 13 percent

TABLE 6.7
Political Status Preference and Attitude toward Civil Rights of Disliked Group*

Activities Permitted	Commonwealth	Independence	Statehood
Right to Associate Freely	69.51	35.70	64.29
Present Candidate	39.40	50.00	35.72
Make Public Speeches	51.00	71.43	65.86
Be a Schoolteacher	40.60	57.71	39.29
Should Be Closely Monitored	68.29	67.85	63.40
Should Have Telephone Tapped	37.50	21.42	35.70
Should Have Dossier Opened	51.52	39.28	46.43

N = 332

*Percentages were computed relative to the total supporters of each political status preference.

respectively). Likewise, intolerance of the Dominican community (or communities) is much less evident in the west (almost nonexistent) than in the metropolitan zone of San Juan (64 percent greater incidence).

The explanation of these findings is possibly linked to a social history differentiated by geography in other times, which apparently still prevails in our process of social integration and fragmentation. Specifically, we suggest that the relative absence of blacks in the central highlands and the relative late arrival of Protestant churches to those areas and a greater isolation because of the lack of highways and roads contribute to the poor integration (and acceptance) of these demographically different sectors. Likewise, we think that the centennial coexistence (both cultural and economic) of Dominicans and Puerto Ricans in the port areas in the west has generated a social integration far removed from the competition for jobs and housing that the more recent immigration of Dominicans to Santurce (a San Juan neighborhood) has caused. In any event, the mentioned results should serve as a warning to those who pretend to turn into national problems what could evidently be more properly attended to at the regional or municipal level. Besides, in the absence of a political will, which recognizes and responds to this reality, there is a basis to the possibility of the rise of different patterns of political persecution throughout the different geographical regions of Puerto Rico.

THE SUBTLE CHARACTER OF
INTOLERANCE IN PUERTO RICO

Some of the studies within the framework of the Puerto Rican political culture conducted in the past have pointed to certain attitudes that although strongly held by ample sectors of the population are not evident at first sight.[17] Specifically, it has been said at different times that not admitting to the existence of racism in Puerto Rico makes it all the harder to combat.

Taking this possibility into account, our questionnaire presented a series of scales concentrating on the tolerance to certain particular groups: women, blacks, Dominicans, gays, persons of different religious preference, and persons of other age groups. One of these scales administered to all participants (N = 541) sought to examine the way in which intolerance of blacks, women, Dominicans, gays, and independence advocates was or was not made evident, as it alluded to situations of social contact with different levels of intimacy. Our expected outcome was that the intolerance not admitted to in a generic situation or of trivial social contact would be made evident in a situation that involved more personal, frequent, or intimate social contact.

To us there is evidence that the apparently greater tolerance of independence advocates in today's Puerto Rico is not necessarily true; this is a different result than those obtained by the studies sponsored by the Commission on Civil Rights twenty-five years ago. The fact that we do not admit to it as readily as we did before is another matter, which will perhaps make it harder to combat an attitude so negative to the development of our civility.

CONCLUSION

We have presented some data, basically descriptive, to offer an idea of a profile of our current political culture. These results illustrate some undeniable tendencies of the manifestation of intolerance in our political culture. The levels of intolerance prevalent in our society certainly threaten the development, if not the survival, of the formal democracy we enjoy. The evidence shows that although the levels of political intolerance vary significantly according to the socio-educational and idiosyncratic characteristics of the participants, as well as the circumstances in which the social relations are carried out, the levels of intolerance are not weakened through them. These results could be indicative of a generalized identity conflict throughout all of the sectors of Puerto Rican society.[18] Although it is true that some of the (openly) nontolerated groups are not the same as those of forty years ago, it also is true that those groups run a greater risk in the event of a new repressive conduct, because they lack strong organizational bases.

Our immediate response, if we believe in the need for a democratic way of life (liberal or based on social equality), should be to alert the most affected groups, both in regard to open political intolerance and to the hypocritical, hidden one, so that they start taking measures to protect their lifestyles and civil and political rights. Also, we should insist on the need to reform our educational system and on the criteria governing our mass communication media to promote civic participation and to question the models of social exclusion, of the good, the bad, and the different, which are still the norm in our country.

NOTES

1. Maldonado Denis 1973; Nieves Falcón 1972; Seda Bonilla 1974; Zenón Cruz 1978: Pabón 1972; Pabón, Anderson, and Rivera Rodríguez 1968; Comisión de Derechos Civiles 1973.

2. Among 632 possible contacts island-wide among Puerto Ricans between age eighteen and seventy, using a multistage, structured random sampling strategy, for a sampling error of $p < .035$. Within each residence, subjects were selected using the Kish random method. All results presented in tables and figures are significant at Chi2 and Lambda $p < .05$, and some are significant at $p < .01$.

3. A good and clear exposition on the concept of "tolerance," as understood in the earlier assessments of the political order in Western thought (Simonides, Socrates, Plato), can be found in the article by Moore (1988). Also, the centrality of the concept in the modern political tradition is well exposed in the works of Riley (1987).

4. Sun Tzu 1993.

5. A good discussion with regard to the way in which the topic is presented in *Leviathan* can be found in the essay by Remer (1992).

6. In my opinion, the best argument in this direction is still the one developed by Locke (1968). However, there are similar discussions in Mill (1974), and as part of the argument on "individual fairness," developed by Rawls (1972).

7. The argument on the classical origin of political tolerance as a key concept in the development of the idea of democracy is evident in the positions assumed by Socrates and Simonides in *Protagoras*. A good discussion on this issue is the one advanced by Mara (1988). The deliberations of Spinoza (1986), as outlined in his *Theological-Political Treaty*, were adopted by the young Marx (1979) in his *Economical and Philosophical Manuscripts*.

8. Wolff, Marcuse, and Moore 1969.

9. Bobbio (1991) addresses the concept of "positive intolerance" which, in his view, may become necessary. He argues that commitment with a democratic state, and our acceptance (as citizens of that state) of the majority rule, presumes that we should be willing to agree with the decisions taken by the majority of the people,regardless of our reasons (ethical or ideological) for objecting to those decisions.

10. De Tocqueville (1961) is very clear on this issue. We should point out that there is some parallelism between the concept of democracy and its obstacles as addressed by de Tocqueville and Montesquieu (1980).

11. Easton 1956; Almond and Verba 1963; Dahl 1989; Bobbio 1991; Negri 1980.

12. The most interesting empirical works, of those examined, are: Bobo and Licari 1996; Gibson 1987a, 1987b, 1982, 1992; Lawrence 1976; McClosky and Brill

1983; Mueller 1988; Sullivan 1982; Barnum and Sullivan 1989; Berlin 1958; Herson 1990; Zalkind et al. 1975; Prothro and Grigg 1960: Shamir and Sullivan 1985.

13. Pabón, Anderson, and Rivera Rodríguez 1968; Pabón 1972. We should state that certain parts of these reports were taken from a report prior to the creation of the *Comisión de Derechos Civiles de Puerto Rico*, or *Informe del Comité del Gobernador para el Estudio de los Derechos Civiles* (Comisión de Derechos Civiles, 1973).

14. We define "political culture" as the political attitudes and behaviors adopted by a particular social group within a specific institutional or cultural context. Therefore, in this definition, the psychological, anthropological, and sociological concerns are brought together within a holistic perspective.

15. Another social object of intolerance frequently mentioned in response to the same questions in the questionnaire was the *espiritistas* (spiritualistic). However, since this was an unexpected outcome, I did not include the necessary follow-up questions for explaining it.

16. For more on the Cerro Maravilla case, see the introduction of the essay by Bosque-Pérez in the present book. For the subversive files case, see Bosque-Pérez and Colón Morera (1997) and *Noriega et al. v. Hernández Colón et al.*, 130 DPR 919 (June 30, 1992).

17. Zenón Cruz 1978.

18. Fetscher (1994) points out that political and cultural intolerance is closely related to feelings of personal insecurity in regard to national or religious identity.

WORKS CITED

Almond, Gabriel, and Sidney Verba. 1963. *The Civic Culture*. Princeton: Princeton University Press.

Barnum, David G., and John Sullivan. 1989. "Attitudinal Tolerance and Political Freedom in Britain." *British Journal of Political Science* 19: 136–46.

Berlin, Isaiah. 1958. *Two Concepts of Freedom*. Stanford: Stanford University Press.

Bobbio, Norberto. 1991. *El tiempo de los derechos*. Madrid: Editorial Sistema.

Bobo, Lawrence, and Frederick C. Licari. 1996. "Education and Political Tolerance." *Public Opinion Quarterly* 42: 345–62.

Bosque-Pérez, Ramón, and José Javier Colón Morera, eds. 1997. *Las carpetas: Persecución política y derechos civiles en Puerto Rico (ensayos y documentos)*. Río Piedras, Puerto Rico: Centro para la Investigación y Promoción de los Derechos Civiles (CIPDC).

Comisión de Derechos Civiles. 1973. *Informes de la Comisión de Derechos Civiles del Estado Libre Asociado de Puerto Rico, Tomo 1*. Orford, N.H.: Equity.

Dahl, Robert A. 1989. *Polyarchy: Participation and Opposition*. New Haven, Conn.: Yale University Press.

De Tocqueville, Alexis. 1961. *Democracy in America*. Vol. 2. New York: Schocken Books.

Easton, David. 1956. *The Political System*. Chicago: University of Chicago Press.

Fetchscher, Iring. 1994. *La tolerancia: Una pequeña virtud imprescindible para la democracia*. Barcelona: Gedisa.

Gibson, James L. 1982. "On the Conceptualization of Political Tolerance." *American Political Science Review* 76: 603–20.

———. 1987a. "The Evolution of Intolerance in the United States." Annual Meeting of the American Political Science Association. Washington, D.C.: American Political Science Association.

———. 1987b. "Homosexuals and the Ku Klux Klan: A Contextual Analysis of Political Tolerance." *Western Political Quarterly* 42: 345–71.

———. 1992. "The Political Consequences of Intolerance: Cultural Conformity and Political Freedom." *American Political Science Review* 86: 238–75.

Herson, Lawrence. 1990. "Tolerance, Consensus, and Democratic Creed." *Journal of Politics* 37: 1007–32.

Lawrence, David G. 1976. "Procedural Norms and Tolerance: A Reassessment." *American Political Science Review* 70: 80–101.

Locke, John. 1968. *A Letter Concerning Toleration*. Oxford: Clarendon Press.

Maldonado Denis, Manuel. 1973. *Puerto Rico: Una interpretación histórico social*. México: Siglo XXI.

Mara, Gerald M. 1988. "Socrates and Liberal Toleration." *Political Theory* 16 (3 August): 468–95.

Marx, Karl. 1979. *Manuscritos económicos y filosóficos*. Mexico, D. F.: Fondo de Cultura.

McClosky, Herbert, and Linda Brill. 1983. *Dimensions of Tolerance: What Americans Believe about Civil Liberties*. New York: Russell Sage Foundation.

Mill, J. S. 1974. *On Liberty*. Harmondsworth: Penguin.

Montesquieu. 1980. *El espíritu de las leyes*. Madrid: Tecnos.

Moore, Gerald M. 1988. "Socrates and Liberal Toleration." *Political Theory* 16 (3 August): 468–95.

Mueller, John. 1988. "Trends in Political Tolerance." *Public Opinion Quarterly* 52: 1–25.

Negri, Antonio. 1980. *Del obrero masa al obrero social*. Barcelona: Anagrama.

Nieves Falcón, Luis. 1972. *Diagnóstico de Puerto Rico*. Río Piedras, Puerto Rico: Edil.

Noriega et al. v. Hernández Colón et al. 130 DPR 919 (June 30, 1992).

Pabón, Milton. 1972. *La cultura política puertorriqueña*. Río Piedras, Puerto Rico: Tiempos Nuevos.

Pabón, Milton, Robert W. Anderson, and Víctor J. Rivera Rodríguez. 1968. *Los derechos y los partidos políticos en la sociedad puertorriqueña*. Río Piedras, Puerto Rico: Editorial Edil.

Prothro, James, and Charles Grigg. 1960. "Fundamental Principles of Democracy." *Journal of Politics* 22: 275–94.

Rawls, John. 1972. *A Theory of Justice*. Oxford: Oxford University Press.

Remer, Gary. 1992. "Hobbes, the Rethorical Tradition and Toleration." *The Review of Politics* 54:1: 5–33.

Riley, Patrick. 1987. *Consent and Political Legitimacy*. New Haven, Conn.: Yale University Press.

Seda Bonilla, Eduardo. 1974. *Requiem para una cultura: Ensayos sobre la socialización del puertorriqueño en su cultura y en ámbito del poder neocolonial*. Río Piedras, Puerto Rico: Editorial Bayoán.

Shamir, Michel, and John L. Sullivan. 1985. "Everybody Hates Somebody Sometime." *Journal of Conflict Resolution* 2: 283–305.

Spinoza. B. 1986. *Tratado teológico-Político*. Madrid: Alianza Editorial.

Sullivan, John. 1982. *Political Tolerance and American Democracy*. Chicago: University of Chicago Press.

Sun Tzu. 1993. *El arte de la guerra*. Bogotá, Colombia: Elektra.

Wolff, Robert P., Herbert Marcuse, and Barrington Moore. 1969. *A Critique of Pure Tolerance*. London: Cape.

Zalkind, Sheldon S. et al. 1975. "Civil Liberties, Personal Attitudes, and Measures." *Journal of Social Issues* 31: 77–91.

Zenón Cruz, Isabelo. 1978. *Narciso descubre su trasero*. Río Piedras, Puerto Rico: Editorial Edil.

SEVEN

Puerto Rican Political Prisoners in U.S. Prisons

Jan Susler

IN THE 1960s AND 1970s, Chicago's Puerto Rican community, like so many other communities in the United States, was rebelling, resisting the violence and brutality of colonialism, racism, and exploitation. Its young leaders sought not only to battle against and expose these evils but to help the community take control of its institutions, to instill a sense of hope. It was a time when anti-colonial, national liberation movements had prevailed throughout the world,[1] and anti-imperialist movements were at war. It was a time when young men were being drafted to fight the Vietnamese people's efforts at liberation. It was a time when the Black Panther Party advocated armed self-defense, when police in Chicago assassinated the party's young leaders. Men and women such as Oscar López Rivera, Ida Luz Rodríguez, Carlos Alberto Torres, and Carmen Valentín led these community struggles and were influenced by events not just in their immediate neighborhood but in the world.

The *Fuerzas Armadas de Liberación Nacional* (FALN) formed during this period.[2] Between 1974 and 1980, the FALN would claim responsibility for bombings of military, government, and economic sites, mainly in Chicago and New York, to call attention to the colonial case of Puerto Rico.[3]

In the early 1980s, Oscar López Rivera, Ida Luz Rodríguez, Carlos Alberto Torres, Carmen Valentín, and many other Puerto Rican women and men were captured in the United States, accused of being members of the FALN and the clandestine movement, convicted, and sentenced to the equivalent of life in U.S. prisons for their actions to end U.S. colonial control over Puerto Rico. After most had served almost twenty years in prison, in an unprecedented act in response to a broad campaign for their release, President Clinton commuted some of their sentences. On September 10, 1999, Ida Luz Rodríguez, Ricardo Jiménez, Carmen Valentín, Elizam Escobar, Alicia Rodríguez, Adolfo Matos, Dylcia Pagán, Luis Rosa, Alejandrina Torres, Edwin Cortés, and Alberto Rodríguez walked out of prison and into the warm embrace of the Puerto Rican people. Oscar López Rivera, Carlos Alberto Torres, Juan Segarra Palmer, and Antonio Camacho Negrón remain in prison.

WHO ARE THE PRISONERS?

Perhaps the most significant aspect of the legal context is the fact that under international law, colonialism is a crime against humanity.[4] For fighting this crime, for taking measures that are absolutely and expressly protected by international law, the Puerto Rican political prisoners have paid with decades of their lives.

The FALN

In 1974, continuing the long history of the Puerto Rican people's resistance to U.S. colonialism, the FALN emerged, a clandestine formation that committed political-military actions inside of the United States. Selecting its targets for their role in the continuing exploitation and oppression of the Puerto Rican people, the FALN explained its armed actions in communiqués and also called for the release of the Nationalist prisoners then in U.S. custody for almost a quarter century.[5]

In the early 1980s, many of its members came to be in the government's custody, some of whom had been the subject of illegal surveillance of their pro-independence activities dating from their years in high school and college. Upon arrest, each declared that she or he was a combatant in an anti-colonial war to free Puerto Rico from U.S. domination and invoked the status of prisoner of war (POW). They asserted that the courts of the United States and its political subdivisions had no jurisdiction to try them as criminals and asked to be remanded to an impartial international tribunal to have their status judged.

While their POW position was to be recognized by international judicial bodies and other international fora,[6] the state of Illinois and the U.S. government refused to recognize their POW status and proceeded to try them for criminal offenses. The prisoners, however, persisted in their refusal to recognize the courts' jurisdiction. In one case, they did not participate at all in the trial; in another, they minimized their participation. They presented no defense and prosecuted no appeals.

On April 4, 1980, among those arrested in Evanston, Illinois, were Carlos Alberto Torres, Ida Luz Rodríguez, Dylcia Pagán, Ricardo Jiménez,

Carmen Valentín, Elizam Escobar, and Adolfo Matos. The arrests were "accidental," occurring because an occupant of a house near where their van was parked reported "suspicious activity." Local police responded, with no idea who they were arresting. Alicia Rodríguez and Luis Rosa were arrested nearby the same day with rental trucks that were reported stolen.

The first seven were tried in state court for possession of weapons found in the van in which they were arrested and for conspiracy to commit the armed robbery of the rental trucks. They were sentenced to eight years in the Illinois Department of Corrections.[7] Alicia Rodríguez and Luis Rosa were tried for armed robbery of the rental trucks, armed violence, and possession of stolen vehicles and sentenced to thirty years in the Illinois Department of Corrections.[8] None of these men and women had previous criminal convictions.

After the state court trials, the federal government charged them with seditious conspiracy—conspiring to use force against the "lawful" authority of the United States to oust it from Puerto Rico—of doing so by membership in the FALN, and of related charges of weapons possession and transporting stolen cars across state lines.[9] They were sentenced to prison terms from fifty-five to ninety years—consecutive to their Illinois sentences—based mainly on the militancy of their statements in court on the day of sentencing. The judge stated his regret that he did not have the power to give them the death penalty.[10]

In 1981, Oscar López-Rivera, who had been named in the aforementioned federal indictment, was arrested after a traffic stop, tried for the identical seditious conspiracy, convicted, and sentenced by the same judge to a prison term of fifty-five years. He received a consecutive fifteen-year term in 1987 for conspiracy to escape—a plot conceived and carried out by government agents and informants and provocateurs.[11]

On June 29, 1983, four independentistas, including Alejandrina Torres, Edwin Cortés, and Alberto Rodríguez, were arrested. The FBI had conducted extensive electronic surveillance, including the use of miniature video cameras with lenses the size of a dime hidden in private dwellings. The government charged them with the same basic seditious conspiracy and with additional related charges of possession of weapons and explosives and transporting a stolen vehicle across state lines.[12] Each of the three received a sentence of thirty-five years in prison.

HARTFORD

On August 30, 1985, hundreds of FBI agents descended on Puerto Rico and staged a predawn raid in the homes and offices of independence activists, arrested thirteen people, including Juan Segarra Palmer, and spirited them away from their country to the state of Connecticut.[13] There they were charged along with three others later arrested, including Antonio Camacho Negrón, with conspiracy to take $7.5 million in government-insured money from a Wells Fargo armored car,[14] an act for which the Puerto Rican clandestine organization, *Los Macheteros* (Machete Wielders), had taken responsibility. The charges included taking the money, transporting the money out of the United States, and giving toys purchased with the proceeds to poor Puerto Rican children.

In preparing for trial, the government revealed that it had conducted extensive, intrusive surveillance, in addition to having seized and analyzed belongings from homes, law offices, and other places. Following years of litigation challenging the constitutionality of such seizures, Juan Segarra Palmer was convicted and sentenced to fifty-five years in prison; Antonio Camacho Negrón was sentenced to fifteen years.

THE TRIALS

The various proceedings against the captured independentistas shared in common a virtual hysteria by the media, law enforcement, and the courts. Many of the arrests were carried out in military regalia, replete with helicopters, snipers, and excessive numbers of FBI agents.

In the earlier arrests, the government sought, and the courts set, prohibitive bail. With the advent of "preventive detention," the government sought, and the courts ordered, no bail at all, and, in the case of Filiberto Ojeda, set the record for the longest preventive detention.[15] Awaiting trial, all of the prisoners were held in the most punitive, restrictive, often unprecedented isolation unless and until some outside intervention occurred—hunger strikes by the prisoners, protests by the independence movement and supporters, lawsuits by the attorneys, and monitoring by Amnesty International.

Newspapers whipped the public—and potential jurors—into an anti-terrorist frenzy, aided by and assisting the marshals' court "security," which not only sent a message to the judges and juries that the accused were guilty but also sought to intimidate supporters.

The courts, open as a forum for the government's political agenda, facilitated and cooperated in acts ranging from permitting the government's use of terms such as *terrorist* and banning the defense's use of terms such as *colonialism*, to convening anonymous juries, to cutting back on traditional limitations on state power, particularly on the right to be free from unreasonable searches and seizures.

THE SENTENCES

LENGTH OF SENTENCE

Puerto Rican independentistas are punished for their beliefs and affiliations, for who they are, not for any act they committed. Government statistics prove that those who commit criminal offenses receive far lesser sentences than do independence fighters. In 1981, the year most of the political prisoners were sentenced, the average federal sentence for murder was 10.3 years.[16] Puerto Rican political prisoners—who were not convicted of hurting or killing anyone—were sentenced to an average of 65.4 years—six times longer than the average. By 1997, with sentence lengths increasing, the average federal sentence for murder/manslaughter was 153 months (less than thirteen years).[17] Their sentences were still about five times longer than the average. Perhaps a concrete application of the sentences will provide insight: Oscar López will be 113 years old if he is made to serve his entire sentence; Carlos Alberto Torres, ninety-eight.

Comparing their sentences to those meted out to anti-independence forces likewise proves the politically punitive nature of the independentistas' sentences. Former Puerto Rican police colonel Alejo Maldonado, an admitted assassin, was paroled from prison after serving less time than most Puerto Rican political prisoners did, when, according to press reports,[18] he participated in police death squads that kidnapped, robbed, extorted, trafficked in weapons, tortured, and killed. The five Puerto Rican police officers who were convicted of the 1978 Cerro Maravilla murders of Carlos Soto Arriví and Arnaldo Darío Rosado received sentences from ten to thirty years. The commander of the intelligence unit responsible for the murders was released on parole after six years in prison.[19]

Comparisons to police cases in the United States lead to the same conclusion. Four white New York City policemen who in 1999 shot forty-one bullets at and killed a West African immigrant were acquitted of all charges—murder, manslaughter, criminally negligent homicide, and reckless endangerment.[20] A white Chicago officer, who killed a black homeless man and fled from the scene, was initially not indicted. After the community came out in force, the prosecution still refused to charge him with murder.[21] Three white Chicago policemen who killed a mentally ill Honduran man in his own home were not prosecuted criminally even after the county's impartial medical examiner concluded that his death was a homicide.[22] The white Detroit police officers who used their flashlights to club to death an unarmed African-American citizen when he failed to follow orders to open his hand won reversal of their twelve-to-twenty-five-year and eight-to-eighteen-year sentences.[23] Upon retrial, their sentences were even lower.[24] A border patrol officer who shot at fifteen Mexicans was to serve no more than ten months in prison.[25]

Sentences given to members of right-wing paramilitary groups pale in comparison to the sentences served by Puerto Rican political prisoners. Militia members faced a maximum of twenty-two years upon conviction of conspiring to stockpile pipe bombs for use against the federal government.[26] Anti-Castro Cubans affiliated with a known paramilitary group, captured in a boat loaded with explosives and weapons and suspected of planning an armed raid on Cuba,

were released without charges.[27] Another group of anti-Castro Cubans caught
in a boat loaded with weapons and ammunition on the way to overthrow the
Cuban government faced a maximum of eight years.[28] A Ku Klux Klan wizard
captured in a boat with an arsenal of weapons and explosives about to invade
a Caribbean nation with hopes of establishing a white supremacist state was
sentenced to three years, paroled after two.[29] A Klan member served six years
for a plot to blow up school buses to avoid court-ordered busing.[30] Likewise, sentences handed out to those who bomb abortion clinics and shoot at physi-
cians,[31] as well as sentences given to government officials,[32] reflect a huge dis-
parity with the sentences served by Puerto Rican political prisoners. Sentences
in political cases in other countries also confirm the disproportionate, politically punitive nature of Puerto Rican political prisoners' sentences.[33]

TIME SERVED

Puerto Rican political prisoners released in 1999 had served sixteen to 19.5
years in prison. In the 1980s, when they were sentenced, the average time actually served in prison by those convicted in state court of serious violent crimes
was "about 2.5 to four years."[34] By the early 1990s, the average time actually
served in prison by those convicted in federal court of violent felonies hovered
just above four years.[35] Department of Justice statistics for the late 1990s estimated that the average time served for state convictions of murder/manslaugh-
ter was 10.5 years; for federal convictions of murder/manslaughter, 10.8 years.[36]

PRISON CONDITIONS

It is a violation of human rights that those who have dedicated their lives to
the freedom of their people, to self-determination—a right protected by
international law—must endure prison, even for one day. But Puerto Rican
political prisoners have endured conditions that are designed to break their
commitment to independence and to break their human spirit, conditions
that violate even minimum standards under international law.

Placement in prisons far from their families meant long-term separation,
contrary to the Bureau of Prisons' stated policy encouraging maintenance of
family and community ties. Adolfo Matos, in Lompoc, California, for the
bulk of his almost twenty years in prison, rarely saw his daughters who live in
New York. Ida Luz Rodríguez's son Damián could afford to see her only infre-
quently. Elizam Escobar's elderly mother, a resident of Puerto Rico, could
travel to see him in Oklahoma only once a year.

Many of the prisoners' parents passed away during their long imprisonment. In spite of the bureau's policy permitting bedside visits and attendance
at funerals, and ignoring letters of support from ministers and elected officials,
prison authorities consistently refused to let the prisoners grieve with their

families. Among others, they rejected requests that Ricardo Jiménez see his mother who died of cancer, that Adolfo Matos attend his mother's funeral, that Carmen Valentín attend her father's memorial service, and that Elizam Escobar be present at his father's bedside and burial.

Officials classified every one of the prisoners as a special monitoring and high-security case, resulting in heightened surveillance and limited programs and movement for all of them. Some were subjected to special control units, isolating them from the prison population, restricting sensory stimuli and human interaction. In 1984, Ida Luz Rodríguez was held for close to a year at Alderson, West Virginia's Cardinal Unit; Alejandrina Torres and other women political prisoners spent two years, 1986 to 1988, at the infamous Women's High Security Unit in Lexington, Kentucky; and Oscar López Rivera was held for twelve torturous years, 1986 to 1998, at the U.S. Penitentiary in Marion, Illinois, and its successor, Florence, Colorado's Administrative Maximum Unit. Such extreme isolation, known to cause psychological and physical deterioration, has been widely condemned as violating international human rights standards.[37]

PAROLE

Parole, or conditional release from prison before the expiration of one's sentence, while available to those convicted of anti-social offenses[38] is not available to Puerto Rican political prisoners. Four of the Puerto Rican political prisoners sought release on parole, approaching the process from various perspectives. The response from the government—oblivious to what approach was used—was to apply a higher standard than most prisoners must meet by assigning them to a unique category to which only 1 percent of all prisoners are assigned, and then to deny parole. Alberto Rodríguez, after accumulating an unprecedented spotless record over twelve years of his thirty-five-year sentence, was told that he must remain in prison until the expiration of his sentence. Dylcia Pagán and Carlos Alberto Torres, who at the time of their hearings had served more than fourteen years of their fifty-five- and seventy-year federal sentences, were told to serve an additional fifteen years before they would be considered for release on parole. Juan Segarra Palmer received the identical response. The documents denying them parole expressly relied on their pro-independence affiliations and activities.

PETITION FOR RELEASE

The Campaign

In November 1993, the campaign for the release of the prisoners submitted a formal application to the U.S. Justice Department asking the president to exercise the constitutional power of pardon to grant the immediate and unconditional release of the prisoners. The pardon process in practice is rather routine, but in fact the president is free to follow whatever process he wants. While the routine requires an individual application from the federal prisoner himself or herself, in this case the campaign made the application not on behalf of a single person but rather fifteen, not all of whom were in the same case and not all of whom were even in federal custody at the time.

In accepting the application, the Justice Department's pardon attorney acknowledged the political nature of the case, indicating that in addition to applying the legal norms of the criminal justice system, she, and more particularly, the president, would have to then evaluate the political consequences of the disposition.

During the time the petition was pending, an unusual phenomenon developed—in the highly contentious political atmosphere in Puerto Rico, a consensus emerged that it was time for the prisoners to come home. Crossing party lines, the leadership of the entire spectrum of Puerto Rican politics asked the president to release them, as did the Speaker of the House and his predecessor, the president of the senate, former three-term governor Rafael Hernández Colón, former governor Roberto Sánchez Vilella, many other elected officials, the Manufacturers' Association and the Puerto Rico AFL/CIO and other labor groups, churches and bishops groups, including the Episcopal Church, the United Evangelical Church, the Christian Church (Disciples of Christ), the Baptist Church, and the Presbyterian Church, community leaders and organizations, lawyers groups, municipalities, university faculties, artists, and so many others.

The call for their release enjoyed wide support in the United States as well, including former president Jimmy Carter, the three Puerto Rican U.S. congressional representatives, Luis Gutiérrez, José Serrano, and Nydia Velázquez, elected officials from municipal, county, and state governments, including the New York City Council, Democratic Party local leaders and activists, countless churches and religious groups, including the National Council of Churches of Christ, the United Church of Christ, the Baptist Peace Fellowship of North America, the General Board of Church, and the Society of the United Methodist Church, women's groups, artists, lawyers associations, professional athletes, Latino coalitions, and more. Wide support also came forth on an international level, including Archbishop Desmond Tutu and ten other Nobel Prize laureates, members of parliament from Australia, human rights organizations from Central America and Africa, labor organizations, lawyers associations, and others.

THE EXECUTIVE GRANT OF CLEMENCY

On August 11, 1999, President Clinton announced his decision—a complicated, conditional offer of clemency that if accepted would amount to immediate release on parole for eleven (prisoners Ida Luz Rodríguez, Ricardo Jiménez, Carmen Valentín, Elizam Escobar, Alicia Rodríguez, Adolfo Matos, Dylcia Pagán, Luis Rosa, Alejandrina Torres, Edwin Cortés, and Alberto Rodríguez), delayed release on parole for two (after an additional five years in prison for Juan Segarra Palmer and after an additional ten years in prison for Oscar López), a remitted fine for one (Antonio Camacho Negrón), and an inexplicable wholesale denial for one (Carlos Alberto Torres).

Declaring that "the prisoners were serving extremely lengthy sentences—in some cases 90 years—which were out of proportion to their crimes,"[39] the president said that he was moved by the support from "various members of Congress, a number of religious organizations, labor organizations, human rights groups, and Hispanic civic and community groups," along with "widespread support across the political spectrum within Puerto Rico," and thousands of letters requesting their release.[40] He also indicated that he was moved by "worldwide support on humanitarian grounds from numerous quarters," pointing specifically to former president Jimmy Carter, Nobel Prize laureate South African Archbishop Desmond Tutu, and Coretta Scott King.[41]

THE RESPONSE

The campaign immediately criticized the president's offer for failing to release all of the prisoners and for attaching conditions; the prisoners and their counsel set about to discuss the complicated offer; and the campaign in Puerto Rico mobilized one of the largest mass marches in the nation's history to press for the unconditional release of all.

In the month following the offer of conditional clemency, as the prisoners weighed their options, the right wing in the United States set about to whip the public into a hysterical frenzy, adopting the issue—with a vengeance and to achieve vengeance—to batter Clinton for having avoided their efforts to remove him from office following the discovery of his affair with a young White House intern.[42] Several committees in both houses of the legislature convened hearings, and both houses overwhelmingly approved a joint resolution condemning the action of President Clinton,[43] in what was thought to be the strongest bipartisan rebuke to Clinton from Congress,[44] accusing him of "making deplorable concessions to terrorists and placing in danger the national security in conceding clemency to Puerto Rican 'terrorists.'"[45] The proximity of presidential elections, with Republicans desperate to regain the White House, led to posturing on the issue by party leaders and candidates.[46] Even the president's wife, herself a candidate for the U.S. Senate, ventured into the fray, challenging her husband.[47] The prevailing atmosphere in the United States during the prisoners' deliberations was hate-filled hysteria that ultimately pressured the president to set a date by which the offer would expire if not accepted.

The conditions attached to the clemency offer included renouncing the "use, threatened use, or advocacy of the use, of violence for any purpose, including the achieving of any goal concerning the status of Puerto Rico."[48] Since the prisoners had submitted a statement to the U.S. Congress in 1997 when it considered legislation to resolve the status, indicating their disposition to participate in an open, democratic process, the renunciation of their use of force gave them no pause. There were hesitations, however, with the prospect of leaving some behind, and also with the conditions of parole, particularly in two aspects: the restriction on association "with persons who have a criminal record" and the restriction on travel. Not only would they be prohibited from seeing each other—problematic enough for the Rodríguez sisters and for all of them for the difficult process of transition from prison—but, in a movement for so long criminalized by the U.S. and colonial governments, many of whose leaders and heroes are former political prisoners, these restrictions would interfere with their participation in the independence movement. The conditions would have given pause due to the sordid trajectory of COINTELPRO, but additional concern arose upon learning of the Justice Department's public opposition to their release,[49] given that this agency was to be responsible for monitoring their compliance with the conditions. Support offered by the *Colegio de Abogados* (Bar Association) in Puerto Rico and the National Lawyers Guild in the United States helped allay some of this concern.[50]

The prisoners, scattered throughout the United States in eleven remote prisons, were not given the opportunity to meet face-to-face to discuss the president's offer.[51] However, in three unprecedented conference calls, they discussed the president's offer as frankly as they could, given the assumption that the calls were being intercepted. The years of separation and arduous prison conditions had not daunted them. With developed political vision, creativity, love, and maturity, they carefully listened to each other and to their movement, and, wholly supporting each other, together decided their course.

RELEASE

On September 10, 1999, eleven women and men became former political prisoners,[52] emerging from prison to be received with a hero's welcome in Chicago, where two returned to their families and communities, in San Juan, where nine went to live, and in New York, even though none of the prisoners appeared there.[53] In Puerto Rico, hundreds of enthusiastic supporters waited hours at the airport for their arrival, greeting them with shouts of "hero, hero."[54] Parents and grandparents, recognizing the significance of the historic moment, brought their children and grandchildren to witness the moment and to learn the importance of their flag and their country.[55]

Not only did San Juan's Catholic archbishop invite them as special guests to participate in mass on Three Kings Day,[56] where he and San Juan's mayor celebrated the prisoners' freedom and integration into the community, but they have been welcomed by churches, civic and religious groups, universities and labor organizations, and family and friends, and offered temporary housing, economic support, and employment. They are seen and respected as "ex-political prisoners," including by the island's largest daily newspaper.[57] They are recognized wherever they go, as people they have never met stop them in the street to embrace them, to show their respect, to thank them for their contribution to the nation, and to express a most heartfelt welcome.

The eleven have fully complied with the conditions that accompanied the president's order, meeting as required with probation officials, submitting reports, limiting their association, and traveling only with permission, granted only rarely. While initially much of their time was spent reuniting with their families and getting acquainted with their new surroundings,[58] after a few short months, most were working and/or attending university.[59] They have established themselves as teachers and mentors, artists, musicians, artisans, and museum guides, media and public relations professionals, and office clerks and handymen. Involved in their communities, caring for their elderly parents and, in some cases, spouses, they are popular on the high school and university lecture circuit, where they are asked for their autographs, their opinions, their advice, and their input. They are public figures, revered, respected, and honored by their people.

Their rapid integration into the fabric of Puerto Rican society is a testament to the president's good judgment in ordering their release, a judgment Clinton said he did not regret, even after the congressional onslaught.[60] The former prisoners' comportment likewise demonstrates that the release of their remaining imprisoned patriots would result in no risk to society—a release actively sought by the same campaign that won the release of the eleven.

SEPTEMBER 11, 2001, AND THE POLITICAL PRISONERS

The necessity of working for their release was only confirmed on September 11, 2001. Within hours of the World Trade Center and Pentagon attacks, various political prisoners throughout the United States, including Puerto Rican political prisoners Carlos Alberto Torres and Antonio Camacho Negrón, were removed from the general population and segregated. Even Haydeé Beltrán, who for over a decade has made clear to the government her withdrawal from the political scene, was swept into segregation.

None of the political prisoners segregated on September 11 was suspected of involvement in the attacks carried out that day. None was suspected of violating prison rules, none was provided with written notice of charges, none was offered a hearing or any other opportunity to defend himself or herself, and none was allowed to communicate with attorneys or family members to inform them what was being done to them.

Antonio Camacho was held so completely incommunicado at the Federal Correctional Institution (FCI) of Allenwood, Pennsylvania, that it took three weeks to learn about his situation. When he asked prison staff why he was segregated, they told him, "You know how the general situation is. You know why you are here" (personal communication). He was allowed no incoming or outgoing mail and no telephone calls, not even with his attorney. The medication for his stomach ulcer was withheld, in spite of his many requests to prison staff. He was returned to the general population on October 2, some ten to fifteen pounds thinner, only to learn that he lost the two-man cell he had occupied and had to move to a six-man cell, and that much of his personal property, including clothing and a radio, had been taken.

Carlos Torres was detained in segregation at FCI Oxford, Wisconsin, for a month. In daily conversations, prison staff, those responsible for his day-to-day supervision, universally expressed to his lawyer their puzzlement at his placement in segregation, given his spotless record in prison. They likewise expressed universal impotence to do anything about it, given that the order came from Washington. An attorney in the office of the Bureau of Prison's general counsel in Washington made it quite clear that his segregation had nothing to do with his prison conduct and everything to do with what she called "national security" and the fact that he was convicted of seditious conspiracy. A journalist reporting this story encountered a similar response from Bureau of Prisons' (BOP) spokesperson Linda Smith: "Were they terrorists?"[61]

Other political prisoners segregated on September 11 include Marilyn Buck, Sundiata Acoli, Yu Kikumura, Raymond Levasseur, and Richard Williams—even Phil Berrigan, a former priest and radical pacifist. Acoli and Williams were so held for four and five months, respectively.

Indefinite, long-term solitary confinement, legitimated by the new regulations, causes psychological and physical deterioration of the sort widely condemned as violating international human rights standards.[62] The devastating consequences to isolated human beings are well documented and well known to the Bureau of Prisons, particularly Puerto Rican political prisoners.

The attorney general has announced on many occasions following September 11 that he fully expects more terrorist attacks. Given his segregation of political prisoners on September 11, in spite of the fact that the government knew full well that they had no relationship to the attacks, the attorneys for political prisoners have asked the government for assurance that such sweeps not recur. Assurance has not been forthcoming. Carlos Torres, Oscar López, and many other political prisoners are serving lengthy, disproportionate sentences the equivalent of life in prison. Torres's projected release date is October 15, 2024; López's, September 27, 2027. There is no assurance that they will not be made to serve these long sentences in total isolation, barred from communication with families, loved ones, and counsel. Instead, there is a new law that ensures their vulnerability to illegitimate political punishment, a vulnerability only confirmed by Attorney General Ashcroft's testimony before the Senate Judiciary Committee criticizing President Clinton for being soft on terrorism, offering the example of his 1999 order granting clemency to the eleven Puerto Rican political prisoners.

As for the former political prisoners, they are not immune from the anti-terrorist hysteria reigning in Washington. After two and a half years of scrupulously complying with all of the conditions, having integrated into civil life, working and supporting themselves, and reunited with their families and loved ones, they are now being subjected to increased supervision, required to submit to urinalysis, with officials telling them that they are likely to make visits to their families' homes (although they do not live with these family members), to their places of work, and to places they are known to frequent.

CONCLUSION

In the month following the president's clemency offer,[63] and in the times of the U.S. Navy's military "exercises" in Vieques—those rare moments when Puerto Rico actually appears on the radar screen of U.S. news—notably missing from the public discourse is any acknowledgment of the colonial case of Puerto Rico or the U.S. Congress' responsibility for resolving the status question.[64] Pro-statehood and pro-commonwealth leaders readily agreed in 1999 that the prisoners' release and the simultaneous, brewing issue of the U.S. Navy's presence in Vieques were "symptoms of a deep-seated problem, the unresolved status of Puerto Rico, that will crop up in other forms in the future,"[65] that they reflect "the frustration and the powerlessness that the people of Puerto Rico feel in their political status,"[66] demonstrating "a persistent deficit of democracy in the current relationship"[67] between Puerto Rico and the United States that detracts from the legitimacy of U.S. sovereignty over Puerto Rico. A White House announcement in 2000 to call for a process to resolve the colonial status[68] seemed more calculated to win support for the administration's decision to keep the navy in Vieques than to envision any legitimate decolonization efforts.

The decade of the 1990s, declared by the United Nations the decade to end colonialism, came and went, with Puerto Rico's colonial status undisturbed. The United Nations Decolonization Committee continues to pass annual resolutions recognizing the right of self-determination of the Puerto Rican people, while successive U.S. administrations consistently take pains to avoid the United Nations' scrutiny, in spite of occasional lip service to the need to resolve the status of Puerto Rico.

Regardless of the prevailing hysteria in the United States, and whether or not the colonial status of Puerto Rico is resolved, eleven women and men who dedicated decades of their lives to the freedom of their country now walk free, contributing, if only by their mere presence and example, to the real potential for independence. Their compatriots remain behind bars, contributing, by their absence and example, to the need for a speedy and just resolution of the status, which would of course result in their release.

In this not-yet-postcolonial era, following the attacks of September 11, much can be gleaned from the astounding pace at which "anti-terrorist" legislation has wiped out many civil liberties, the government's frontal attack on the most harmless dissent,[69] the increase in domestic spying,[70] and the utter disregard for domestic and international law in the treatment of those being held in Guantánamo.[71] This historical moment promises to be difficult for the remaining Puerto Rican political prisoners—and all political prisoners—as well as for the movements they represent.

NOTES

Portions of this chapter were part of a presentation at the International Seminar "Liberation of Puerto Rican Political Prisoners and Prisoners of War," October 13–16, 1995, San Juan, Puerto Rico.

1. "The independence of Ghana (1957), the agony of the Congo (Lumumba was murdered in January 1961), the independence of France's sub-Saharan colonies following the Gaullist referendum of 1959, finally the Algerian Revolution (which might plausibly mark our schema here with its internal high point, the Battle of Algiers, in January–March 1957, as with its diplomatic resolution in 1962)—all of these signal the convulsive birth of what will come in time to be known as the 60s." Fredric Jameson, "Periodizing the 60s," in The 60s without Apology, ed. Sohnya Sayres et al. (Minneapolis: University of Minnesota Press, 1980), p. 180.

2. Armed Forces of National Liberation.

3. "Terrorists without a Cause," Chicago Tribune editorial, March 18, 1980, sec. 2, p. 2. ("Most of the incidents have involved bombs, fortunately so placed and timed as to damage property rather than persons. . . . But again the terrorists were out to call attention to their cause rather than to shed blood").

4. In 1960, the United Nations General Assembly called for "a speedy and unconditional end [to] colonialism in all its forms and manifestations" (Resolution 1514 [XV]). By 1970, that same body declared that "further continuation of colonialism in all its forms and manifestations is a crime which constitutes a violation of the Charter of the United Nations, the Declaration on the Granting of Independence to Colonial Countries and Peoples, and the principles of international law" (Resolution 2621 [XXV]). The latter resolution recognized the right of colonial peoples to do precisely what the thirteen colonies that would later comprise the United States had done: "to struggle by all necessary means at their disposal against colonial powers which suppress their aspiration for freedom and independence." The same United

Nations, through its Decolonization Committee, established to monitor the implementation of its resolutions mandating an end to colonialism, has repeatedly declared that Resolution 1514 (XV) applies to the case of Puerto Rico.

5. For example, a 1977 FALN communiqué following bombings of multinational corporations in New York explained the choice of targets as "they best characterize and represent Yanki imperialism. These corporations are using underhanded and barbaric tactics to explore and exploit our natural resources, especially land and off-shore petroleum and minerals such as copper and nickel." In *Towards People's War for Independence and Socialism in Puerto Rico: Documents and Communiques from the Revolutionary Public Independence Movement and the Armed Clandestine Movement*, ed. Sojourner Truth Organization (Committee in Solidarity with Puerto Rican Independence, May 19 Communist Organization, October 30 Organization, January 1979).

6. See, e.g., Verdict of the Permanent Peoples' Tribunal, Session on Puerto Rico (Barcelona, 1989); Verdict of the Special International Tribunal on the Violation of Human Rights of Political Prisoners and Prisoners of War in United States Prisons and Jails (New York, 1990); Verdict of the International Tribunal of Indigenous Peoples and Oppressed Nations in the U.S.A. (San Francisco, 1992).

7. *People of the State of Illinois v. Carlos Torres et al.*, No. 80-4794 (Circuit Court of Cook County).

8. *People of the State of Illinois v. Mary Rodriguez and Luis Rosa*, No. 80-2479 (Circuit Court of Cook County).

9. *United States v. Carlos Alberto Torres et al.*, No. 80 CR 736 (N.D. Ill.).

10. At the sentencing hearing, which took place soon after the holiday marking George Washington's birthday, Federal Judge Thomas McMillen made the following retort to an observation by one of the prisoners about the irony of the occasion: "You mentioned George Washington. You know, if George Washington had been captured by the British during the American Revolution he wouldn't have been put in the penitentiary or jailed; he would have been executed. And that, as a matter of fact, is the penalty which should be imposed on Count 1 [seditious conspiracy] in this case." *U.S. v. Carlos Torres*, Transcript of Sentencing Hearing, February 18, 1981, p. 20.

11. *United States v. Oscar Lopez et al.*, No. 86 CR 513 (N.D. Ill.).

12. *United States v. Alejandrina Torres et al.*, No. 83 CR 494 (N.D. Ill.).

13. Others arrested include Jorge Farinacci, Hilton Fernández Diamante, Isaac Camacho Negrón, Orlando González Claudio, Yvonne Meléndez Carrión, Luis Colón Osorio, Roberto José Maldonado, Norman Ramírez Talavera, Carlos Ayes Suárez, Luz Berríos Berríos, and Filiberto Ojeda Ríos. The first four, in a negotiated plea with the government, admitted to having committed acts in the name of Puerto Rican independence considered crimes by the United States, and they received prison sentences of five years to be followed by five years of parole. In an earlier plea agreement, Luz Berríos pled guilty and received a five-year prison sentence. Yvonne Meléndez received a sentence of probation following trial, and Carlos Ayes was found not guilty. Roberto José Maldonado and Norman Ramírez were found guilty and sentenced to five years in prison. Juan Segarra and Antonio Camacho were found guilty, as indi-

cated earlier. Filiberto Ojeda, who had been released on bond after almost three years in pretrial detention, was tried in Puerto Rico for defending himself and his home when FBI agents opened fire during his arrest. A Puerto Rican jury acquitted him. Before trial in Connecticut, in 1990, he left his electronic ankle bracelet to be delivered to the FBI in Puerto Rico with a note that he was returning to clandestinity. He was tried in absentia and sentenced to fifty-five years. Over the years since his departure the FBI has offered an ever-increasing reward for information leading to his arrest. See Hiraldo de León, "$150 mil por captura Ojeda Ríos: FBI duplica recompensa." El Vocero, March 25, 2995, p. 4; Rosita Marrero, "$500,000 por hallar a Filiberto: FBI subirá la recompensa" Primera Hora, January 7, 1999, pp. 1A, 10A.

14. *United States v. Victor Gerena et al.*, No. H-85-50 (D. Conn.).

15. *United States v. Filiberto Inocencio Ojeda Rios*, 846 F.2d 167 (2d Cir. 1988).

16. Administrative Office of the United States District Court, *Sentences Imposed Chart for Year Ended June 30, 1981* (Washington, D.C.), p. 145. See also, Alice Vachss, "Megan's Law Won't Reduce Sex Crimes," *New York Times*, July 31, 1995, p. A9 ("According to the most recent Bureau of Justice report, the national average sentence for convicted violent felons was less than eight years, of which they served less than four in prison.").

17. Kathleen Maguire and Ann L. Pastore, eds., *Sourcebook of Criminal Justice Statistics 1997* (Washington, D.C.: U.S. Department of Justice, Bureau of Justice Statistics, 1998), table 5.57, p. 430.

18. *"Acuerdo esclarecería Caso Muñiz Varela,"* Claridad, August 4–10, 1995, p. 3; Marilyn Pérez Cotto, *"Justicia no puede descansar en testimonio Alejo,"* Claridad, August 11–17, 1995, p. 3.

19. Ortiz Luquis, *"Ignacio Rivera: Un agente encubierto de abogado,"* Claridad, November 29–December 5, 1991, p. 3; Ortiz Luquis, *"Cartagena desmiente a Romero e involucra al FBI,"* Claridad, November 29–December 5, 1991, p. 5. According to *United States v. Moreno Morales et al.*, 815 F.2d 725 (1st Cir. 1987), the commander was indicted in 1984 and tried in 1985. Given that his sentence was twenty years, this means his 1991 release on parole occurred immediately upon becoming eligible.

20. Tara George, "4 Diallo Cops Go Free: Albany Jury Acquits Officers on All Counts in Bronx Death," *New York Daily News*, February 26, 2000, p. 2.

21. Andrew Martin, "Becker Now Indicted in Killing: New Evidence Is Cited by O'Malley in Shooting Death of Homeless Man," *Chicago Tribune*, September 28, 1995, p. 1.

22. Andrew Martin, "Probe of Police Sought in Humboldt Park Death," *Chicago Tribune*, November 26, 1996, section 2, p. 3.

23. "Ex-Detroit Officers Will Go to Prison for Beating Death," *New York Times*, October 13, 1993, p. A1; also see http://www.larrynevers.com (accessed June 15, 2003).

24. See, e.g., "New Trial Convicts Larry Nevers of Manslaughter: Appeal Planned," Law Enforcement Legal Defense Fund, *With Justice For All: Protecting Those Who Protect* 2:1 (Summer 2000); also see http://www.leldf.org/Newsletters/jun2000-p.1.html (accessed June 15, 2003).

25. "Border Shootings," *USA Today*, September 9, 1994, p. 3A.

26. "3 Militia Members Guilty in Bomb Plot," *Chicago Tribune*, November 7, 1996, sec. 1, p. 8.

27. "U.S. Seizes Armed Anti-Castro Squad off the Florida Keys," *Chicago Tribune*, January 24, 1996, sec. 1, p. 11.

28. "Mississippi Boat Is Linked to a Plot against Castro," *New York Times*, December 26, 1995, p. A13.

29. James Ridgeway, "Hard Time: Why the Left Goes to Jail and the Right Goes Home," *Village Voice* (December 11, 1990).

30. Mark Starr, "Violence on the Right," *Newsweek* (March 4, 1985): 25.

31. See, e.g., "Guilty Plea Expected in Fires at Clinics," *New York Times*, June 4, 1995, p. Y16 (ten-year sentence for attempted murder of doctor); Sue Anne Pressley, "From Prison Back to P.G. Pulpit," *Washington Post*, July 26, 1989, p. B1 (man guilty of bombing ten health clinics and causing over $1 million in damage sentenced to ten years, released after serving 3.8 years).

32. See, e.g., Linda Campbell, "Poindexter Gets 6 months in Iran-Contra," *Chicago Tribune*, June 12, 1990, p. 1; George Lardner Jr., "Abrams Sentenced to 2 Years' Probation, Fined $50: Former Official at State Department Withheld Iran-Contra Information from Congress," *Washington Post*, November 16, 1991, p. A20 (among those prosecuted and convicted for the Iran-Contra government arms for hostages scandal, the longest prison sentence was six months); "The Luckless Watergate Four," *Newsweek* (November 19, 1973): 45–46; G. V. Higgins, "Judge Who Tried Harder," *Atlantic* (April 1974): 83–92 (anti-Castro Cuban Watergate "plumbers" sentenced to six years for burglary; Watergate executives received lighter sentences for lesser offenses).

33. See, e.g., Tina Rosenberg, "Force Is Forever," *New York Times Magazine* (September 24, 1995): 44 (former leaders of the Chilean DINA, or intelligence police, sentenced to terms of six and seven years in prison for U.S. car bomb assassinations of Salvador Allende's former cabinet minister, Orlando Letelier, and his assistant, one of whom refused to surrender to custody); Stephen Kinzer, "3 Ex-East German Leaders Convicted," *New York Times*, September 17, 1993, p. A3 (former East German officials responsible for deaths of seven people killed as they tried to cross to west, sentenced to 5.5 and 7.5 years in prison, eligible for 50 percent reduction of sentence).

34. Herbert Koppel, *Time Served in Prison: Bureau of Justice Statistics Special Report* (Washington, D.C.: U.S. Department of Justice, Office of Justice Programs, Bureau of Justice Statistics, 1984), p. 1. As of 1991, state prisoners convicted of violent offences, including murder, manslaughter, and sexual assault, could expect to serve an average of 5.8 years. See *Survey of State Prison Inmates, 1991* (Washington, D.C.: U.S. Department of Justice, Bureau of Justice Statistics, March 1993), p. 7.

35. *Federal Criminal Case Processing, 1980–89 with Preliminary Data for 1990: A Federal Justice Statistics Report* (Washington, D.C.: U.S. Department of Justice, Office of Justice Programs, Bureau of Justice Statistics, October 1991), p. 18 (between 1985 and 1990, for violent offenses, the average time served until first release ranged from

a low of 48.8 months (4.0 years) to a high of 54.2 months (4.5 years); see *Sourcebook of Criminal Justice Statistics 1993*, table 6.92.

36. Kathleen Maguire and Ann L. Pastore, eds., *Sourcebook of Criminal Justice Statistics 1997* (U.S. Department of Justice, Bureau of Justice Statistics: Washington, D.C., 1998), table 5.57, p. 431. See also, *Sourcebook of Criminal Justice Statistics 1993*, table 6.92, p. 652 (average time served in federal prison for murder, 5.4 years); *National Corrections Reporting Program, 1992*, p. 34 (average time served in state prison, eight years); Michael Pollan, "How Pot Has Grown," *New York Times Magazine* (February 19, 1995): 32 ("An American convicted of murder can expect to spend, on average, less than nine years behind bars.").

37. Amnesty International, *Allegations of Ill Treatment in Marion Prison, Illinois, USA* (May 1987): 15 ("[w]ithin Marion, violations of the [United Nations] Standard Minimum Rules [for the Treatment of Prisoners] are common. . . . There is hardly a rule in the Standard Minimum Rules that is not infringed in some way or other."); L. C. Dorsey, *Marion Prison: Progressive Correction or Legalized Torture?* (New York: National Interreligious Task Force on Criminal Justice), p. 6 ("The absence of balance in the procedures at Marion prison, where security measures override the individual need for human contact, spiritual fulfilment, and fellowship, becomes an excuse for the constant show of sheer force. The conditions of Marion prison . . . constitute, in our estimation, psychological pain and agony tantamount to torture."); *Prison Conditions in the United States* (New York: Human Rights Watch, 1991), pp. 3, 75–77 (noting the proliferation of state maximum security prisons modelled after Marion, condemning as dangerous the trend toward "Marionization" of prison in the United States).

38. The majority of those who seek parole are released. See, e.g., *Sourcebook of Criminal Justice Statistics, 1993*, p. 658, reflecting that in 1993, 70 percent of those applying were freed.

39. William J. Clinton letter of September 21, 1999, to Rep. Henry Waxman, p. 2 [hereinafter "Waxman letter"].

40. Waxman letter, p. 2.

41. Waxman letter, p. 2.

42. Marco Antonio Rigau, *"Es la colonia, estúpidos,"* *El Nuevo Día*, September 14, 1999, p. 105; see also, José Javier Colón Morera, *"¿Qué esperar del Congreso estadounidense en el 2000?"* *Claridad*, January 14–20, 2000, pp. 8–9.

43. Lina M. F. Younes, *"Continúa debate sobre perdón de Clinton,"* *El Mundo*, September 19, 1999, p. 9. See also, Robert Friedman, "Clinton Attacked from All Sides As Clemency Debate Continues," *San Juan Star*, c. September 1999.

44. Robert Friedman, "U.S. Senate Approves Censure of Clinton," *San Juan Star*, September 15, 1999, p. 5.

45. Ibid.

46. See, e.g., Robert Friedman, "U.S. Senate to Vote on Censure Today," *San Juan Star*, September 14, 1999, p. 5; James Anderson, Associated Press, *"A flote el status ante la clemencia,"* *El Mundo*, September 12, 1999, p. 8.

47. See, e.g., Ana Mendieta and Lynn Sweet, "Freed Puerto Ricans Hailed," *Chicago Sun Times*, September 12, 1999, p. 3A.

48. U.S. Department of Justice. "News Advisory." Wednesday, August 11, 1999. http://www.usdoj.gov/opa/pr/1999/August/352dag.htm. Accessed August 12, 1999.

49. See, e.g., Katharine Q. Seelye, "Director of F.B.I. Opposed Clemency for Puerto Ricans: A Sign of a Fierce Debate," *New York Times*, September 22, 1999, p. 1 ("The FBI 'unequivocally opposes' President Clinton's offer of clemency to the 16 Puerto Rican nationalists, affirming that the liberation of the majority of the prisoners would reinvigorate their terrorist movement.").

50. John M. Broder, "12 Imprisoned Puerto Ricans Accept Clemency Conditions," *New York Times*, September 8, 1999, p. 1.

51. John McPhair, "Justice Nixes P. R. Inmates' Request for Joint Session," *San Juan Star*, August 14, 1999, p. 4.

52. Juan Segarra Palmer also accepted the conditional clemency, which provided for his release five years hence.

53. No author, *"Recepción de héroe,"* *Primera Hora*, September 11, 1999, p. 3A. See also Milvia Archilla, *"Fustiga CRB timidez sobre el terrorismo: En convención PNP,"* *Primera Hora*, September 13, 1999, p. 4A; Ana Mendieta and Lynn Sweet, "Freed Puerto Ricans Hailed," *Chicago Sun Times*, September 12, 1999, p. 3A; Richard Sisk, "11 in FALN Freed," *New York Daily News*, September 11, 1999, p. 6; Helen Peterson and Salvatore Arena, "Cheers Welcome Returning FALN Members," *New York Daily News*, September 12, 1999, p. 5.

54. Agnes J. Montano, *"Multitudinaria bienvenida,"* *El Nuevo Día*, September 11, 1999, p. 62.

55. Ibid.

56. Mireya Navarro, "Freed Puerto Rican Militants Revel in Life on the Outside," *New York Times*, January 27, 2000, p. A14.

57. Ibid.

58. Daisy Sánchez, *"En busca de un nuevo destino: Hablan los ex prisioneros políticos,"* *Diálogo*, November 1999, p. 34.

59. See, e.g., Benjamín Torres Gotay, *"Navidad sin rejas para los ex presos políticos,"* *El Nuevo Día*, January 4, 2000, p. 32; Benjamín Torres Gotay, *"Difícil la reintegración de los ex prisioneros,"* *El Nuevo Día*, January 3, 2000, p. 26.

60. Francine Kiefer and James N. Thurman, "Race, Pardons, and a Small Boy from Cuba," *Christian Science Monitor* (January 20, 2000): 1.

61. Anne-Marie Cusac, "You're in the Hole: A Crackdown on Dissident Prisoners," *The Progressive* (December 2001); see also http://www.progressive.org/0901/amc1201.html (accessed June 14, 2003).

62. See note 36.

63. José Garriga Picó, *"El sentir del Congreso,"* *El Mundo*, September 12, 1999, p. 35.

64. Lina M. F. Younes, *"Próxima semana vista sobre clemencia a presos,"* El Mundo, September 17, 1999, p. 12.

65. Robert Friedman, "Bill Ordering Navy Withdrawal To Be Filed," *San Juan Star*, September 16, 1999, p. 5, citing the then pro-statehood Governor Rosselló.

66. Ibid.

67. Rafael Hernández Colón [former governor of Puerto Rico], *"Presos Políticos en U.S.A.,"* El Nuevo Día, September 8, 1999, p. 133 (translated from the original Spanish).

68. Leonor Mulero, *"En este mismo año la consulta,"* El Nuevo Día, February 8, 2000, p. 20; Lina M. F. Younes, *"Denuncian inacción del Congreso: Sobre status,"* El Vocero, September 20, 1999, p. 13.

69. Neil A. Lewis, "Ashcroft Defends Antiterror Plan and Says Criticism May Aid Foes," *New York Times*, December 7, 2001, p. 1A. "Mr. Ashcroft told the Senate Judiciary Committee, 'To those who scare peace-loving people with phantoms of lost liberty, my message is this: your tactics only aid terrorists.'"

70. Carolyn Skorneck, "House OKs More Money for Spying," Associated Press, December 12, 2001.

71. See, e.g., Schey, Peter A. 2002. "In Pursuit of Justice: Taliban Prisoners in Guantanamo Have Geneva Convention Rights," posted in the Interfaith Communities United for Justice and Peace website (http://www.icujp.org). Accessed August 30, 2002.

EIGHT

Puerto Rican *Independentistas*

Subversives or Subverted?

Alberto L. Márquez

INTELLIGENCE WORK, the second oldest profession in the world (or maybe the first, at the beginning of the planet), is the most abundant in myths, confusions, and illusions. It has been existentially defined "as a wilderness of mirrors,"[1] and perhaps the twentieth century will be known not as the Age of Enlightenment but as the Age of Intelligence, in its triple sense of institution, process, and product (and by no means as an intellectual or ethical endeavor of the human race). Never before in the long history of so pervasive an activity, though not much addressed in traditional texts, have so many millions been spent, or so many bureaucracies been created, institutions which, because of their initials, FBI, CIA, MI5, MI6, KGB, SDECE,[2] resemble those alphabet soups we had as children.

This esoteric discipline needs to be approached without paranoia but also without naiveté, with an awareness of its omnipresence but also that it is, to a great extent, inapprehensible. Its effects are felt yet it is hardly ever seen, despite the fact it has been a constant force in Puerto Rican history since interpreter-spy Juan González managed to infiltrate the councils of the *taínos* and discover the preparations for a rebellion, to the technical interception of meetings and conversations of *The Macheteros* prior to the arrests of August 1985, and even to the future.

In the last three decades, approximately, some of the effects or consequences of the dual process of intelligence and repression can be noted. First, a significant, talented, and productive part of our population was prevented from participating in public life; I refer to the hundreds, possibly thousands of *independentistas* (Puerto Rican independence advocates) who were not able to reach their potential of participation in political work. Some spent years in court, even in prison, for the only "crime" of being part of pro-independence, student, community, or labor organizations. Others retreated from the political struggle because of the false accusations, the continuous and obsessive vigilance, and the illegal questioning of neighbors, relatives, and even employers by agents, in short due to all of the forms of repression that were practiced against them. Many were not able to counteract the effects of harassment, which resulted in their inability to find or maintain jobs, or of family pressure, because of their beliefs. These circumstances, of incalculable consequences to the development of independence movements or the democratic process of the country, were acknowledged by a not too progressive institution, the Supreme Court of Puerto Rico, in the famous "subversives files" cases.[3]

Just as serious, or maybe more so, was the series of crimes committed by the so-called security forces, the Police of Puerto Rico and the FBI,[4] which culminated in the entrapment and double murder at Cerro Maravilla[5] and which, in several ways, contributed to the development of the criminality problem from which we suffer.[6] The impunity, by a series of illegal techniques, with which independence advocates were persecuted, created a sense of arrogance and invulnerability in the repressive forces. Convinced that they were above the law, some members of said forces went from committing political to common crimes; they formed several "death squads," the most notorious being that led by Alejo Maldonado,[7] though by no means the only one.

The final report resulting from the Puerto Rico Senate's investigation of the events at Cerro Maravilla yields valuable information on the death squads. It reads, in one of its parts, as follows:

> The Commission investigated and was able to obtain sufficient evidence to establish the existence of illegal civilian-military groups trained, abetted, armed, and protected by some federal authorities in Puerto Rico. These groups, commonly called death squads, operated under the protection of sectors of the U.S. government and outside the law, just as was the case in some Latin American countries. The main purpose of these civilian military groups was to repress, by harassment, persecution, fabrication of cases, and murder, the activists of the Puerto Rican movement.[8]

Later on, it states:

> These groups acted outside the law. They had their own methods of gathering information about the members of the pro-independence groups they meant to repress. Mostly they shielded themselves behind the official positions held by their members in the security agencies of the Commonwealth and the Federal Government.

We concluded that people in those federal and local public positions systematically violated the rights of many independence advocates, using special weapons of the U.S. Marshall Service assigned to the Federal District Court for the District of Puerto Rico, the U.S. Navy, personnel, equipment, and funds from local and federal agencies and the intelligence files of the Federal Agencies and the Commonwealth of Puerto Rico.[9]

The report expands on one of the groups in particular and its modus operandi:

This group, formed by the then Federal Marshall, José A. López, Julio César Andrades, at the time Chief of the Special Arrests Division of the Police of Puerto Rico, and personnel assigned to both divisions, from 1978 to 1980 put in practice the lessons learned in Panama's School of the Americas, taught by members of the Special Forces of the U.S. Army. [. . .] The group was composed of groups of civilians, ex-military personnel, ex-policemen, and volunteers [who operated] as a sort of vigilantes, if necessary. For example, Juan Dalmau, a weapons expert and armorer who worked at the Police's U.O.T.[10] was in contact with Marshall López and was the person in charge of altering the Federal Agent's weapons which would be used for the illegal activities of the group. The weapon used by Luis Reverón Martínez in Cerro Maravilla to kill Arnaldo Darío Rosado was one of those altered by Juan Dalmau. Andrades received the guns, property of the U.S. Government, from Marshall López in mid-1979, and gave them to his lawyer, Ignacio Rivera, in the beginning of 1984, so that he would deliver them to the FBI.

Andrades thinks the task of keeping an inventory of the Federal Marshall's guns fell on some Administrative Judge of the Federal Court. Said arms had been retired from regular service for the office of Federal Agents, but were numbered and inventoried, and were supposed to be kept in the vault at the Office of Federal Agents.[11]

Within the Intelligence Division of the Police of Puerto Rico, another death squad was created, several of whose members were prosecuted for the crimes at Maravilla. Despite these accusations, one of the presumed "intellectual authors" of the illegal group, Desiderio Cartagena Ortiz, at one time chief of the Police of Puerto Rico, was never prosecuted and escaped all sanctions, as happened with other officers known to have participated in illegal, repressive acts, such as the aforementioned federal marshall, José López, and Lieutenant Alex de la Zerda,[12] of the U.S. Navy.

The ideological characteristics of these groups are reflected in the following fragment:

The philosophy of this group was that to defend Democracy, [certain] persons had to be identified, kept under observation and eliminated, if necessary. When using the term eliminate, they meant assassination. According to Ignacio Rivera, this was the mentality of the terrorist police groups, operating in

South America, such as the "Death Squads" of Brazil and Argentina that were the role models much talked about in the group. They studied and even had books by the Servicio de Inteligencia Brazileiro [sic] (Brazilian Intelligence Service). In due time, the supposedly anti-terrorist group turned into a terrorist one. In their operations, they were going to use the Riot Squad, directed by Coronel Enrique Sánchez and the guns property of the Marshall Service.[13]

The transition from illegal activities against the independence movement to illegal activities in general was not long to come. The aforementioned Puerto Rico Senate report states it thus: "In a given moment, the group degenerated, and went from allegedly defending Democracy to generating illegal income, through common crimes, stealing, giving and selling protection."[14]

The most renowned example of this is the group led by Alejo Maldonado. The Senate report already referred to has, among other things, the testimonial of an ex-member of the gang:

Other testimony that tends to corroborate the nature of these clandestine "vigilante" groups is that of Juan "Payo" Fuentes Santiago. Juan Fuentes Santiago was a member of the so-called "Gang" of then police agent Alejo Maldonado and, along with Maldonado deputy, César Caballero, committed a number of serious crimes, abetted by officers of the Police of Puerto Rico and a group of Cuban exiles. In 1982, the FBI intervened with Fuentes, in relation to the kidnapping of jeweler Consuegra's son. [. . .] Fuentes, after turning into a witness for the Federal Government, was protected by the Federal Authorities. [. . .] Alejo Maldonado and many of the persons who committed crimes with him were members of a death squad that César Caballero called "Los Duendes" (The Elves). The purpose of this squad was to eliminate persons for ideological reasons. Associated with this group were Maldonado, Andrades, U.S. Marshall López, another one identified as "a certain (La) Cerda" [sic], two FBI agents stationed in Roosevelt Roads Naval Base, and others. This group, as told to him by César Caballero, had contacts with a group of Cuban-American agents who allegedly were related to the Central Intelligence Agency (CIA).[15]

The sense of impunity and arrogance we spoke of earlier is shown in another part of the report:

This group, "Los Duendes," followed orders from above to create a climate of violence in Puerto Rico, as Alejo Maldonado told Fuentes. They were under orders from "higher up" levels. Even during the Consuegra kidnapping case, Alejo Maldonado kept saying the FBI couldn't touch him because he was the FBI's instrument to deal with independentistas.[16]

Although the development of drug trafficking transcends the subject with which we are dealing, and it is an almost worldwide phenomenon, in

Puerto Rico, in the first stages, it had a disproportionate rise because a group of Cuban exiles involved in drug dealing, directly or indirectly, was used as shock troops in paramilitary operations against the independence movement, giving them a *de facto* immunity for their other criminal acts.

HOW HAS INTELLIGENCE WORK OPERATED IN PUERTO RICO?

Intelligence work precedes, directs, and orients repression; this two-pronged approach has had, in Puerto Rico, the following characteristics (which are not exhaustive):

1. The presence of intelligence work has been constant, even since before the 1898 U.S. invasion.
2. Repression has been relatively selective, with the exception of the periods 1934–1939 and 1950–1954.[17]
3. The operation and the effects of intelligence work in its repressive phase have been of a predominantly preventive nature, of intimidation in the socioeconomic levels, which has resulted in relatively bloodless repressive operations, especially when compared to other liberation processes in the Third World.
4. Intelligence and repression forces have tried to prevent confrontation between Puerto Ricans and U.S. personnel and institutions, using the Police of Puerto Rico and other structures as a shield. They try to repress Puerto Ricans with other Puerto Ricans. This has undergone a modification in the last ten years, with the "federalization" of the repressive apparatus and a more open and flagrant operative role of the FBI, Drug Enforcement Administration (DEA), Border Patrol, and other repressive forces.
5. The local repressive organisms have always been dominated, infiltrated, and controlled by the United States. The best example is the penetration of the local police by the FBI.[18]
6. Nongovernmental social sectors, such as Cuban exiles and right-wing extremists of the NPP (New Progressive Party, pro-statehood party), have been used for clandestine or undercover paramilitary operations against the independence movement but were always led and controlled by U.S. civilian or military agencies, especially the FBI, the ONI (Office of Naval Intelligence), and the Military Intelligence Division (MID) of the U.S. Army.
7. The strategic objectives of the intelligence-repression two-track approach have been and continue to be the following:
   a. Isolate the pro-independence organizations from the rest of the people and divide them internally, to disarticulate and disintegrate them.

b. Isolate the independence movement from the autonomist movement, steering the latter to colonialist positions.
c. Criminalize the organizations that have pushed for social change, particularly those that have proclaimed or practiced forms of armed struggle.
d. Criminalize the ideals and practices that proclaim national liberation and social change in the eyes of the rest of the Puerto Rican population.

MORE SUBVERTED THAN SUBVERSIVE

Historically, the periods of acute and open repression have prevented the Puerto Rican independence movement from developing strategies, structures, and styles to counteract the enemy intelligence work. The conspiratorial tradition and practice so painstakingly elaborated in the nineteenth century, especially by Ramón E. Betances and his group,[19] and even then interrupted in different stages, suffered a significant setback with the "98 trauma" from which it would not recuperate until the irruption in Puerto Rico's political life of Pedro Albizu Campos and the Nationalists, on the one hand, and the Puerto Rican Communist Party, on the other hand. The enemy did not give them respite or time to develop the structures to withstand the repressive onslaught. Albizu, unlike Betances after the 1868 *Grito de Lares* uprising, was not able to change from direct to indirect confrontation. The enemy prevented him from doing so.

Not all was lost, nevertheless; a link was maintained between the Nationalist's practice and what was later called the "new struggle," through oral transmission and the example set by organizations such as *Acción Patriótica Unitaria* (United Patriotic Action) from 1954 to 1960. The individual work of patriots coming from nationalism and communism should be noted. Among the Nationalists, to name only a few, were Ramón Medina Ramírez, Juan Gallardo Santiago, Domingo Vega Figueroa, and Félix Feliciano Morales. Among the Communists who also undertook such an important task were Félix Ojeda (senior), César Andreu Iglesias, Juan Santos Rivera, and José Enamorado Cuesta.

Those patriot's efforts managed to rescue, for the political action after 1960, the need for intelligence strategies, at least in theory. Nevertheless, objective and subjective conditions in those decades prevented the pro-independence organizations from taking into account and using efficiently that important type of political struggle.

First, it was constantly proclaimed that free speech and democratic rights prevailed in Puerto Rico. Large segments of the population, many independence advocates included, were blinded by this propaganda and did not even think about protecting themselves from the schemes of the intelligence repression agencies. Second, the lack of theory and practice concerning this issue and the lack of an ongoing, solid tradition in conspiracy and the gathering and filing of information about enemy personnel and methods also were obstacles for the development of intelligence sources.

The most obvious example of these deficiencies that still plague the independence movement is the reaction of many people when it was confirmed, between 1987 and 1992, that the state kept political files on so many citizens: a mixture of surprise, lack of knowledge, ignorance, naiveté, pessimism, and paranoia. Reactions gravitated to two extremes: from "repression is over" to "nothing was gained in Puerto Rico; they handed over something worthless because they already have it on microfiche, and because at this moment independence is not a threat." In view of all of this, it does not seem an exaggeration to say that in Puerto Rico, the intelligence and repression machinery of the colonial powers have managed to make us more subverted than subversive. But there are many things to be done to change that fact, and it becomes more urgent every day to start doing so.

THE AGENDA FOR THE FUTURE

When examining other struggles and reflecting upon ours, we will see that when a contender is weaker or strategically defensive, the more important it becomes to obtain the best possible intelligence about an adversary and to protect what it wants to know about us. The intelligence process consists of the detection, acquisition, and analysis of the data useful for making political, economic, and military decisions.[20] One has adequate intelligence about an adversary if one complies with the following:

1. Have an accurate knowledge about the enemy's strengths and weaknesses, especially the weaknesses.
2. Be able to protect one's own secrets, whether by concealment, disinformation, or a combination.
3. Be able, with the data obtained, to surprise the enemy, as well as to prevent the enemy from surprising us.

The product of intelligence work can be classified as static, dynamic, strategic, and tactical:

1. Static: the description of the enemy's political, military, and economic means and its forces.
2. Dynamic: changes in doctrine, leadership and administration, production and technology, and the development of initiatives or events.
3. Strategic: the analysis of the enemy's capacity; what it can do and its long-term intentions.
4. Tactical: what the enemy is doing, its way of operating, everyday moves, and short-term reactions.

Given the fact that the pro-independence movement has historically been referred to as "subversive," let us define this term, which is closely related to intelligence measures. Subversion is the attempt to exercise political influence in favor of one of the contenders, in a given situation, both in peace and in war, without the other contender being wise to it and without it appearing as having been generated by its enemy. It aims to persuade some persons or groups to convince others to act in the benefit of the country or group that favors a given act without the very persons who so act being aware of it.

As a matter of fact, whoever can obtain intelligence also can subvert. Conversely, whoever has inadequate means to obtain intelligence is to a good extent unable to subvert. Subversion as a political activity consists, among others, of the following techniques: positively influence in favor of the adversary, propagate rumors and disinformation, increase the latent or existing contradictions, and weaken the influence of key individuals or sectors in the enemy camp. In some liberation processes, intelligence was a key factor in the outcome,[21] as is the case in Vietnam, Ireland, and Palestine. It is an inescapable conclusion, upon the study of our reality, that the independence movement in Puerto Rico cannot succeed without the development of the doctrine, structures, and methods that create and develop intelligence and information resources.

Building those resources, let it be emphasized, is not urgent only to those of us who advocate independence but to everyone living here. Different threats loom over our country, for example, the contaminating activities of industrial capitalism, with projects such as the Armed Forces Radar, the possible exploitation of the copper mines, projects from Congress that are adverse to our economy, the use of Puerto Rico as a base from which to attack other countries, the last two chronological examples being Grenada and Panama, and the transfer of the U.S. Army South Com, which is the military structure in charge of planning, commanding, and coordinating that type of intervention. An obvious conflict exists between the people's right to know about things pertinent to their survival and the interests of the metropolitan power, the colonial state, and the military-industrial complex.

Organized efforts to provide the people with the available information can be carried out, without having to play at being spies. Truth be told, nearly 80 percent of the pertinent information can be obtained from open sources and is accessible to any investigative group. Nevertheless, and may this be understood by those who should, working in isolation and without foresight, it is very difficult, if not impossible, even to collect this information, much less to analyze it and make it accessible to those who need it without the proper structures and education. Let us remember the advice from Betances, our founding father, applied to the current colonial power, appearing in the New York paper *La Revolución* on July 19, 1870, where he said it was necessary to

. . . prepare slowly, in silence, without boasting, without indiscretions or imprudence, with all the reserve of the weak, with all the precautions of those who are unsure of their strength, with all the steadfastness of those obliged to risk all to chance, to rid themselves of the yoke, to cleanse the leprosy, to separate from Spain.[22]

NOTES

This chapter is a revised version of a presentation at the Third Annual Meeting of the Puerto Rican Association of Historians, October 6–7, 1995, Río Piedras Campus, University of Puerto Rico.

1. The reference to the world of intelligence and espionage as a "wilderness of mirrors" is commonly attributed to James Jesus Angleton, who was the head chief of counterespionage of the Central Intelligence Agency (CIA) for a long period of time. In fact, there is a book about Angleton, in which the author used this phrase as the title (Martin 1980). See also Polmar and Allen 1997.

2. FBI: Federal Bureau of Investigation, United States; CIA: Central Intelligence Agency, United States; MI5: Military Intelligence 5, counterespionage, Great Britain; MI6: Military Intelligence 6, espionage, Great Britain; KGB: *Komitet Gosudarstvennoy Bezopasnosti*, Russia; SDECE: *Service de Documentation Extérieure et de Contreespionnage*, France.

3. *Noriega et al. v. Hernández Colón et al.* 122 DPR 650 (November 21, 1988) and 130 DPR 919 (June 30, 1992).

4. For more information about the FBI, see Kessler 1993; about provocation and police activities, see Chevigny 1972.

5. Suárez 1987.

6. In a press article published at the end of the 1970s, for example, it is mentioned that the level of attention that was given to leftist clandestine groups (some of them made up by the police itself, as will be known later) is as follows: "The police has given priority to the tracking of these groups, even more than the gangs and the groups devoted to drug dealing and the organized crime in general." See José Rafael Reguero, *"Conoce la policía 25 grupos clandestinos,"* El Nuevo Día, October 10, 1978, p. 6.

7. For more details about Alejo Maldonado's gang actions, see Senado de Puerto Rico 1992. See also the book by journalist José Rafael Reguero (1992).

8. Senado de Puerto Rico 1992, 8–9.

9. Ibid., 26–27.

10. Acronym for *Unidad de Operaciones Tácticas* (Police Tactical Operations Unit), also known as *Fuerza de Choque* (Riot Police).

11. Senado de Puerto Rico 1992, 27–28.

12. On Alex de la Zerda's links, see, for example, the Senate's Report, which states:

The group's contact in the Navy was Alex de la Zerda, who was the Public Relations Official for the Commander of the Navy in the Caribbean. His importance was that he provided munitions and equipment to the group. [. . .] According to Ignacio Rivera, the group participated in many acts: the placement of a bomb at the Puerto Rico Bar Association by Alex de la Zerda, Abraham Arzola, and U.S. Marshall José López; the import or export of some illegal arms to Santo Domingo approved by the Dominican Army, and the illegal use of arms and federal equipment. Senado de Puerto Rico 1992, p. 30.

13. Ibid., 29.

14. Ibid.

15. Ibid., 31–32.

16. Ibid., 32.

17. Concerning this last period in particular and the Gag Order, see Acosta 1987.

18. For more on the FBI-Police of Puerto Rico connection, see the chapter by Bosque-Pérez in this book.

19. Delgado Pasapera 1984.

20. Regarding intelligence work and war, see Copeland 1974; Miller and Foss 1987; Seaborg and Codevilla 1989; Sun 1994.

21. For details regarding these cases, see, for example, Bowyer Bell 1993; Coogan 1992, 1993; Livingstone and Halevy 1990; Lockman and Beinin 1989; Schif and Ya'ari 1990.

22. Betances 1985, 175.

WORKS CITED

Acosta, Ivonne. 1987. *La Mordaza: Puerto Rico 1948–1957*. Río Piedras, Puerto Rico: Editorial Edil.

Betances, Ramón Emeterio. 1985. *Cuba en Betances: Selección e introducción de Emilio Godínez*. La Habana, Cuba: Editorial de Ciencias Sociales.

Bosque-Pérez, Ramón, and José Javier Colón Morera. 1997. *Las carpetas: Persecución política y derechos civiles en Puerto Rico (ensayos y documentos)*. Río Piedras, Puerto Rico: Centro para la Investigación y Promoción de los Derechos Civiles (CIPDC).

Bowyer Bell, J. 1993. *The Irish Troubles 1967–1992*. New York: St. Martin's Press.

Chevigny, Paul. 1972. *Cops and Rebels: A Study in Provocation*. New York: Curtiss Books.

Coogan, Tim Pat. 1992. *The Man Who Made Ireland: The Life and Death of Michael Collins*. Niwot, Colo.: Roberts Rinehart.

———. 1993. *The IRA: A History*. Niwot, Colo.: Roberts Rinehart.

Copeland, Miles. 1974. *Without Cloak or Dagger*. New York: Simon and Schuster.

Delgado Pasapera, Germán. 1984. *Puerto Rico, sus luchas emancipadoras*. Río Piedras, Puerto Rico: Editorial Cultural.

Kessler, Ronald. 1993. *The FBI*. New York: Simon and Schuster.

Livingstone, Nell C., and David Halevy. 1990. *Inside the PLO*. New York: William Morrow and Co.

Lockman, Zachary, and Joel Beinin, eds. 1989. *Intifada: The Palestinian Uprising against Israeli Occupation*. Boston: South End Press.

Martin, David C. 1980. *Wilderness of Mirrors*. New York: Harper & Row.

Miller, David, and Christopher F. Foss. 1987. *Modern Land Combat*. New York: Basic Books.

Polmar, Norman, and Thomas B. Allen. 1997. *Spy Book: The Encyclopedia of Espionage*. New York: Random House.

Reguero, José Rafael. 1992. *Alejo y los niños de sangre azul*. Río Piedras, Puerto Rico: Editorial Cultural.

Schiff, Ze'ev, and Ehud Ya'ari. 1990. *Intifada*. New York: Simon and Schuster.

Seaborg, Paul, and Angelo Codevilla. 1989. *War: Ends and Means*. New York: Basic Books.

Senado de Puerto Rico. 1992. *Informe Final de la Investigación del Senado de Puerto Rico Sobre los Sucesos del Cerro Maravilla*. Estado Libre Asociado de Puerto Rico, 11a Asamblea Legislativa, 11na Sesión Extraordinaria (December 31).

Suárez, Manuel. 1987. *Requiem on Cerro Maravilla*. Maplewood, N.J.: Waterfront Press.

Sun Tzu. 1994. *Art of War*. Boulder, Colo.: Westview Press.

PART III

The Vieques Case

NINE

Vieques

To Be or Not to Be

Jalil Sued-Badillo

VIEQUES IS ONE of the municipalities of the Commonwealth of Puerto Rico; it is located some six miles off its southeastern coast and measures close to fifty square miles. For over 5,000 years, it has been an integral part of Puerto Rico, in political, cultural, and economic aspects. This fact has come about as part of a long, haphazard history, but it has been basically unavoidable because of its proximity and social interaction with Puerto Rico and the Virgin Islands. Its location imparted Vieques its historical role of the threshold to all migratory movements from the Eastern Caribbean to the Greater Antilles.

In the last decade, Puerto Rican archaeologists have identified traces of the first human settlement in the Puerto Rican archipelago; these traces were found in Puerto Ferro—on the southern coast of Vieques—and date back nearly 4,000 years A.D. (Chanlatte 1985). Several thousand years later, Vieques was once again the doorway to Puerto Rico of successive migrations from South America, made up of people with pottery and agricultural skills (Chanlatte and Narganes Storde 1983; Centro de Investigaciones Arqueológicas 1984). These groups brought to Puerto Rico, and eventually to all of the Western Caribbean, the agricultural way of life, the language, and the rudiments of the material and intellectual culture, which prevailed until the coming of the Spaniards, some 1,500 years later. Yet Vieques was not merely a route or a waiting station in these initial stages. It was the first stable settlement for these early cultural groups, and thus the geographic scenario for an important transition stage: from noninsular ways of life to

the social demands placed upon them by a land with diverse ecologic components such as Puerto Rico.

The lengthy time that the different migratory groups stayed in Vieques
before moving to Puerto Rico is evidence that the island had the necessary
resources to satisfy the needs for food, shelter, and safety of these early
groups, contrary to what had been their experience in many of the smaller
windward and Virgin Islands. Archaeological evidence also suggests that
Vieques became an important political scenario during the period when agricultural and pottery lifestyles expanded to Puerto Rico in the first three centuries of the era. The archaeological sites of Sorce and La Hueca were clearly
the foundation beds of a geocultural expansion, which lasted three or four
centuries (Chanlatte 1981). These pre-Columbian movements, which originated on the South American continent, stayed in Vieques and Puerto Rico
for many centuries; they were absorbed, in a manner of saying, by a geography that satisfied their vital needs. Centuries later, their descendants would
move once again to new lands out to sea, taking agriculture and pottery
techniques to Haiti, Jamaica, Cuba, and the Bahamas and thus closing a
process of centuries.

In other words, Vieques and Puerto Rico were the lands in which the
original South American immigrants were culturally transformed into insular
peoples. That is why those lands are important archaeological regions for the
study and comprehension of all of the Caribbean's early history. In the areas
in Vieques, today under the domain of the U.S. Navy, hundreds of archaeological sites have been identified that await confirmation of their cultural
importance (Tronolone et al. 1984; Curet 1987). In terms of academic
research, Vieques is Puerto Rico's most important archaeological province,
and Puerto Rico is one of the Caribbean's most important archaeological
regions, due to the number of settlements, the stages represented, the existing archaeological remains, and the relative chronologies.

THE SPANISH CONQUEST

When the Spaniards invaded in 1508, Vieques was part of one of the most
important native political chieftainships in Puerto Rico, which had its center on the southern coast. This is why when the *caciques* in the big island
rebelled against the Spaniards, the two caciques in Vieques promptly joined
the resistance. One of them, Cacimar, is identified in early chronicles as
accosting the lands of a woman cacique, Luisa, who was collaborating with
the invaders, and whose lands were in the northeastern part of Puerto Rico.
In one of the attacks, Cacimar was killed, and his brother, Yahureibo, intensified the attacks against the farms and mining camps in Puerto Rico. In May
1513, Vieques *tainos* participated in burning down Caparra (the then Spanish capital), and in the attacks against the settlements of caciques allied with

the Spaniards and came dangerously close to the royal estate in the Toa region. This participation by Vieques inhabitants was confirmed when the island suffered the terrible retaliation measures taken by Viceroy Diego Colón, who was in Puerto Rico during those months. Colón ordered his political lieutenant, Cristóbal de Mendoza, to attack and depopulate Vieques. The punitive expedition took place in October of that same year, 1513. Mendoza oversaw the massacre of hundreds of natives and the imprisonment of the survivors, who were later sold in public auction in San Germán (Fernández de Oviedo y Valdés 1959, 102–3).[1] Vieques thus suffered its first condemnation for existing as a social community, and its first death sentence as a human society.

With such drastic measures, the Spaniards strived to offset support for the rebellion in its weakest flank, as the conquerors were not fully in control of most of the Puerto Rican territory until almost the end of the eighteenth century, and the easternmost regions were always the least populated and most susceptible to external incursions. That explains why Vieques was considered early on a threat to the safety of the European settlements. The policy established by the Spaniards to protect their conquests in land was to depopulate nearby regions that had proved hard to occupy or guard. Throughout the Caribbean, those lands where no gold had been found, and therefore were not targeted for colonization, were referred to as "useless islands."

Puerto Rico, having been one of the first mining settlements in the colonial Caribbean, suffered early on from this policy of depopulation and relocation of the natives in the conqueror's zeal to supply a working force to the mine sites. Vieques also was a target of the relocation of its indigenous communities, one of the true reasons for Cristóbal de Mendoza's orders to depopulate Vieques in 1513.[2] Yet the depopulation measures were ultimately counterproductive, because they created power vacuums, ungovernable and indefensible spaces that were susceptible for the use—as in effect they were— of opposing political groups, outcasts, and eventually foreign enemies. The depopulation measures taken in Vieques and in a great part of Puerto Rico spread to the Virgin Islands and numerous other islands in the Eastern Caribbean. Vieques was just one more of the many Caribbean islands affected by the Spanish slave policies since the second half of the sixteenth century.

A close study of the documents of the time shows that Vieques had become an inevitable stop for any smuggler who eventually went to the ample southeastern coast of Puerto Rico in search of deals and contracts; the small Vieques isle had ceased being a historical community and became a stepping-stone in the routes of smugglers, a clandestine stopover for pirates, escaped slaves, European privateers, and even for Indians and *mestizos*, who, for longer than has been credited, came and went with relative ease. The Lesser Antilles had been a constant target of the expeditions to capture slaves for the Puerto Rican gold mines, so a certain amount of escapees was to be expected, those who would most likely go via Vieques to their islands of origin (Cárdenas Ruiz 1980).

Although the Spanish conquest was the precipitating factor for the dissolution of the indigenous community in Vieques, as was the case for most of those populating the Antillean archipelago, the demographic collapse of the next two centuries was the true aggravating circumstance. Given the scarce population of Puerto Rican lands, the different marginal groups looking up and down for a space away from colonial powers in which to operate were not in need of unpopulated islands in order to go unnoticed. The coastal farms had always provided enough space and protection, even for the occasional foreigners seeking refuge in Puerto Rico. That is, at the time Vieques became formally uninhabited, the same could be said of ample regions of Puerto Rico, both inland and on the coasts, where the populations had been dramatically reduced or had disappeared altogether.

In the course of the uninhabited stage, Vieques seems to have reconstituted itself ecologically speaking, because when other groups eventually set their sights on the island once again, they expressed much praise for its natural beauty and resources. In the *Memoirs*, or *Report of 1582*, by Governor Melgarejo, he added that Vieques had "many sheep without owner." The town council in San Juan occasionally gave permits to some to hunt the sheep there (Fernández Méndez 1976, 134). Said *Memoirs* also mentioned Vieques supposedly being used by "Carib" *marauders*, in direct reference to the indigenous communities of Dominica, whose inhabitants were coveted by the sugar plantation owners always looking for new sources of cheap labor. The *Memoirs* cannot exaggerate the occasional visits of windward indigenous groups looking for resources such as the sheep.[3] In fact, just a few years later, in 1587, members of John White's fleet, momentarily detained in Saint Croix, visited "Beake" island to confirm the rumors of its "sheep riches." This was White's fourth trip to Virginia, where he was one of the first settlers (Quinn 1955, 519).

In the seventeenth and eighteenth centuries, Puerto Rico and Vieques were truly floating forests with great extensions of timber trees for medicinal or aromatic purposes, for fine and strong constructions, or, at worst, for firewood. The trees were hardly used in their places of origin, while they were much in demand by the Eastern Caribbean for their burgeoning sugar plantations, run by slaves. Its native or acquired fauna also turned them into lands with good food, not only for their inhabitants but also for the fleets cruising the Atlantic, which were in need of food, water, and firewood. Vieques also was notorious for its banks of hawksbill turtles, an appetizing meat source up until recently. Furtive visits from foreigners in search of these resources were the norm during the eighteenth and nineteenth centuries. Between 1755 and 1756, for example, corsairs based in Puerto Rico captured five schooners in

Vieques or its neighboring waters, belonging to English settlers coming from the nearby islands of Tortola or Virgin Gorda. The cargo consisted of small rowboats for fishing, cut wood for carpentry jobs, forty-seven hawksbill turtles, and two black slaves (Feliciano Ramos 1990).

THE EUROPEAN TAKEOVER OF THE CARIBBEAN

Since 1625, different European nationals organized in commercial companies—English, French, Dutch, and Danish—began occupying the parts of the Caribbean that the Spaniards had left uninhabited for over a century. Little by little, first with the Lesser Antilles, and then with some of the Greater Antilles (Jamaica, Haiti), a switch of power took place. Toward the last twenty-five years of the seventeenth century, the insular Caribbean was already a multi-European sea or, as Juan Bosh (1970) called it, an "imperial frontier." Spain unsuccessfully tried to avoid it, failing to reign supreme in most cases. Using both ordinary and extraordinary measures, Spain tried fiercely to prevent its competitors from establishing themselves near Puerto Rico.

Puerto Rico had never been an important military base for the Spaniards, not even to defend itself. This was demonstrated not only by the two English attacks of 1585 and 1598 but also by the Dutch occupation of 1625, when the fragile insular defenses were exposed by the enemy. By this last date, the English, coming from Barbados, began accosting the islands of Saint Croix and Saint Christopher at the beginning of a long era of hostilities and occupation of the Virgin Islands near Puerto Rico. Once again the Spanish armed forces stationed in Puerto Rico were unable to prevent the takeover of their sea space. The unsuccessful defense of the islands of Saint Croix, Saint Thomas, and Saint John (all considered part of the Puerto Rican archipelago since the conquest) also is illustrative of the inadequacy of the metropolitan military forces in Puerto Rico. Spain mobilized the fleets, which were passing through, such as that of Fadrique de Toledo, who expelled the English and the French from St. Christopher in 1629 but demonstrated that without such extraordinary resources, it was unable to keep the persistent enemy at bay.

In 1633, the Spaniards from Puerto Rico expelled the Dutch from St. Martin in a final attempt to establish a commanding presence in the eastern Caribbean and kept a precarious garrison until 1648, when an epidemic forced them to withdraw. By then, the English, the French, and the Dutch had occupied a great part of the windward islands, including one as close to Puerto Rico as St. Croix, which was the first demarcation border traced by Spain to contain the encroachment of its rivals. Possibly occupied by English from Barbados, and later reinforced by the French and the Dutch, the Spaniards expelled them by force on numerous occasions, but never permanently. After 1650, the French prevailed in the occupation until they voluntarily abandoned it, occupying instead the more profitable St. Domingue. In 1671, the Danes occupied St. Thomas, an island that would in a few decades substitute St. Croix commercially, as well as the Virgin Island of St. John.

By the end of the seventeenth century, Spain had lost Jamaica, Haiti (St. Domingue), and all of the Eastern Caribbean, except Puerto Rico and Trinidad; the strategic Puerto Rican colony had only Vieques as a defense. Yet in this history of Caribbean geopolitics, of Spanish defeats and European advancements, there is an aspect that has remained hidden in much of the Caribbean historiography, that being the effects and consequences of all of these turnovers and struggles in the state of mind and in the disposition of the native Creoles. It is common to use European genteelism when referring to the inhabitants of the islands without taking into account that on many occasions, the main protagonists were not necessarily European nationals but the island natives themselves. When speaking of matters where loyalty to the land is at stake, differences in origin are very important. Many of the Lesser Antilles occupied by Europeans had a scant or nonexistent indigenous population, and most of its population consisted of groups not born in the land. It was the other way around in the islands dominated by Spain, such as Puerto Rico, where by the seventeenth century there already existed an eminently native Creole society. Therefore, when speaking of Puerto Rico, the distinction must be made between the disposition and goals of the Creoles as opposed to those of the Spanish foreigners so as not to confuse them. By the eighteenth century, of course, other eastern Caribbean islands also developed native Creole populations.

Until the Dutch attack to the city of San Juan in 1625, the defense of Puerto Rico relied mainly on the garrison headquartered in the city, which had to be comprised of Spanish military personnel, never natives. The native militia, badly armed and unpaid, dispersed in other areas of the island, had played a very marginal military role until then. But the advancement of well-trained and well-armed European enemies was too much for the regular Spanish forces in Puerto Rico, who by 1625 proved unable to defend not only the island from direct attacks but also the surrounding archipelago. As Spain was unable to reinforce the troops in Puerto Rico with Spanish-born soldiers, it was forced to recruit Creoles to the exclusive city garrison—at first with the sons of Spanish officers and soldiers—and to depend on Creole troops for the defense of the island and the region. The first company made up of free blacks also was created in those days, and eventually all of the racially mixed groups flourishing on the island were admitted into the military. It was coincidentally in the battles to retain St. Croix and the Virgin Islands where the native troops showed their military skills and began to develop a sense of loyalty toward the Puerto Rican archipelago.

The use of native soldiers in overseas expeditions was not only a success but also a surprise to the Spanish government. The until then undisciplined

Puerto Rican peasantry proved a pertinacious, aggressive, and efficient soldier and sorely needed in those precarious days for the lands dominated by Spain. Puerto Rican soldiers were used since 1635, during the second attempt to expel the English from St. Croix. Two years later, after a second incursion to said island, the bishop of Puerto Rico wrote to the king:

> . . . in short, our forces did not reach fifty, while the enemy were over two hundred, but while only one of ours was dead in the field, over forty of theirs died, [. . .] and some twenty prisoners were held, because the people who went, named peasants, did things which exceeded the fabulous. (Murga Sanz and Huerga 1988, 281)

That same year the Metropolitan War Council of the Indies formally included the new policy to embrace natives in the overseas expeditions, putting an end to a long tradition of exclusion of the Creoles.[4] The short-term success of the incursions against rivals in St. Croix led to considering their use in the eviction of the Dutch from Curacao, but this excursion was not carried out, so the Creole troops continued training during the occasional attacks to the very coasts of Puerto Rico. In 1642, Juan de Bolaños wrote to the king:

> . . . this island, in the enemies' constant attempts to invade it, has been attacked twice in the coasts, [. . .] trying to ransack Cuamo [. . .] and San German, and were met with a force . . . only two injured in our side, and more than forty of theirs dead [. . .] they left.[5]

The defense of Puerto Rico was now in the hands of Puerto Ricans.

VIEQUES PURSUED

The seventeenth century was the time in which the pieces on the chessboard were placed. The military occupation and population of the different lands was simply the preamble to an eminently commercial game. The struggle—still among commercial enterprises rather than nations—was barely beginning, and the name of the game was the commercial control of the colonies in the Caribbean (Morales Carrión 1974; Williams 1984). In that preliminary scenario, Vieques hardly played a part but was not overlooked either. In 1647, British settlers tried the first incursion led by John Pinard but were violently evicted by native soldiers (Brau 1975, 137), who later also evicted the French from St. Croix. The invaders were poor European settlers looking for better lands in which to settle. But Vieques was already considered part of Puerto Rico, and the Creoles trained to defend it spared no effort to avoid it from falling into enemy hands.

Forty years later, not to be left behind in the European race to ensure colonial bases in the Caribbean, the Brandenburg-Prussia state claimed

Vieques, but the Danes, who already controlled St. Thomas and St. John (with Spain's apparent consent), opposed it. By strange geopolitical designs, the Danes considered themselves—diplomatically speaking—the legitimate claimants of Vieques (Williams 1984). Nevertheless, international rights have always been determined by force, or by political convenience, and a few years after the Prussian claim, in 1687, English and French settlers from St. Christopher (St. Kitts) again invaded Vieques. This time around, the Spanish government designated corsairs established in Santo Domingo to evict the invaders, because a recent epidemic on the island had greatly reduced the Puerto Rican peasantry. The use of privateers and mercenaries at the service of the different colonial governments was already widespread (in the Spanish colonies since 1675); the mercenaries in time were among the direst of participants in the game to control the Caribbean.

The order to drive the invaders out of Vieques had been given before to the viceroy of New Spain, using the Barlovento fleet, and it also was decreed that Vieques be razed to make it inhospitable to new settlers.[6] This dramatic measure was never carried out, but it hung as a sword of Damocles over Vieques, its existence as any type of society constantly threatened. More than 300 British settlers and their families were evicted on said occasion, and their properties were destroyed. The settlers had been attracted to the better soils, the impressive wood resources, and the rich bank of sea tortoises. Besides, with the Dane colonies close by, the exploitation of the resources in Vieques seemed a good business. In 1689, some eighty prisoners taken in Vieques turned up in Santo Domingo, working on the construction of its wall. Others were probably sent to Puerto Rico to perform similar tasks. Yet in 1691, those detained in Santo Domingo were sent to Jamaica (now in the hands of the British) amidst a controversial decree, which probably involved bribery.[7]

At the dawn of the eighteenth century, it was evident that both the British and the Danes coveted the strategic island of Vieques, although aware of the difficulties to conquer it due to its proximity to Puerto Rico and the obstinate defense of its inhabitants. Vieques already was regarded as an important station for the increasing clandestine traffic of Curacao and St. Thomas with Puerto Rico. Morales Carrión (1974) states that Vieques had the reputation of being the "best of all of the Virgin Islands, maybe even better than all of them together." On the Spanish side, the importance of Vieques was not underestimated, and although contraband was tolerated, the idea of a foreign base only six miles away was not acceptable. But Spain did not have the resources to populate it either, not even to maintain a garrison there. This detente would seal the island's fate for the next 150 years. Not one of the parties involved—the Spaniards, Brits, or Danes—would renounce its interest in the island despite recognizing its inability to take and defend it. The British found the battles against Creole soldiers and privateers particularly aggravating; they bitterly complained about their martial methods and ethno-racial composition. In the 1688 deposition regarding the British defeat in Vieques the previous year, Manning Rogers expressed the following:

> . . . yet the enemy compossed their design by treachery such as honest heathens, pagans or mahometans would have been ashamed to practice. But nothing better is to be expected of the Spanish in the West Indies, for however brave their ancestors may have been, they have degenerated into a bastardly and mongrel herd of mullatos, mustees and other spurious mixtures and are now certainly become the very scum of mankind.[8]

Racial conflict was now added to a commercial war.

The eighteenth century was a continuation of the previous one in terms of incursions to Vieques and violent evictions, which increased in intensity as Spain and Great Britain fought formal wars. This chapter will not distinguish the extra-Caribbean variables or purely regional moves that affected life in Vieques in all of the episodes of this century but will clearly establish the differences between the metropolitan interests and those of the rich and poor settlers—the locals of the different islands—who all along had been engaging in illicit and uninterrupted commerce. Puerto Ricans, still demographically depressed, preferred Vieques free of state controls, because it allowed the much-needed contraband, whether in the sale of products or the acquisition of manufactured goods.

The vehemence of the Puerto Ricans defending Vieques whenever foreign attempts to conquer were made is indicative of their political preferences. It was simply not deemed beneficial or convenient for it to fall under foreign hands. For over a century, Puerto Ricans had trafficked extensively with Europeans and Creoles within their very coasts. The relationship with foreign smugglers was of caution, not trust. There were too many factors differentiating or distancing all parties involved, despite the fact that necessity and common interests forced contact. It is very probable that Puerto Rico's ethnic and protonational identity was stoked by this long history of contacts and conflicts with foreign groups, of which the British seem to have been the most frequent. But this long history of clandestine relations only surfaced when a conflict arose among the parties. Many so-called "pirate attacks" probably concealed conflicts between associates in contraband. In the first five years of the eighteenth century, many such conflicts occurred: in 1702, Arecibo was attacked by the British (or at least the native settlers of the British colonies); in that same year, Dutch and British crews from St. Thomas attacked Loíza; in 1703, similar crews moved against Guayanilla. Years later, the situation was the same, and British crews from Curacao attacked Ponce and Guánica in 1742. All of these cases illustrate the extent to which illicit commercial contact crossed Vieques to intervene in the lands of the mother island. López Cantos (1998) relates that in the beginning of the eighteenth century, the Danes lost eight of their ships to privateers stationed in Puerto Rico, but that ". . . most were not caught at sea, but when they were chopping wood or fishing in Vieques or the San Juan Keys." It should be pointed out that a great part of the island of Puerto Rico was not in effect under efficient political or military control. The riots in 1704 of militiamen in Ponce and Guanica confirm this, which is why the conflicts with foreign groups, as well as those regarding Vieques, should be looked at closely and not dismissed as mere state military conflicts.

In Puerto Rico, as in all colonies, contraband was an activity in which not only the poor, marginal groups participated but most prominently the affluent sectors and the peninsular military authorities. The colony's precarious economic condition, as well as a policy favoring the commercial exclusivism of the mainland, impoverished many and led the Creole sectors to join forces in smuggling. It was nothing less than a claim for free commerce. In 1706, the governor of Puerto Rico dramatically stated the following:

> Given that the orders [. . .] to impede the deals and commercial transactions
> carried out by the inhabitants with enemies of the crown have not sufficed,
> nor the troops designated for that purpose, and it being imperative to stop
> such grave inconveniences [. . .] and the perpetrators receive grave and rig-
> orous punishment.[9]

Spain had limited military forces in the Caribbean and thus depended on the use of corsairs (*corsos*), that is, naval mercenaries, to confront formal enemy threats and to combat the smuggling activities of the population, but this predictably backfired, because corsairs in fact encouraged smuggling. Unlawfulness overlaid the whole colonial scenario, from the highest social structures to the hidden camps in Vieques. Said unlawfulness, which we have insisted was a reaction against the monopolistic practices and exclusivist policies of the metropolis—a reaction not unlike that in the ports of Boston that gave way to the struggle for independence of the thirteen British colonies in North America—had once again intertwined Vieques to the most intense experiences of the mother island. If the Puerto Rican soldiers were adamant in keeping foreigners out of Vieques, they did so not to keep Vieques for Spain but under Puerto Rican control. In 1718, poor settlers from Anguilla again occupied lands in Vieques. Puerto Rican peasant lancers, commanded by José de Andino, forced them out. López Cantos documents the events:

> 1. All the settlers were British. 2. They came from St. Christopher, Barba-
> dos, Antigua, Tortola, and mostly from Anguilla. 3. Before reaching
> Vieques, they had all stopped in St. Thomas. 4. The two ships in which they
> traveled were the property of the king of England. . . . 5. That they had been
> in Vieques for almost two months. 6. That the governor was from Anguilla.
> 7. The population consisted of 70 white men, 40 black men, and two white

women. 8. That they had built a sort of fort, in a palisade, overlooking the
port. 9. They had 6 or 8 cannons. 10. There were three houses in the palisade, and the rest lived in the hill. (1998, 272)

They were attacked by a troop of 290 Puerto Ricans, who killed thirty
Brits after losing one of their own. The remaining prisoners were liberated
and placed in a sloop with enough supplies for fifty-nine persons.

Both Puerto Rican soldiers and corsairs were implacable in their efforts
to stop foreigners from invading Vieques. In 1752, under Governor Ramírez
de Estenós, Puerto Rican militias again evicted British and Dutch settlers
insisting on populating Vieques and including it among the commercial
interests of St. Thomas. This time they had gone so far as to name a governor, Carlos Macales.

By mid-century, the Dutch had commercial control of the Caribbean,
and St. Thomas was one of its strongest bastions. Spain had capitulated to
Dane pressure and had sold St. Thomas, as it would sell others. St. Thomas
had both legal and illegal commercial activities with Puerto Rico, a growing
market as the island recovered demographically. Vieques, aside from supplying St. Thomas with firewood for its sugarcane furnaces, with fine woods,
and with hawksbill turtle meat, represented a good base for commerce. Spain
tolerated commerce with the Dane colonies but feared the fall of Vieques to
British hands, who were the real rivals and the actual commercial agents in
St. Thomas. Spanish policy against smuggling was irregularly reinforced, as
was the patrolling of Vieques. Instructions to the corsairs had been precise:
". . . search the whole island of Vieques and seize any ships you find,"
". . . any ship found in the ports of this island or that of Vieques, of whatever
nationality, shall be seized, without harming the prisoners, or hiding any
thing, and led in convoy to San Juan" (López Cantos 1998, 328–29).
Between 1716 and 1733, corsairs stationed in Puerto Rico captured twenty
smuggling ships in the region and confiscated 175 slaves. Only seven of
them were captured from two pirogues in Vieques waters (López Cantos
1998, 113). Clearly, more ships evaded vigilance than were captured. But
the incident also identifies Vieques as one of the routes for slave trade in the
beginning of the eighteenth century.

For its part, England viewed Vieques as it did Gibraltar, that is, with a
commercial eye and as a poke in the enemy's eye. But in that part of the
Caribbean, England's enemy was not Spain but the Puerto Rican mercenaries.
According to López Cantos (1998), during the eighteenth century corsairs stationed in Puerto Rico captured 279 vessels, of which eighty-one were British
and forty-seven had sailed from St. Thomas. The saga of Miguel Enríquez colored the whole first quarter of the century. Enriquez was a nightmare to British
commerce and illustrates the danger that the island represented for them
(López Cantos 1998). It should not come as a surprise, therefore, that England

considered, more than once, the capture of all of Puerto Rico or its exchange for Gibraltar (Morales Carrión 1974). But while that dream was not realized, Vieques was a second option.

In the European diplomatic scenario, the intercolonial battle followed its own course. In 1722, England included Vieques in the claim for the islands of St. Thomas and St. John. In 1728, Spain unsuccessfully ordered the evacuation of foreigners from these same islands. Diplomatic moves totally alienated the real power struggle in the Caribbean, which had no effect whatsoever. Likewise, in 1733, France "ceded" St. Croix to the Danes and included Vieques in the deal; in 1763, and again in 1788, Denmark claimed Vieques as its property, as reparation for damages to its naval commerce.[10] Everyone claimed jurisdiction over Vieques, while being perfectly aware that the prize went to whoever was able to retain it. In 1716, the British governor of the leeward isles made this interesting observation about Vieques:

> . . . attended with this inconveniency that it lyes [sic] so very right [. . .][11]

In other words, other than the proximity to Puerto Rico, the other important factor to take into account was the Puerto Rican peasantry—the eighteenth-century *jíbaro*—then involved in the furtive hunt of cattle. They were precisely the ones who made up the militia that had repeatedly rescued Vieques from foreign hands, but they also were important participants in the generalized smuggling activities.

The British reduced their attempts to forcefully occupy Vieques after their 1752 adventure. They chose to penetrate commerce with Puerto Rico and eventually became one of the principal providers. Even though Danish neutrality and the participation of the North Americans in Caribbean trade hampered their commercial supremacy, the British seem to have protected their interests—despite even the formal war conflicts—and retained as unfinished businesses the hope of an eventual takeover of Vieques. In 1771, they again claimed Vieques as their property, and the Spaniards seriously considered ceding it to the Danes to avoid it going to British hands. But there was no need. The British took over Surinam in 1789 and Trinidad in 1797 but suffered a colossal loss in their last attempt to occupy Puerto Rico that same year. Puerto Rican militias defeated them, not the Spanish army. It also was Puerto Rican civilians led by Captain Casimiro Dávila who threw out the British from Vieques for the last time, after their brief stay in 1797.

Toward the end of the eighteenth century, the following factors were at play in Puerto Rico: a noticeable demographic growth, a greater demand for lands, more liberty for free commerce, and increased commerce with the British and the Danes. Their defeat in 1797 notwithstanding, contraband with the loyal rivals of the Spanish state remained intact. In a letter dated March 6, 1799, the governor of Puerto Rico wrote the following:

... there is reason to believe [. . .] that the enemy is trying to establish in
that island [Vieques] a resting place with cattle for the troops, cattle that
they can only get in that island and in the southern coast from Loyza to
Guayama, where clandestine shipments are constantly carried out, with the
leniency of many of the territorial judges.[12]

By the end of the eighteenth century, it was clear that the course of
action to take in the colony was determined neither by the distant monarchy,
nor at the elegant military quarters in Madrid, but by the interests and needs
of the different Creole groups.

THE COLONIZATION OF VIEQUES

Until the first decades of the nineteenth century, Vieques remained officially uninhabited. The furtive groups of hunters or fishermen, woodcutters,
escaped slaves, and military deserters that had always found refuge in
Vieques soil were not the best example of popular movement to the island.
But they were the most sought after by the colonial authorities. In 1806,
Anastacio Guevara was captured in Puerto Rico. He is described as the "captain of the *bandidos* in Vieques, where he stayed for over twelve years, he also
took a stolen boat, and they say it is in Guayama; he is a two times deserter
from the Spanish Regiment *(Regimiento Fijo)*." Also captured was Jose
Gutierrez, ". . . for providing foodstuff to the refugees in Vieques and harboring deserters."[13]

The commercial war and the new hardships brought about by the
Napoleonic Wars in Europe moved Spain to strengthen its defenses in the
Caribbean. Vieques was cause for worry to the government in San Juan,
because it also served as a refuge to the insurgent corsairs, who had made
their appearance in Caribbean waters due to the Continental independence
wars. Let us not forget that no other than Simón Bolívar had been there in
passing in 1816. Also, since 1804, Spain was at war with England and a year
later suffered defeat at Trafalgar, where it would lose many of its naval
resources. It again resorted to privateering as a defense measure. The coasts
of Vieques would once again be witness and site of numerous events associated with these external conflicts, which could easily be confused with the
more common, everyday activities of smuggling and unlawfulness of a more
local nature.

Vieques also became the target of the patrols of the new U.S. Navy, sent
to protect its merchant ships both from pirates and corsairs. Between 1821
and 1824, some seven U.S. ships had been intervened and sequestered on
Puerto Rican coasts by privateers at the service of Spain, under suspicion of
illicit traffic, and in that same period, an American ship was attacked by
pirates in Vieques waters. In 1824, a U.S. fleet entered the port in Fajardo

and threatened the authorities in a show of force.[14] In 1822, adventurer Doucoudray Holstein sailed from the East of the United States to supposedly liberate the island of Puerto Rico. In 1825, American warships, after patrolling the coasts of Vieques and chasing a "piratical sloop boat," captured Roberto Cofresí, a Puerto Rican pirate, and his whole crew, because they were considered a threat to Yankee trade. The North Americans had come to the Caribbean to stay.

The first population statistics appearing for Vieques date to 1811. A report from the period refers to twenty-one inhabitants dispersed through the coasts, cutting woods "in form of joists, dedicated to the construction of wood for domestic use."[15] The report also refers to the "expedition to Vieques," a clear reference to the first government attempt to start the process of effectively controlling the island. These attempts were carried out under the governorship of Salvador Menéndez Bruna (1809–1820) with the purpose of "establishing a settlement with a regular government to impede the harboring of criminals, and make the territory—beautiful and fertile— respectable" (Bonnet Benítez 1977, 33). We are aware that a year later a post of guards was stationed there, composed of ten agents and a commander, Juan Roselló, responding to the Fajardo headquarters, under the orders of Commander Don Ramón de Aboy.[16] The British government vehemently opposed this attempt to inhabit Vieques with Spanish subjects and sent warships to Vieques to intimidate.

Little is known of the administration feats of this character, who was succeeded by his brother, Francisco Roselló, and who, between the two, led the destiny of Vieques for twenty-six years. In 1823, a French exile, Leguillou, or Le Guillen, who had resided in Santo Domingo, was hired to help drive out the more uncontrollable elements from the island (mostly singled out as pirates). But this does not seem to have been very successful. The fact that the Roselló brothers participated in administrative corruption by stealing the customs revenues did not contribute to a more stable community. A memoir written in 1828 by the commander in Fajardo states that under the Roselló brothers, the population in Vieques hardly grew, reaching 120 free persons and forty slaves; among the first, some twenty-five men and twenty-seven women and their thirty-two children were considered principal inhabitants; the seventy-three remaining persons were workers and peons. The guard consisted of three or four agents. The cultivated lands did not surpass 124 acres, of which most (sixty-eight) were dedicated to plantains, a very insignificant ten acres dedicated to sugar cane, and forty-six to raising cattle, and not in large numbers. The main economic activity was still woodcutting:

Trade is mainly of fine woods [. . .] for construction of ships, houses, sugar mills. The houses and farms are dispersed. The ports used to embark wood are: Mulas and Punta Arenas in the North, Puerto Ferro, Mosquito and

Ensenada Honda in the South. [. . .] The lower lands are of better quality, and the higher ones are covered with forests and much appreciated wood trees. (de Córdova 1968, 409–12)

Eleven years later, in 1839, 10,000 acres of land had been handed out, but only 1,447 were being farmed for internal consumption. This means that under the Roselló administration, the wood industry, possibly managed by foreigners, was the main beneficiary. During this period, England and Denmark made their last claims on Vieques. The incidents involved timid threats of military force from the British and the threat from Denmark to populate the island with thousands of settlers from Tortola (Bonnet Benítez 1977, 36–37). The claims would eventually be lost in the European chanceries but in the short term had the effect of intimidating the Spaniards, who did not formally incorporate Vieques to Puerto Rico for fear of British intervention. This would explain both the period of government by the Roselló brothers and that of Leguillou.

In 1832, Leguillou was named civil and military commander of Vieques, with sufficient authority to enforce a better occupation than that miscarried by the Roselló brothers. Leguillou became a force to be reckoned with, the first landowner on the island, conducting business throughout the Caribbean. Under his rule, Vieques kept a great deal of autonomy from the insular fiscal regime, except from the military control, and progressively turned to sugar production, the same main economic activity in Puerto Rico. Soon many sugar plantations cropped up, with mainly French owners. The names of those plantations are a giveaway as to which power circle prevailed during those times: Quittance, La Patience, St. Jacques, Marquisat, Le Pistolet, La Chere, La Reussite. The Leguillou regime lasted twelve years, from 1832 to 1843. By 1845, the population reached 1,036: 249 whites, 411 free mulattos, and 368 slaves. Half of the population was made up of farmers working in the 203 acres dedicated to the production of sugar and rum and an ample variety of products such as plantain, yams, corn, tobacco, yucca, and coconut palm trees. There was a potentially rich future in raising cattle and poultry. There were sixty-six wooden houses and 241 huts, indicative of the prevailing class division. There were three steel mills and two distilleries. But still the Vieques enterprise operated out of the formal Puerto Rican gubernatorial frame. In 1841, Quartermaster Antonio Maria del Valle recommended the following:

> But while it is in the interests of this island to protect the population of Vieques island, said protection should not be understood to mean the free extraction on its part of the produce that owes taxes upon exportation, because as Vieques is a free port without restrictions of any kind, it would happen that everyone would use that port for their annual exportations, that is, unless His Majesty decrees the order of free exportation of local produce I

have asked for [. . .] [and he added] to agree on the precautionary measures
needed to stop contraband from that island [. . .] it might be better to send
an aide or Receiver to guide what comes to that island. (Sonesson 1990, 295)

In other words, with time it became increasingly difficult to keep Vieques
out of the Puerto Rican fiscal system, and thus government policy strove for
inclusion. British reaction was immediate. On November 9, 1846, the U.S.
consul in San Juan wrote to his superiors the following:

> This government has lately fortified "Vieques" or Crab Island at the east of
> this, and as the British Governor say[s,] this is contrary to the agreement
> under which they (the Spanish government) are allowed to hold it. The
> British Admiral on the West India Station, Sir Francis Austin, is expected
> to come here and look into the matter. (U.S. State Department 1982, 191)

In time, the British stopped resisting the firm actions of the Spanish to
formally incorporate Vieques into the Puerto Rican tax system, which began
in the fiscal year 1869–70. The visit to Vieques from the governor of Tortola
in 1864 would seem to confirm our suspicions that the British received concessions from the Spanish to allow for the migration of workers from Tortola
to Vieques. The next decade saw the end of the special exportation conditions from the ports in Vieques, and a full customhouse was created. Until
then, Vieques only contributed to the church and clergy and to attend to the
municipal expenses (De Hostos 1990, 716). After 1860, as the commercial
and political status was stabilized, the population started growing and reached
3,000 inhabitants. Most were nonwhite immigrants from the nearby British
and Dane colonies, such as Tortola.

According to the U.S. consul, English was widely spoken in Vieques, a
practice that probably was encouraged by the free trade—while it lasted—
with foreign countries. More interesting yet was the decline of the slave population in Vieques, which by 1867 was a mere ninety-eight, most domestic
servants. It seems that the abundance of free workers coming from other
lands discouraged the reproduction of an economic system based on slavery,
as had been the case in most parts of Puerto Rico. That same year, the population in Vieques had doubled to close to 6,000 inhabitants, of which 1,700
were white and 4,000 nonwhite (U.S. State Department 1982, 39–40). Commercially, the United States had become the major buyers of Vieques produce, but Danish St. Thomas was still the main supplier of goods.

By 1870, Vieques also had become a producer of sugarcane, having ten
plantations, of which seven relied on vapor and three on oxen, and 109 farms
of minor products. Other than sugar, molasses, coffee, cotton, tobacco,
woods, fruits, rice, horses, and cattle were exported. Return on its capital was
superior to that of forty municipalities in Puerto Rico. In 1865, the year in
which its civil war ended, the United States named Mr. Garben as its first

consular agent in Vieques. In those same years, the British stopped claiming Vieques as theirs and instead got their petition to name Francisco Cooper, son of the British consul in San Juan, as vice consul in Vieques. In a short time, Danish and French consular agencies also were established, giving testimony to the commercial well-being in Vieques.

In 1870, Spain permitted the construction of the first church and school for Protestants. The town of Isabel II, founded around 1842, had a population of close to 2,500 by 1878, most foreigners. The ethnic diversity of the population may have given way to bouts of discrimination, especially under the government of tyrant Laureano Sanz. In 1873, Tortolan workers staged a violent confrontation with the Civil Guard. The next year, a military detachment was sent to Vieques and stayed there over the next nine years. The repressive measures against workers spurred diplomatic complaints from Great Britain, which led to amnesty for those accused of rioting. Conflicts with foreign workers had occurred before, in 1866, inducing the government to introduce changes in the island's administration.[17] By 1880, commercial franchises in Vieques were suppressed (De Hostos 1990, 716). We suspect that behind these events lay a surreptitious intent to encourage control of the island by the immigration of laborers, or at least that is what the Spanish authorities feared. In keeping with this idea, it is probable that the practice to exile many Puerto Rican liberals to Vieques was their way of assuring that those of Spanish origin or ancestry prevailed over the other ethnic components, notwithstanding that this was done with politically dissident elements (Cruz Monclova 1970). In any event, by the end of the century, those conflicts had been surpassed. The population, by then close to 6,642 inhabitants, was 59.6 percent nonwhite natives, 38.3 percent white natives, and only 2.1 percent white non-natives. There is no mention of nonwhite foreigners, which leads us to think that the immigration movement of British workers from Tortola depended on the sugarcane production work calendar, and with the collapse of sugar production, they all returned to their island of origin. The sugar crisis—which also hit the island of Puerto Rico—explains as well the general demographic decrease observed in Vieques as the nineteenth century came to an end (U.S. War Department 1900).

In the dawning of a new century, Vieques had been transformed into an additional Puerto Rican municipality, *en tiempos buenos y malos*, an intrinsic part of the Puerto Rican nation.

NOTES

1. Also *Archivo General de Indias* (AGI) México 302-Probanza de Juan González, 1532.

2. Because of its participation in the resistance against Spanish colonization, Vieques also was criminalized as a *Caribe* island. This was used as a justification for the

depopulation of the island and the enslavement of its inhabitants. Colonial literature insisted on projecting a foreign and threatening view of Vieques. For examples of the official views promoted on Vieques, see, for instance, the Melgarejo Memoir, in Fernández Méndez (1976, 107).

3. On the matter of *Caribe* Indians and Puerto Rico, see Sued Badillo 1978.

4. AGI Indiferente General 2536.

5. AGI Indiferente General 1887.

6. AGI SD-R.C. December 8, 1685.

7. AGI Santo Domingo 973.

8. British Museum Library, Colonial Papers, 1669–1674, Vol. VII.

9. Letter from Governor Juan López de Morla (December 7, 1706), AGI SD 544.

10. AGI Santo Domingo 2370.

11. As quoted in Morales Carrión (1974, 102).

12. *Actas del cabildo de San Juan*. March 6, 1799, letter.

13. *Archivo General de Puerto Rico*, GF caja 18-*Relación de reos para conducir a la capital*. 1806.

14. Minutes, Court of Inquiry, Commodore David Porter, Washington, D.C., 1825.

15. Report of May 6, 1811, as quoted by Barragán (1996, 96).

16. *Actas del cabildo de San Juan*. March 9, 1812, 199. Also see Bonnet Benítez (1977).

17. *Archivo Histórico Nacional*. Inventario de la Serie Gobierno de Puerto Rico. 1972. Madrid (p. 66).

WORKS CITED

Barragán Landa, Juan José. 1996. *Los Benitez: Raíces de una familia hacedora de historia*. Río Piedras, Puerto Rico: N.d.

Bonnet Benítez, Juan Amédée. 1977. *Vieques en la historia de Puerto Rico*. San Juan: F. Ortiz Nieves.

Bosh, Juan. 1970. *De Cristóbal Colón a Fidel Castro: El Caribe, frontera imperial*. Madrid: Alfaguara.

Brau, Salvador. 1975. Historia de Puerto Rico. San Juan: Editorial Coquí.

Cárdenas Ruiz, Manuel. 1980. *"La primera narración francesa sobre las Antillas: El diario de navegación de la campaña del General de Cahuzac." Revista/Review Interamericana* 10:1: 46–82.

Centro de Investigaciones Arqueológicas, Universidad de Puerto Rico, Recinto de Río Piedras. 1984. *Catálogo: Arqueología de Vieques*. Text and photos by Luis A. Chanlatte Baik. Río Piedras, Puerto Rico: Universidad de Puerto Rico.

Chanlatte Baik, Luis A. 1981. *La Hueca y Sorce (Vieques): Primeras migraciones agroalfareras antillanas.* Santo Domingo, Dominican Republic: N.d.

Chanlatte Baik, Luis A., and Yvonne M. Narganes Storde. 1983. *Asentamiento poblacional Agro-I: Complejo cultural-La hueca-Vieques, Puerto Rico.* San Juan: N.d.

Chanlatte, Luis. 1985. *Arqueología de Guayanilla y Vieques.* Río Piedras, Puerto Rico: Museo de la Universidad de Puerto Rico.

Cruz Monclova, Lidio. 1970. *Historia de Puerto Rico, siglo XIX.* Río Piedras, Puerto Rico: Editorial Universidad de Puerto Rico.

Curet, L. A. 1987. *The Ceramic of the Vieques Naval Station Reservation: A Chronological and Spatial Analysis.* Masters degree thesis, University of Puerto Rico.

De Córdova, Pedro Tomás. 1968 [1831]. *Memorias.* San Juan: Editorial Coquí.

De Hostos, Adolfo. 1990. *Tesauro de datos históricos: Indice compendioso de la literatura histórica de Puerto Rico, incluyendo algunos datos inéditos, periodísticos y cartográficos.* Río Piedras, Puerto Rico: Editorial de la Universidad de Puerto Rico.

Feliciano Ramos, Héctor R. 1990. *El contrabando inglés en el Caribe y el Golfo de México (1748–1778).* Sevilla: Excma. Diputación Provincial de Sevilla.

Fernández de Oviedo y Valdés, Gonzalo. 1959. *Historia general y natural de las Indias.* Madrid: Ediciones Atlas.

Fernández Méndez, Manuel. 1976. *Crónicas de Puerto Rico: Desde la conquista hasta nuestros días (1493–1955).* Río Piedras, Puerto Rico: Editorial de la Universidad de Puerto Rico.

López Cantos, Angel. 1998. *Miguel Enríquez.* San Juan: Ediciones Puerto.

Morales Carrión, Arturo. 1974. *Puerto Rico and the Non-Hispanic Caribbean: A Study in the Decline of Spanish Exclusivism.* Río Piedras, Puerto Rico: Editorial Universidad de Puerto Rico.

Murga Sanz, Vicente, and Alvaro Huerga. 1988. *Episcopologio de Puerto Rico.* Ponce, Puerto Rico: Pontificia Universidad Católica de Puerto Rico.

Quinn, David B., ed. 1955. *The Roanoke Voyages, 1584–1590: Documents to Illustrate the English Voyages to North America under the Patent Granted to Walter Raleigh in 1584.* London: Hakluyt Society.

Sonesson, Birgit. 1990. *La Real Hacienda en Puerto Rico: Administración, política y grupos de presión, 1815–1868.* Madrid: Instituto de Cooperación Iberoamericana, Sociedad Estatal Quinto Centenario.

Sued Badillo, Jalil. 1978. *Los caribes: Realidad o fábula.* Río Piedras, Puerto Rico: Editorial Cultural.

Tronolone, Carmine A., et al. 1984. *Cultural Resource Reconnaissance Survey for the Vieques Naval Reservation.* Norfolk, Va.: Department of the Navy, Ecology, and Environment.

U.S. State Department. 1982. *Despachos de los cónsules norteamericanos en Puerto Rico, 1821–1899 [Dispatches from U.S. Consular Representatives in Puerto Rico, 1821–1899].* Río Piedras, Puerto Rico: Editorial de la Universidad de Puerto Rico.

U.S. War Department. 1900. *Report on the Census of Porto Rico, 1899.* Washington, D.C.: Government Printing Office.

Williams, Eric. 1984. *From Columbus to Castro: The History of the Caribbean, 1492–1969.* New York: Vintage Books.

TEN

Expropriation and Displacement of Civilians in Vieques, 1940–1950

César J. Ayala and Viviana Carro-Figueroa

THE ORIGIN OF THE CONFLICT in Vieques lies in the expropriation of civilian lands during the 1940s to build military facilities for the U.S. Navy. These expropriations took place in two waves: 1942–1943 and 1947–1950. At present, the facilities in Vieques are part of a larger military complex known as "Roosevelt Roads," which spans eastern Puerto Rico and the island of Vieques. Roosevelt Roads is one of the largest U.S. naval bases outside of the Continental United States. It was built during World War II with the capacity to house the British Navy in case it became necessary during the war (Veaz 1995, 166). Since the 1940s, the western part of Vieques is used as a munitions depot, while the eastern part serves as a target range for combined sea-air-ground maneuvers. The U.S. Navy rents the island of Vieques to the navies of other countries for target practice (Langley 1985, 271–75; Giusti 1999b, 133–204). For six decades, the civilian population has been constrained on the center of the island, surrounded by the ecological devastation produced by navy bombardments.

In this chapter, we examine navy expropriations in Vieques during the 1940s, utilizing two sources of original data. We have examined the tax record data for all properties located in Vieques in the fiscal years 1940, 1945, and 1950.[1] The profile of land-ownership in Vieques allows us to set comparisons of social and economic conditions before and after the first and second rounds of expropriation. The records can be matched owner by owner so the data yield exact quantitative information on who suffered the expropriations, how much land they lost, and the location of each property.[2] In addition to the land tenure data based on archival sources, we present here some of the results of a set of interviews with residents of Vieques who experienced expulsion from the land in the 1940s. In 1979, under the sponsorship of the Youth Exchange Project of the American Friends Service Committee (later to become the *Proyecto Caribeño de Justicia y Paz*, Caribbean Project for Justice and Peace, hereafter *PCJP*), fifty-three personal interviews were conducted with a sample of Viequenses who were—themselves, their parents, grandparents, or close relatives—affected by the expropriations of the navy during the 1940s. Two additional interviews with former large landowners of Vieques also were carried out in Puerto Rico as part of that study. The survey was conducted by a team of seventeen Viequenses and eight persons from the main island of Puerto Rico.[3] The mean age of those interviewed was sixty-seven years in 1979.

In the more than twenty years that have passed since the initial *PCJP* research on the expropiations of Vieques lands by the navy, several accounts have been published that depict many issues that in the late 1970s were unclear to both activists and researchers. After the 1999 killing of David Sanes Rodríguez by a stray bomb, the struggle to oust the navy from Vieques has become a national and global issue of justice and respect for human rights. Television and newspaper reports ocassionally portray the memories of old Vieques residents who lived through the traumatic expropriation experience, or the account of second-generation relatives who have kept their stories alive for present-day Viequenses.

One of the basic findings that both kinds of data yield is that land was extremely concentrated in Vieques at the time the U.S. Navy took over. For this reason, the data on land tenure imply a limitation in that they give us insight into only those who owned property. It leaves out of sight all of the rural workers and *agregados*[4] who did not have title to lands but who were nevertheless expelled from the land when the titled owners were expropriated by the U.S. Navy. Thus our approach is twofold: on the one hand, we reconstruct the disappearance of the landowners of Vieques as a result of the expropriations. On the other hand, we try to assess the broader social impact of the expropriations by looking into the experience of those who did not own land but who were nevertheless displaced.

LAND CONCENTRATION IN VIEQUES

The degree of land concentration in Vieques at the time of the expropriations is in large part due to the existence of a sugar-plantation economy since the nineteenth century. Concentration of land-ownership is typical of all sugar plantation regions in the Caribbean. At the beginning of the twentieth century, Vieques had four sugar mills (*centrales*): the Santa María, the Arcadia, the Esperanza, also known as "Puerto Real," and the Playa Grande

(Bonnet Benítez 1976, 126). Central Arcadia produced sugar in the years 1907 to 1910 but ceased operations sometime before 1912. *The Book of Porto Rico*, edited by Eugenio Fernández García, gives production figures for Puerto Rico's sugar mills between 1912 and 1922. The sugar output of *centrales* Puerto Real, Playa Grande, and Santa María is listed in the municipality of Vieques, but not that of the Arcadia mill (Fernández y García 1923, 544; Bonnet Benítez 1976, 126). Possibly the Arcadia stopped grinding between 1910 and 1912. The Santa María mill is listed in Fernández García's book until 1923, displaying small outputs of sugar, and Bonnet Benítez states that it produced in its distillery a brand of rum, the Santa María. Nevertheless, in 1930, the Santa María mill is not listed in Gilmore's *Sugar Manual* (1930), an indication that it had either stopped grinding, or that its sugar production was negligible. The Puerto Real mill ground its last crop in 1927. After that date, some of the cane was ground at the Playa Grande mill (Bonnet Benítez 1976, 126), and some was shipped by ferry from Vieques to the Pasto Viejo mill in Humacao.[5] By 1930, the Playa Grande mill enjoyed "the distinction of being the surviving sugar factory on the island of Vieques" (Gilmore 1930).

The 1930s were years of a terrible crisis in the sugar industry in the entire Caribbean (Ayala 1999, 230–47). By 1940, the sugar industry of Vieques was in sharp decline. The number of *cuerdas* planted in cane had decreased from 7,621 in 1935 to 4,586 in 1940. Cane yields had dropped from twenty-four tons of cane per *cuerda* in 1910 to twenty-two in 1935 and nineteen in 1940. During the 1930s, the control of the great landowners over land resources reached its peak. The Eastern Sugar Associates owned 11,000 acres of land, of which 1,500 were planted in cane. The cane was shipped to Pasto Viejo (Picó 1950, 209–11). Puerto Rican geographer Rafael Picó argued in 1950 that toward the end of the 1930s, more than two-thirds of the land planted in cane in Vieques was in the hands of the Benítez Sugar Company, owner of the Playa Grande mill, and the Eastern Sugar Associates. Thus according to Picó, "the evils of land concentration and absentee ownership, prevailing in most sugar cane lands in Puerto Rico, were deeply intensified in Vieques. The bulk of the population was landless, a part of the 'peon' class" (Picó 1950, 209).

The Playa Grande sugar mill, owned by the Benítez family, went bankrupt in 1936 and was under receivership to the Bank of Nova Scotia until 1939, when it was purchased by Juan Angel Tió. In the tax assessments of 1940, however, the Benítez family still appears as the principal owner of the lands. The taxes charged were small compared to those paid by the Eastern Sugar Associates, probably because of the state of bankruptcy of the Playa Grande corporation, its doubtful legal standing, or litigation in court and competing claims by the bank and the new owners. Despite the fact that Tió started to operate the Playa Grande mill in 1939, in the tax records for 1940,

the members of the Benítez family were still listed as the principal landowners of Vieques, owning almost half of the land in the island municipality.
Dolores Benítez, Carlota Benítez and others, Carmen Aurelia Benítez
Bithorn, and María Bithorn Benítez each appear as the owner of 3,636 *cuerdas*, while Francisco and J. Benítez Santiago are listed as the owners of a tract
of 1,191 *cuerdas*. In sum, the above-mentioned members of the Benítez family "owned" 15,735 *cuerdas* of land out of a total of 36,032 *cuerdas* assessed for
taxation, or 44 percent of the land of Vieques. These 15,735 *cuerdas* were
assessed at $47,410 for tax purposes in 1940, or $3.01 per *cuerda*. In contrast
to the situation of the Benítez family, the 10,043 *cuerdas* of the Eastern Sugar
Associates were assessed in the same year at $661,400, or $63.95 per *cuerda*,
twenty times more per *cuerda* than the lands of the Benítez family.

According to the census of 1930, two owners of more than 1,000 acres
controlled 71 percent of the farmland in the municipality of Vieques. Only
in Santa Isabel, a municipality controlled by a U.S. corporation, the Aguirre
Sugar Company, and in Guánica, a municipality controlled by the South
Porto Rico Sugar Company, was there a structure of land concentration more
unbalanced than that of Vieques. One farm of over 1,000 acres owned 87 percent of the farmland in Santa Isabel. In Vieques, farms of over 100 acres occupied 93 percent of the area, while in Santa Isabel the corresponding figure
was 98 percent. According to the *Census of the Puerto Rico Reconstruction
Administration*, in Vieques, the average farm spanned 393 acres, while in all
of Puerto Rico, the average farm size was thirty-six acres. In more than 70
percent of Puerto Rico' s municipalities, the average farm size was below fifty
acres, and there were only eight municipalities with average farm sizes larger
than 100 acres (Puerto Rico Reconstruction Administration 1938, 124).
Vieques was the third most extreme instance of land concentration in Puerto
Rico and was surpassed only by the *municipios* (municipalities) controlled by
the South Puerto Rico Sugar Company (Guánica) and the Aguirre Sugar
Company (Santa Isabel). There is no doubt that the problem of land concentration dominated the social and economic landscape of Vieques, to a
much greater degree than in the majority of the *municipios* of Puerto Rico.

The U.S. Navy's accounts of the expropriations generally emphasize that
most of the land was acquired from a handful of owners.

Of the 21,000 acres, 10,000 acres or nearly half were acquired from Juan Tio,
owner of Playa Grande mill and sugarcane lands in the western, central, and
eastern sectors. Another substantial portion, nearly 8,000 acres, was
acquired from Eastern Sugar Associates who had owned and operated the
Esperanza sugar mill and lands in the east central sector. Lands of two other
major families, Benítez and Rieckehoff, brought the total to over 19,000
acres, or 90% of this first series of acquisitions. (Department of the Navy
1979, vol. 1, sect. 2, p. 199)

EXPROPRIATION OF THE LANDOWNERS

The tax records offer a glimpse into rural life in a plantation society dominated by a few landowning families. For example, the farm of "Carlota Benítez and others," located in the *barrio*,[6] Punta Arenas, spanned 3,082 acres. There were "62 houses" among the improvements listed in 1940. The farm of Francisco and J. Benítez Santiago in Punta Arenas, which spanned 558 acres, contained sixty houses. The Eastern Sugar Associates had sixty-two houses in one of its properties. Another farm owned by Carlota Benítez in Barrio Llave, spanning fifty-four acres, had a cockpit in addition to a number of houses (*AGPR, DH* 1940). These were *ranchones* or *barracones*, which housed some of the poorest workers. Even cockfights, which were an important part of rural community life, took place on the land of the great landowners. The land and the houses were listed in the tax records as belonging to the landowners, who paid the corresponding taxes. The workers, having no titles, were removed without legal obstacles when the large landowners sold their properties. The ease of eviction was due, to a large degree, to the degree of rural landlessness among a rural population whose only possession was, as they say in Vieques, "the day and the night" (Pastor Ruiz 1947, 196).

Tax records provide no insight, nevertheless, on how big landowners experienced the expropriations, or how this process differed from the plight of small farm owners and *agregados*. As part of the 1979 study, the team interviewed one of the members of the Tió family—the largest landowning family of Vieques in 1941, controlling more than 10,500 *cuerdas* at that time—on the expropriation proceedings and the position taken by the family during the process.[7] Together with the testimonies of descendants of other large landowners and information gathered during the research process on the litigation followed in the federal court, an outline emerges of the expropriation experience and its significance from the point of view of the landowning class.

As it already has been portrayed in this chapter, the sugar economy of Vieques was in critical condition by 1941. The Playa Grande mill, the only one still grinding cane in Vieques at the time, had been acquired by the Tió family from the Bank of Nova Scotia just two years earlier. The Tiós had been able to operate only during three harvests before the entrance of the United States into World War II. They acquired not only the lands and the mill from the bank in 1939, but they also inherited the *agregado* system, which was "already established in the land at the time of purchase."

Agregados were rural workers who lived on the plantations and exchanged labor services for usufruct over the land. Relations of *agrego* existed in Puerto Rico since the nineteenth century and developed initially in the interior highland region that specialized in coffee production (Bergad 1983). In its origins, *agrego* relations served landowners as a means of securing workers in a context

TABLE 10.1

Principal Landowners of Vieques in 1940–1941 and their Properties in 1944–1945

Last Name	Name	Cuerdas 1940	No. Farms 1940	Cuerdas 1945	No. Farms 1945	Cuerdas: Difference[1]	Value of Land 1940	Value of Land 1945	Land Value Difference	Improvement Value 1940	Improvement Value 1945	Improvement Value Difference
Eastern Sugar	Associates	10,343	15	1,825	1	-8,518	662,210	121,010	-541,200	77,720	0	-77,720
Benítez	Dolores	3,636	2	0	0	-3,636	2,720	0	-2,720	0	0	0
Benítez	Carlota y otros	3,636	2	0	0	-3,636	0	0	0	12,870	0	-12,870
Benítez Bithorn	Carmen Aurelia	3,082	1	0	0	-3,082	20,300	0	-20,300	0	0	0
Bithorn Benítez	María	3,082	1	0	0	-3,082	19,590	0	-19,590	0	0	0
Benítez Santiago	Francisco y J.	1,191	2	0	0	-1,191	0	0	0	6,080	0	-6,080
Benítez Bithorn	Carmen Amelia	554	1	0	0	-554	3,800	0	-3,800	10	0	-10
Bithorn Vda. Benítez	María	554	1	0	0	-554	3,720	0	-3,720	10	0	-10
Simons	Miguel	2,129	4	1,308	4	-821	83,770	54,320	-29,450	12,230	610	-11,620
Díaz Sabino	Esteban	678	16	0	0	-678	37,250	0	-37,250	5,190	0	-5,190
Rieckehoff	Ana	468	1	0	0	-468	17,150	0	-17,150	150	0	-150
Bermúdez	Juan	441	4	108	4	-333	7,920	7,920	0	3,100	3,100	0
Haristory	Justine y M.	347	1	0	0	-347	34,740	0	-34,740	2,150	0	-2,150
Díaz	Esteban	333	4	0	0	-333	10,740	0	-10,740	10	0	-10
Quiñones Imodóvar	Manuel	293	3	105	1	-188	7,950	3,150	-4,800	0	0	0
Rivera Sucn.	Sixto A.	243	1	243	0	0	19,600	19,600	0	50	50	0
Rivera	Sixto A.	242	3	243	3	1	13,740	13,740	0	100	100	0
Ramírez	Tomás	210	2	315	3	105	6,300	10,500	4,200	0	0	0
González Mercedes	Jovito	190	2	0	0	-190	9,110	0	-9,110	300	0	-300
Quiñones Almodóvar	Natividad/otros	181	2	0	0	-181	10,000	0	-10,000	90	0	-90
Brignoni Vda. Pérez	Rosa	180	8	182	9	2	12,240	12,350	110	140	140	0
Brignoni Mercado	Juan	167	1	0	0	-167	11,620	0	-11,620	0	0	0
Cruz Vélez	Eulogio	166	18	0	0	-166	12,140	0	-12,140	2,070	0	-2,070
Quiñones Sucn.	Epigmene	146	2	0	0	-146	3,112	0	-3,112	530	0	-530
Díaz Esteban y	Belén Carcaño	129	1	0	0	-129	3,870	0	-3,870	100	0	-100

Benites Castano	Carlos	124	1	0	0	-124	6,430	0	-6,430	0	0	0
Emeric	José	115	1	0	0	-115	4,200	0	-4,200	80	0	-80
Brignoni Mercado	Inés	110	1	110	1	0	8,280	8,280	0	60	60	0
Acevedo Guadalupe	Antolino	108	1	0	0	-108	1,250	0	-1,250	0	0	0
Brignoni Huertas	José	108	1	0	0	-108	1,260	0	-1,260	0	0	0
Fix Alais	A.	105	1	0	0	-105	3,150	0	-3,150	0	0	0
Picó Mora	Arturo	105	1	6	1	-99	4,200	600	-3,600	1,450	1,400	-50
Fix	Nargaret D.	105	1	0	0	-105	3,150	0	-3,150	0	0	0
Carle Dubois	Carlos	103	2	24	1	-79	9,110	2,400	-6,710	1,070	1,330	260
Jaspard	Carlos	100	2	0	0	-100	8,480	0	-8,480	20	0	-20
TOTAL		33,705	110	4,469	29	-29,236	1,063,102	253,870	-809,232	125,580	6,790	-96,670
Familia Benítez		15,736	10	0	0	-15,736	50,130	0	-50,130	18,970	0	-18,970
Familia Benítez (%)		47%	9%	0%	0%	54%	5%	0%	6%	15%	0%	20%
Eastern Sugar (%)		31%	14%	41%	3%	29%	62%	48%	67%	62%	0%	80%

Source: AGPR, DH 1940–1950.

The total for this column exceeds the total expropriated by the navy, because some landowners not included in this table actually acquired land between 1941 and 1945.

Note: One cuerda = .9712 acres.

TABLE 10.2
Summary of Naval Land Acquisitions

	Approximate Acreage[1]	Approximate Price[2]	Price in $ per Acre[4]	Number of Parcels	Approximate Number of Parties[3]
Naval Land Acquisition, 1941–1943					
Civil Action No. 2300	10,209	379,300	37	6	30
Civil Action No. 2443	97	18,200	188	18	55
Civil Action No. 2487	687	56,900	83	34	150
Civil Action No. 2604	1,234	66,600	54	6	15
Civil Action No. 2714	7,937	423,800	53	2	4
Civil Action No. 3211	13	1,200	92	1	10
Civil Action No. 3254	140	21,500	154	7	25
Civil Action No. 3361	696	74,000	106	42	0
Subtotal	21,013 (21,020)	1,041,500	50	116	489
Navy Land Acquisitions 1950					
Civil Action No. 6108	4,340	530,400	122	9	40
Totals	25,353	1,561,900	62	125	529

[1]Acreages derived from U.S. Navy P.W. Drawing No. 1952 and U.S. Navy Files. Acreage for Civil Action No. 6108 derived by subtraction using interrogatories 20–24, supplying total acreage for selected years. Numbers in parentheses indicate acreage according to U.S. Navy Interrogatories (1978) for the appropriate years.

[2]Derived from U.S. Navy Interrogatories 20–24, August 1978.

[3]Many individuals and banks were parties involved in a number of parcels. Estimate attempts to avoid double counting and is considerably less than the total number named for each action. It also appears that tenants were in some cases made parties in the court actions.

[4]Calculated by Ayala and Carro-Figueroa.

Source: Department of the Navy 1979, vol. 1, sect. 2, p. 200.

of labor scarcity by offering land, sometimes a house, cows for milk, and so on. As the landless population and the supply of labor increased in the nineteenth century, the terms of *agrego* deteriorated for the workers, and by the twentieth century, many *agregados* were in practice undistinguishable from rural workers. In Vieques, the traditional usufruct was not taken into account during the expropriations, and the navy compensated the owners of the properties without being concerned about the fate of the *agregados* and rural workers who were settled on the land on terms defined by traditional relations of *agrego*.

The expropriation process began several months before Pearl Harbor, but the attack was the event that made landowners accept the decision without further litigation. According to the Tiós' recollections, a marshal from the federal court brought a notification to the family that explained that the navy was expropriating most of their lands and had already deposited in the federal court the amount of money deemed reasonable compensation for their property. Initially, the family tried to defend their assets by contesting the condemnation decree and trying to prove in court that the allocated compensation did not correspond to the real market value of their property. But the pace of the process was too rapid to allow them to organize a better defense.

The Tió family remembers how immediately after the notification, the navy asked for permission to start the construction of military installations in Monte Pirata, the highest elevation of Vieques, located within their fields. Subtle intimidation of the family by the commander in chief of the base followed. The expertise of A. Tió, an engineer, was sought by the navy to assemble a map of the island's properties and their legal owners. As recorded in the 1979 transcript of our interview with A. Tió, his cooperation was secured in the following manner:

> Commander Johnson, chief of the base came to talk with Tió. He already had in place several study brigades to measure the island of Vieques. He asked Tió to draw for him a landholding map, as best as he could, and to have it ready in 30 days. The only way to accomplish this task was to take some measurements, and by putting into a bigger map all of the already existing maps of the island. Tió replied to Johnson that, how was he going to do this if they were going to use this map to expropriate him? The commander told him that if he didn't do it he was going to recruit him, make him a lieutenant, and then order him to do it. This was said half jokingly and half seriously, but more seriously than jokingly. This was a few days before Pearl Harbor, and when the attack occurred, he went to the federal court, settled the case, and finished with everything. He did the map, as best as he could, exactly enough.[8]

Tió remarked that his family did not participate in any way in the process of notifying or removing the *agregados* from the property. The navy took charge of everything. The principal way in which his family was affected was in economic terms. They had sizable capital losses that were difficult to deduct from their income tax. They had to sell in a hurry 2,000 head of cattle, which grazed in the expropriated lands, and since they did not have enough lands to keep them, they had to accept whatever price was offered by the purchasers. The family concluded that pursuing their case in the federal court would only increase their final compensation by 10 percent, and that amount was not enough to justify putting up a struggle during the war emergency. Although several landholding families opted for litigation, apparently, by 1942, most of the cases were settled.

EXPULSION OF AGREGADOS AND WORKERS

> Surrounded by the beauty of the ocean and the green cane fields, a man starved to death. The ocean, rich in mysteries and hidden wealth, could not help him. The soft and whispering cane field was a sight to behold. But that was all [. . .] the ocean and the cane-field have no heart. (Pastor Ruiz 1947, 199)

The existence of a plantation economy and society in Vieques had important repercussions during the expropriations. As in many other plantation regions, there was no geographic separation between workplace and place of residence. The workers lived and worked on the land of the large landowners. This gives plantation life a kind of "total" character that is different from the situation of most urban wage workers.[9] When the expropriation of the large landowners took place, workers lost in one single blow both their jobs and their houses. To urban workers, this would be the equivalent of being fired from the job and evicted by the landlord on the same day.

Workers who lived on the land of the landowners typically had subsistence plots as part of the usufruct characteristic of the traditional arrangement known as *agrego*. In Vieques, the small amounts of land for planting available to those who described themselves as *agregados* indicate that the function of the plots was principally the production of subsistence garden crops rather than commercial agriculture. For example, Matilde Bonaro indicated that at the time of the navy's expropriations, she was an *agregada* in Playa Grande who had at her disposal half a *cuerda* of land. Francisco Colón López had two *cuerdas* available in Barrio Mosquito, Ventura Feliciano Corrillo had one *cuerda*, and Teodora Velázquez and Juan Sherman had one and a half *cuerdas* each as *agregados* (PCJP 1979). On this scale, it is not possible to make a living without recourse to wage labor in the sugar fields at harvest time. Clearly the function of usufruct was to facilitate the reproduction of labor power while guaranteeing a supply of laborers to the landowners. The frontier between *agrego* as a sort of tenancy or sharecropping arrangement and rural proletarianization is therefore blurred, so it is not possible to speak clearly of "tenants," on the one hand, and "workers," on the other hand. Among the forty-one Viequense *agregados* interviewed in 1979 who reported farm size, the median size of the plots held in usufruct was two *cuerdas*.[10]

Subsistence plots were particularly important during the idle season of the sugar industry, which lasted from June to November. During these months of *tiempo muerto*, most sugarcane workers were unemployed. In Vieques, people who lived during the epoch of the sugar plantations refer to the dead season as *la bruja* ("the witch"), and the term *pasar la bruja* means "to survive the idle season." In other areas of Puerto Rico, the relation of rural peasant/proletarian communities to the ecology has been amply documented (Giusti-Cordero 1994). In Vieques, this aspect has yet to be studied, but it has undoubtedly conditioned the claims of the communities which, based on traditional rights of *agrego* relationships, understood that they had certain rights of possession and usufruct over the land. This explains the double reality of lack of titles, on the one hand, and the widespread feeling of rural disposession after the houses, built by the workers themselves, were leveled during the expropriations, on the other hand. The U.S. Navy itself acknowledges, concerning the land title issues extant in the resettlement areas of Vieques, that traditional usufruct associated with Puerto Rican *agrego* relations has conditioned the expectations of the civilian population regarding their right to have a place to live: "For those who now live in Vieques and who once lived on Navy land, a sense of 'ownership' and therefore desires for return *pertains to their former rights of access and use of land*" (Department of the Navy 1979, vol. 1, sect. 2, p. 213, emphasis in original).

The existence of usufruct also affected the expelled populations who could not count on subsistence plots in the resettlement plots provided by the navy and whose means of subsistence were thus radically curtailed.

> For many *agregado* families, the loss of animals and subsistence crops was traumatic, because it represented a family's insurance policy against hard times. Doña Nilda reflected on this experience. She and her family were evicted from their home in the second wave of military expropriations in 1947. "Those who were living as *agregados* . . . I was also living as an *agregado* when the Navy came," Doña Nilda explained, "The land we lived on the owners of the land gave us to live on. But we didn' t receive money [when the land was expropriated]. I had chickens, pigs, all of this I had to let go. I had to let the animals go, because in Tortuguero there was no place to raise the animals. As *agregados* we could raise them on the land." "How did you learn of your eviction," I asked Doña Nilda. "The owner of the land told us," she responded. "As we were *agregados* they just told us to leave." (McCaffrey 1999, 77–78)

After the July 2001 referendum in which Viequenses voted to request the immediate withdrawal of the navy, the New York press ran stories referencing the decline of usufruct. Ninety-one-year-old Nazario Cruz Viera was quoted saying that before the expropriations, "There were farms and the landowners needed many people to work them. They even gave you a place to live. We had everything. We lacked nothing" (González 2001). *Newsday* featured an article about seventy-four-year-old Severina Guadalupe, who was thirteen years old when the bulldozers razed her family's home in Vieques. Even though the Guadalupes were small landowners and not *agregados*, when we interviewed her in Vieques, Ms. Guadalupe emphasized the transition from the rural economy, where food was abundant, to the squalor of life on the Santa María resettlement tract (Associated Press 2001; Ayala 2001). The transition from an *agregado* settled on the land to an urban dweller settled on a navy resettlement tract in Montesanto or Santa María produced an increase in the number of families living in poverty and a deterioration of living conditions. The Rev. Justo Pastor Ruiz described the transition experienced by the dispossessed as follows: "Those who had garden plots or lived happily on the landowner's land surrounded by farmland and fruit trees, live today in overcrowded conditions and lack even air to breathe" (Pastor Ruiz 1947, 206).

Thus the impact of the navy's expropriations was much broader than one might suppose by considering only the property owners of the island who were evicted through the navy' s condemnation proceedings. Seventy-seven percent of those interviewed by the *Proyecto Caribeño de Justicia y Paz* in 1979 described themselves at the time of the expropriations as *agregados* (PCJP 1979). In addition to landowners large and small, the families of the *agregados* and rural workers who lived in the land of the property owners were affected by the expropriations. They were expelled from the land and relocated to the central parts of Vieques. Thus it would seem necessary to distinguish between the process of *expropriation* as such and a much wider process of *evictions (desalojos)*, which affected not only landowners but *agregados* and rural workers as well. In measuring the social impact of the expropriations, the fate of the landowners who received compensation must be sorted out from the situation of the *agregados* who generally did not receive any compensation.[11] The navy's own conservative estimate is that altogether, "Navy land acquisitions dislocated an estimated 4,250 to 5,000 people or 40 to 50% of the total population and resettled, with Navy assistance, 27% of the population, altering both the social structure as well as the economy" (Department of the Navy 1979, vol. 1, sect. 2, p. 204).

CONDEMNATION PROCEEDINGS

In 1979, the editor of *Sea Power Magazine* wrote an apologetic article defending the navy against the accusations made by a community movement led by fishermen.[12] The fishermen complained that navy bombardments curtailed their livelihood. In the battle of words over the origins of the problems in

Vieques, and as part of a public relations campaign, the article argued that the United States did not "expropriate any property on Vieques." The navy, continued the argument, "purchased" the land over a nine-year period (Hessman 1979, 14). However, a scholarly study produced by the navy in the same year talks of "expropriations" and "displacement" and mentions that the urgency of the war situation necessitated "condemnation proceedings" to move the civilian population. According to the navy, "Condemnation was the method of acquisition at this time and was utilized because of the haste necessitated by wartime conditions" (Department of the Navy 1979, vol. 1, sect. 2, p. 199). What is at stake is not whether property owners received some compenstion but the element of compulsion in the sale.[13]

The initial stage in the eviction of the Vieques population from their land took place between 1941 and 1943 and began in the western section of the island, the region closest to the Isla Grande (Puerto Rico), for which the navy had immediate occupation plans. Most of the families (74 percent of those interviewed in 1979) were notified by a letter with a heading from the Naval Station Officer-in-Charge of Construction, informing them that the United States had acquired the house and land occupied by the tenant's family, and that the property had to be abandoned in no more than ten days after receiving the notification. Still, over 30 percent of those interviewed reported that this written notification was delivered only twenty-four to forty-eight hours in advance of their actual eviction. The former manager of the Central Playa Grande, immediately employed as a field manager by the navy, delivered most of the letters accompanied by "an American or soldier." Those who lived closer to the eastern section of Vieques were given, according to our interviewees, more time to move out. In case the family had nowhere else to go, the navy offered to relocate them on a plot of land, provided that they agreed to abandon this place again, with only twenty-four-hour advance notification and to surrender any future claims. No cement dwellings were to be constructed in these plots, according to the navy's instructions recalled by our informants. This latter condition increased the insecurity felt by most families, then and over the years, since no matter how long they had been living in the navy resettlements or how many improvements they had made to their houses as time went by, they felt that they could again be evicted from one day to the next without any legal rights to protect them.[14]

The recollections of how the actual expulsions took place were still vivid in the memory of the dislodged families and their relatives. In the words of one informant (our translation): "A truck was sent with a carpenter in charge of tearing down the dwelling. Our things were thrown into the assigned plot." Those who had more than twenty-four-hour notice recalled: "We gathered our animals and began to tear down the house," and "Our things were thrown out in the new lot and we had to begin to clear out the brush." Another family remembers that after tearing the house down, the truck did not arrive that day, and they had to sleep out in the open. Others related that after their houses were torn down, they were taken to the assigned lots, given a tarpaulin, and lived under those conditions for three months, until the navy brought wood planks to their new place.

The situation of female-headed households with children and of expectant mothers in the community was singled out by our interviewees as being particularly pitiful: "Women with their children were brought here under the rain and were left with just a zinc plank above."; "Many gave birth under those zinc boards."; "My sister was pregnant and ill. She got wet during the eviction and died soon after." The fields that were converted into residential plots evidently lacked any previous conditioning, water, or basic sanitary provisions. "They were bitten by scorpions and rats. Water and food were lacking. Their skin was swollen," and "We arrived during the rainy season. Many contracted the flu. They were carried in hammocks to the hospital" (PCJP 1979).

The massive eviction evoked feelings of sadness, bitterness, and impotence in the majority of those interviewed for this study. "My mother cried and cried. She arrived in Santa María with her face covered with a towel."; "I was heartbroken."; "I thought I was not going to be able to survive."; "Even a hurricane would have been better than the expropriations." Others, however, believed that their situation was not too different from before and, in fact, improved in the short term. "In the Tió farm [where they lived as *agregados*] there was no water. Besides, a house was given to us in the new plot."; "We were sad, but they promised so much lasting work . . ."; "When the navy arrived in Vieques, the sugar mill stopped grinding cane. The construction of the base created at least some jobs."

One of the principal effects of the expropriations was the destruction of the sugar latifundia, replaced by concentrated military landholdings in the hands of the U.S. Navy. Would the process of expropriation have taken the same course had there been a numerous settled peasantry with property over the land? Would the removal of the families from the land, farm by farm, have been as easy? Perhaps a numerous peasantry would have responded with social movements of resistance, but the actual process took another course.

Generalized distress was not translated into an open kind of resistance. Many reported talks among their neighbors of refusing to leave, but their determination was weakened by several conditions: they were *agregados*, not the owners of the land, and they felt that if their landlord was willing to comply and received money, then there was little they could do. "People were afraid of the navy and scared of being jailed."; "They were *agregados* and respected the federal government. They believed the Americans would send them to Devil's Island." The bulldozers used to clear the expropriated lands scared the population and became an effective deterrent to any action. "I was afraid of the bulldozers. The marines were evil."; "We had seven children, they threatened us with the bulldozers . . ."; "The law was more stringent then, you had to obey. I was scared of the bulldozers."

Yet equally important was perhaps the general understanding that they were ill equipped to face forces too superior for them, and that they would be alone in any type of struggle chosen. "There was nobody backing us. There was fear because of the language [English]. It was mandatory [to leave]."; "We were disoriented. Those who could offer any help were in favor of the navy. Nobody paid any attention if anyone protested." Reflecting on the question of the lack of resistance, one last interviewee summarized the general outlook as follows: "There was a lot of opposition, but people were afraid to express themselves openly. The government and all the powerful were Americans. We had no support. We were slaves. We had no rights."

THE DISAPPEARANCE OF THE BARRIOS

The two successive processes of expropriation in Vieques affected the western barrios first and then the eastern barrios. The condemnation proceedings that began in late 1941 affected all of Punta Arenas, Llave, Mosquito, and some of the lands of Puerto Ferro, Puerto Diablo, and Florida. The navy acquired by its own reckoning 21,020 acres, or approximately two-thirds of the island, in the period 1941–1943. In a second wave of expropriations, the navy acquired an additional 4,340 acres in the eastern portion of Vieques, principally in Puerto Diablo (Department of the Navy 1979, vol. 1, sect. 2, p. 193). According to the municipal taxation records, the barrio of Punta Arenas totally disappeared during the first wave of the expropriations of the navy. Llave lost 95 percent of its land, Mosquito lost 91 percent, and 76 percent of the lands of Puerto Ferro was taken during the first round of expropriations. Due to the high degree of land concentration, the largest haciendas spanned two or more barrios, and for this reason it is difficult to establish with precision what percentage of the large farms belonged to which barrio. For example, during the period 1940–1941, the tax records list 5,856 *cuerdas* of land belonging jointly to the barrios of Puerto Real and Puerto Ferro, without listing which part of the land belonged to which barrio. In 1945, as a result of the expropriation of the lands of Puerto Ferro, some of the land that had previously been listed jointly now appeared to belong solely to Puerto Real. Due to this statistical effect, Puerto Real appears to have had more land in 1945 than in 1940. On the entire island of Vieques, the Department of the Treasury of Puerto Rico assessed for taxation purposes 36,032 *cuerdas* of land during the period 1940–1941, but only 9,935 in 1945. The difference of 26,097 *cuerdas* (72 percent of the land of Vieques) is greater than the figure cited by J. Pastor Ruiz of 22,000 *cuerdas* expropriated by the U.S. Navy during this period (the navy figure is 21,020 acres or 21,415 *cuerdas*).[15]

In the second wave of expropriations, the number of *cuerdas* registered in the municipal taxation records decreased from 1,204 in Florida in 1945 to 369 in 1950, a decrease of 69 percent. In Puerto Diablo, the corresponding decrease was from 3,921 to 2,791 *cuerdas* (a 29 percent decrease), and in Puerto Real, the number of *cuerdas* taxed by the municipality decreased from 4,238 to 1,689 (a 60 percent decrease). In Vieques as a whole, the total area under civilian control according to the taxation records decreased from 9,934 *cuerdas* in 1945 to 5,685 in 1950, a 43 percent decrease from the land area available in 1945. If we consider the original taxation figure of 36,032 *cuerdas* in 1940, before the first wave of expropriations, and 5,685 in 1950, the municipality of Vieques was taxing only 16 percent as much land in 1950 as in 1940. This is a dramatic decrease in the civilian land area, and even allowing for some error in the municipal taxation figures of 1940, this means that in 1950, civilians had in the best of cases one-fifth of the land they had in 1940. This is a remarkable figure if one considers that the population of Vieques did not decline proportionally. In 1950, there were 9,228 persons in Vieques, compared to 10,037 in 1940. In other words, 89 percent of the civilian population remained on the island during the 1940–1950 decade, but civilians retained only 16 percent as much land in 1950 as in 1940. Land available to civilians decreased from 3.6 *cuerdas* per person in 1940 to 0.6 *cuerdas* per person in 1950. It does not take much of an imagination to visualize the effects of this change on a society that had been fundamentally rural and agrarian in 1940.

The fifty-three persons interviewed in 1979 came from all parts of Vieques. Most, however, lived in the western barrios, which were the most populous before the expropriations. Only eight of the fifty-three lived in the eastern sectors. Many were *agregados*, and they listed as their place of residence communities whose names are difficult to locate on today's maps. In the interviews, Viequenses who experienced expulsions from the land were asked not only where they lived before the expropriations but also where they went after the expropriations. Fifteen were relocated to Montesanto and twenty-one to Santa María, the rest moving to various other places in Vieques and even to the main island of Puerto Rico. The navy's version of events concedes that the population of *agregados* and workers (i.e., those who were not property owners) was larger than that of the property owners. This is what one would expect given the degree of concentration of landed property in Vieques and the rates of rural landlessness.

A larger population living on the acquired lands, who were not property owners, were resettled to Montesanto (a tract isolated from the other acquisitions) and to Santa María (a tract at the northeastern edge of the Eastern Sugar Associates acquisition and close to Isabel Segunda). Resettlement to these areas was proposed and accomplished in a relatively short period of time. Records indicate that a proposal of December 1942 to relocate "aggre-gados" [sic] from the Naval Ammunition Facility to Montesanto was a real-ity by August 1943, and that the Santa María tract had also been estab-lished. Those now in Vieques who were among the resettled recall an extremely rapid resettlement. Although recollections of the types of Navy assistance vary widely, the moves appear to have been accomplished with some Navy assistance. The numbers of tenant families affected range from about 500 at a minimum to 1,300 at a maximum, with 800 the most fre-quently cited number. (Department of the Navy 1979, vol. 1, sect. 2, p. 201)

With an average family size of approximately five persons in Vieques, 500 families translates into 2,500 individuals, or one-quarter of the popula-tion of Vieques. The figure of 1,300 families translates into 6,500, or 65 per-cent of the population of Vieques. Between these two extremes, the "most frequently cited" number of 800 families means 4,000 individuals, or 40 per-cent of the population of Vieques. The number of those affected by the evic-tions ranges between a quarter and 65 percent of the population of the island. Thus the expulsions had a much greater social impact than the expropriations per se, which affected only the minority, property-owning population of Vieques.

RECONCENTRATION

The population of Florida, a central barrio of Vieques, doubled during the decade of 1940–1950 due to the settlement, in the vicinity of Isabel II, of the population expelled from Punta Arenas, Mosquito, and Llave. However, the population of Florida was already on the rise at the time of the expropriations and had increased during the period 1935–1940 due to a 1937 resettlement project of the Puerto Rico Reconstruction Administration, which provided plots of two *cuerdas* to 199 homesteaders (Department of the Navy 1979, vol. 1, sect. 2, p. 190). In Punta Arenas, the population declined by 100 percent, in Mosquito, it dropped by 98 percent, and Llave lost 89 percent of its popu-lation during the period 1940–1950. The increase in the central sector of Vieques is the counterpart to the decrease in the barrios affected by the expropriations. According to Rev. Justo Pastor Ruiz, "The barrios of Tapón, Mosquito, and Llave disappeared. All the neighbors and small owners disap-peared and formed new barrios in Moscú and Montesanto" (Pastor Ruiz 1947, 206). The navy's version of events is not very different.

> Both personal recollections of the relocation and naval records substanti-ate that those who lived in barrio Llave (including the Playa Grande set-tlement), Resolución, the Monte Pirata area, and Punta Arenas were moved to Montesanto. The records of lot assignments to Montesanto reveal that of 383 tenant families who lived in the western and southern

TABLE 10.3

Civilian Ownership of Farms in Vieques, by Barrio, 1940, 1945, 1950

Barrio	No. Farms in 1940	Cuerdas in 1940	No. Farms in 1945	Cuerdas in 1945	No. Farms in 1950	Cuerdas in 1950
Florida	41	1,475	23	1,204	18	369
Llave	80	4,152	30	218	28	164
Mosquito	10	95	2	9	2	9
Puerto Diablo	24	7,539	23	3,921	18	2,791
Puerto Ferro	27	915	15	220	15	505
Puerto Real	193	2,418	165	4,238	155	1,689
Punta Arenas	7	13,369	0		0	
Florida and Puerto Ferro	0		1	124	1	124
Florida–Puerto Real	2	3	0		0	
Puerto Real and Llave	0		0		0	
Puerto Real and Puerto Ferro	1	5,856	0		0	
Unknown	2	210	0		6	34
Total	387	36,032	259	9,934	243	5,685

*Some farms spanned more than one barrio, and it was not possible to assign portions of farms to specific barrios. We retained the classification of the original documents. Urban land lots are not included.

Source: AGPR, DH 1940–1950.

TABLE 10.4
Population of Vieques, by Barrio

Barrio	Population 1899[a]	Population 1910[a]	Population 1920[b]	Population 1930[b]	Population 1935[c]	Population 1940[d]	Population 1950[d]	Population 1960[e]	Population 1970[e]
Town (Isabel II)[1]	0	3,158	3,424	3,101	2,816	2,678	3,085	2,487	2,378
Florida[1]	2,645	565	603	775	659	1,253	2,638	1,989	2,381
Llave[1]	1,059	1,610	1,715	1,583	1,683	1,776	191	89	73
Mosquitos[1]	0	748	847	818	785	851	20	4	
Puerto Diablo[1]	0	854	584	505	687	548	894	693	709
Puerto Ferro[1]	879	638	1,041	839	776	570	723	507	884
Punta Arenas[1]	0	922	1,102	833	884	901	0		30
Puerto Real[2]	1,344	1,930	2,335	2,128	1,747	1,785	1,677	1,441	1,312
Vieques, Total	5,927	10,425	11,651	10,582	10,037	10,362	9,228	7,210	7,767

[1]Not counted separately in 1899.
[2]Identified as Puerto Real Arriba and Puerto Real Abajo in 1899.

Sources:
[a]U.S. Department of Commerce, Bureau of the Census 1913, 1190.
[b]U.S. Department of Commerce, Bureau of the Census 1932, 131.
[c]Puerto Rico Reconstruction Administration 1938, 12.
[d]U.S. Department of Commerce, Bureau of the Census 1952, quoted in Veaz (1995, 202).
[e]Department of the Navy 1979, vol. 1, sect. 2, p. 187.

TABLE 10.5
Barrio and Sector of Residence at the Time of the Expropriations
(No. of Persons Interviewed = 53)

Barrio	Sector	No. of Cases	%
Florida	Total	3	5.66%
	Bulfo	2	
	Peña	1	
Llave	Total	14	26.42%
	Unspecified	1	
	Central Playa Grande	7	
	Martínez—GPG*	4	
	Pocito— CPG*	2	
Punta Arenas	Total	12	22.64%
	Resolución—CPG*	7	
	Ventana**	4	
	Colonia Uvero	1	
Mosquito	Total	12	22.64%
	Berro	1	
	Comp. Benítez	2	
	Palma	5	
	Santa Elena	1	
	Perseverancia	2	
	Unspecified	1	
Puerto Real	Total	4	7.55%
	El Pilón**	3	
	Unspecified	1	
Puerto Diablo	Total	8	15.09%
	Unspecified	2	
	Finca Genoveva	1	
	Finca de Enrique Cayeres	1	
	Campaña	3	
	Puerto Negro	1	
Total		53	100.00%

*The Playa Grande estate included different sectors such as those mentioned here. However, not all were located in the Llave barrio.

**The communities known as Ventana and El Pilón are meeting points of several barrios. Ventana is located on the border between Llave and Punta Arenas. El Pilón is a sector common to Florida, Puerto Real, Llave, and Mosquito. Therefore, our classification of these sectors in Punta Arenas and Puerto Real is somewhat arbitrary.

Source: PCJP 1979; Vieques, Archivo Fuerte Conde de Mirasol, Expropiaciones, Generalidades, #9.

TABLE 10.6
Barrio Where Relocated after the Expropriations
(No. of Persons Interviewed = 53)

Barrio	Sector	No. of Cases
Pueblo	Total	3
	Unspecified	2
	Morropó	1
Puerto Diablo	Total	22
	Santa María	21
	Leguillou	1
Puerto Ferro	Total	2
	El Destino	2
Florida	Total	21
	Montesanto	15
	P.R.R.A.*	1
	Tortuguero	5
Total		48

Two individuals did not respond.
One individual did not live in the expropriated property, so there was no resettlement.
Two individuals moved to the larger island of Puerto Rico.

*Puerto Rico Reconstruction Administration

Source: PCJP 1979; Vieques, Archivo Fuerte Conde de Mirasol, Expropiaciones, Generalidades, #9.

sector, 284 resettled in Montesanto, and the remaining 99 chose to go elsewhere. The 17 tenants who had lived in Montesanto prior to the establishment of the resettlement tract were also assigned lots. Records and recollection confirm that families who lived in the Mosquito area (Barrio Mosquito and portions of Florida) on land associated with the Benítez sugar family were moved to Santa Maria. Tenants in the eastern sector lands owned by Eastern Sugar Associates and by Juan Tió were also apparently relocated to Santa Maria. Estimates of the number relocated there range from 180 to 200 families, but estimates of the number who may have lived on the affected lands would be considerably higher. A 1943 investigating committee places the total number of affected families in both tracts as high as 825. (Department of the Navy 1979, vol. 1, sect. 2, p. 201)

A study carried out by the Agricultural Experiment Station of the University of Puerto Rico (1943, 1) states: "The total number of families affected is undoubtedly larger than the 825 families mentioned above."

LONG-TERM POPULATION EFFECTS

The long-term effects of the expropriations on the population levels of Vieques cannot quite be described as catastrophic. The situation that emerged was rather one of stunted growth. The population of Vieques peaked in 1920, when the census counted 11,651 persons living on the island. During World War I, the price of sugar soared to unprecedented levels, and it remained high until it dropped precipitously in October 1920, ending the famous "Dance of the Millions," which made the sugar mill owners of the Caribbean fabulously wealthy during the European armed conflict. During this sugar boom, the population of Vieques increased, but with the drop of the price of sugar in the 1920s, some locally owned sugar mills in Puerto Rico (and in Vieques) began to experience difficulties. The population of Vieques remained stable at around 10,000 people for the next twenty years. The precise figures are 10,582 persons in 1930; 10,037 in 1935, and 10,362 in 1940. This means that even before the expropriations, Vieques could not support an increasing population, and each year a number of Viequenses emigrated, some to Puerto Rico, others to the neighboring island of St. Croix, which is located only a few miles to the northeast. In the mid-1940s, the majority of Puerto Ricans living in St. Croix were from Vieques.

To be exact, between 1930 and 1940, 26 percent of the population of Vieques emigrated (2,749 persons), most of them to St. Croix. In 1947, there were more than 3,000 Puerto Ricans living in St. Croix, most of them from Vieques. Despite the fact that the economy of St. Croix had been experiencing a protracted contraction and a long-term population decline, from about 26,681 persons in 1835 to 11,413 in 1930, the residents of Vieques migrated to St. Croix because the employment situation in Vieques was even worse. In his 1947 study, Clarence Senior pointed out that migrating to an island such as St. Croix seemed like "jumping out of the frying pan into the fire."[16] Nevertheless, the residents of Vieques moved there due to lack of employment in the sugar industry of the Puerto Rican island. The expropriations affected an island that already had problems supporting the population level it had reached in 1920.

CAPITAL ASSETS, EMPLOYMENT,
AND HOW TO MAKE A LIVING

The wealth assessed in Vieques had several components: land, improvements to land, and movable or "personal" property, which included cattle and vehicles. The taxable value of the land decreased by 74 percent as a result of the expropriations, from $1,248,512 in 1940 to $328,772 in 1950. During the same period, the value of improvements to the land decreased by 32 percent, from $294,770 to $201,500. The value of personal property,

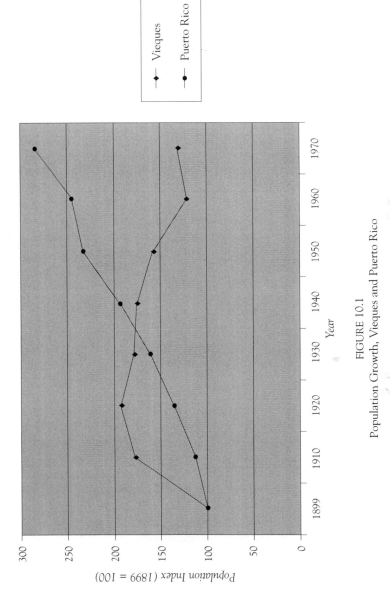

FIGURE 10.1
Population Growth, Vieques and Puerto Rico

Sources: U.S. Department of Commerce, Bureau of the Census, 1913, 1932; Veaz 1995; Department of the Navy, 1979.

which includes vehicles and cattle, increased by 2 percent between 1940 and 1945, from $368,300 to $375,780. This probably reflects the inventories of local merchants who sold goods to the troops and to workers who had employment in construction during the war. The value of personal property then dropped dramatically between 1945 and 1950 to $268,720 (a decrease of 27 percent). The drop between 1945 and 1950 probably reflects the decline in the commercial sector once construction activity ceased in Vieques and the war ended.

The net effect of the expropriations was a decrease in the amount of capital available to generate income. Since the decrease in property value was more extreme than the decline in population, total assets per person decreased from $186 to $86 per capita. This means that Viequenses were left in 1950 with less than half of the assets per person they possessed in 1940, that is, with less than half of the capacity to generate income.[17]

Before the expropriations, rural stores in the Vieques neighborhoods were known as *pulperías* and *colmados*, in addition to company stores in the sugar mills known as *tiendas de raya*. The sale of alcohol was not specialized but took place instead together with the sale of foodstuffs and supplies. Between 1940 and 1945, the number of *pulperías* on the tax lists decreased from six to three, and the establishments that sold *"Provisiones y Mercancía"* decreased from three to two. Against this trend, in 1945 there appeared a number of establishments dedicated exclusively to the sale of alcohol: one *"Bar y Hospedaje,"* one *"Cafetín y Rancho Chico,"* ten *"Cafetines,"* one *"Bar, Cafetín, y Mesa de Billar* [pool table]," one *"Bar,"* and one *"Cafetín y Establecimiento Comercial Independiente."* Not one of these businesses appears on the list in 1940. Their existence reflects the new purchasing power introduced by the military personnel in Vieques. Likewise, the number of civilian automobiles registered in Vieques increased from forty-two in 1940 to seventy-four in 1945 (AGPR, DH 1940–1950). Many of these were used to transport the population from the military base to town and back. During the same period, prostitution thrived in Vieques. The neighborhood known as *"El Cañón,"* near the old Vieques cemetery, became forbidden to the troops, because the prostitutes lived and practiced prostitution there.[18]

During the war, despite the catastrophic decline in land and improvements to the land in civilian hands, the value of personal property remained relatively stable. The number of stores of all kinds remained stable, and their value increased by 27 percent. The number of automobiles increased by 76 percent and their value by 278 percent between 1940 and 1945.[19] The number of bars, pool halls, restaurants, and hostels increased. The prosperous period of 1942–1943, during which the Mosquito pier was built, reduced the negative economic impact. Since landlessness and poverty had been so extreme in Vieques before the expropriations, the social profile of the island did not seem as dramatically different as one might expect when one considers that the navy took four-fifths of the land. Evidently there was a sector of the population for whom employment in military construction meant a good source of income, at least before the cessation of all construction in 1943.

The increase in the number of jobs in construction and other sectors promoted by military contracts during the Second World War compensated for the decline of employment in the sugar industry. In addition, the new jobs paid better wages. Pastor Ruiz refers to the years 1941–1943 as the period of the "fat cows." Between 1941 and 1943 in Vieques, according to Pastor Ruiz, "the town swam in gold for a couple of years" (Pastor Ruiz 1947, 206). This explains why the decline in population was not proportional to the decline in available land, in a society that had been fundamentally agrarian before the expropriations.

The construction of the pier and the Mosquito base generated payrolls to civilians of $60,000 a week and reached at one point the sum of $120,000 weekly, which was "a fantastic amount," according to Rev. Justo Pastor Ruiz. These were the years of the "fat cows," of employment at better salaries than under the old sugar plantation regime, a period of feverish economic activity (Pastor Ruiz 1947, 205). However, in the summer of 1943, Viequenses marched with black flags to protest the lack of employment. This signaled the beginning of a period of squalor for the majority of the population. After 1943, German submarine activity in the Caribbean faded, the focus of the war moved to North Africa and Europe, and construction practically came to a halt in Vieques. While it is true that the first two years of the war were the period of "pharaoh's cows," when the court of the pharaoh withdrew, Vieques was overtaken by the period of the "thin cows." The protests with black flags during the summer of 1943 signaled a new consciousness concerning the impact of the expropriations: the future looked bleak, there were no jobs, and there was no land.

Unemployment became rampant. Most of the workers in Vieques had been in one way or another involved in the sugar industry. Among the fifty-three persons interviewed, thirty-two (60 percent) had jobs in the sugar industry or related to it. Secondly, the wave of expropriations during the period 1947–1950 further reduced the civilian land area from 9,939 *cuerdas* in 1945 to 5,685 in 1950. Capital assets, including land, taxed by the municipality shrank from $1,911,582 in 1940 to $798,992 in 1950 (see Table 10.9). The military base never generated enough employment in Vieques but only temporary jobs during maneuvers.

The great sugar-producing landed estates disappeared, and so did the sugar industry, during the first expropriations. Some ranching interests remained on the island, but they were the object of the second round of expropriations by the navy in 1947 (Veaz 1995, 185). All attempts to restore sugar production were unsuccessful. An experiment to substitute the production of sugar with pineapples did not meet with great success. The navy's expropriations of 1947 dislocated pineapple production and cattle ranching (Picó 1950, 216–17). As of 1950, the scenario in Vieques was of a reconcentrated population, without the agricultural economy that had existed before the war, without an alternative economy to replace what was lost, surrounded by a military base that generated no employment and that restricted the access of the community to most of the seashore and mangroves, to most of the coconut groves, and in short, to most of the rich, tropical ecology of Vieques.

The situation in 1950 was therefore dramatically different from that of 1943. Not only did landed assets and improvements to land decrease dramatically because of the expropriations, and then even more because of the second round of expropriations in 1947–1950, but the value of movable or "personal" property declined as well. The commercial sector of Vieques, which had been able to hold its own during World War II, also had collapsed by 1950. If the taxation records indicate anything, they point to the catastrophic economic scenario of a reconcentrated population without assets to make a living and without the kind of insurance against hunger that *agregado* usufructs used to provide before the expropriations. To top it off, the interaction with the local ecology was barred, as Viequenses could not access most of the coastline for fishing, or the mangroves, which provided sources of fish, crabs, and mangrove wood for charcoal making. Even the coconut groves were destroyed by the navy during maneuvers in February 1950 (McCaffrey 1999, 122; Harris 1980, 20). Faced with such a catastrophic scenario, and lacking alternative sources of employment, Viequenses took to the sea. A Vieques fisherman eloquently expressed the dilemma: "The only factory that has its door open to whomever wants to work is the sea" (McCaffrey 1999, 149).[20]

TABLE 10.7
Vieques: Civilian Land Ownership in 1940, 1945, 1950

Farm Size in Cuerdas	Cuerdas, 1940	1940 %	Cuerdas, 1945	1945 %	Cuerdas, 1950	1950 %
Less than 5	166	0.46%	88	0.89%	83	1.47%
5 to 9	284	0.79%	222	2.23%	206	3.62%
10 to 19	464	1.29%	191	1.92%	151	2.66%
20 to 49	913	2.53%	521	5.24%	597	10.50%
50 to 99	485	1.35%	357	3.59%	345	6.06%
100 to 174	1,690	4.69%	1,096	11.03%	508	8.94%
175 to 499	3,129	8.68%	1,331	13.39%	2,362	41.55%
500 to 999	694	1.93%	2,237	22.51%	1,433	25.20%
Over 1,000	28,208	78.28%	3,896	39.20%		0.00%
Total	36,033	100.00%	9,939	100.00%	5,685	100.00%

Source: AGPR, DH 1940–1950. *Departamento de Hacienda, Registro de Tasación de la Propiedad (1940, 1945, 1950).*

CONCLUSION

It would be inaccurate to characterize the economy and society of Vieques before the expropriations of World War II as a prosperous and an egalitarian paradise. Society in Vieques was highly stratified in specific ways characteristic of plantation societies. The land belonged to a chosen few, and the majority of

TABLE 10.8
Vieques: Non-Farm Property in 1940, 1945, 1950

Type of Property	Value in 1940	(%)	Value in 1945	(%)	Value in 1950	(%)
Stores	$47,380	13%	$60,070	17.23%	$46,310	17.23%
Cinema	$1,220	0.34%	$1,220	0.35%	$1,220	0.45%
Boats	$1,600	0.44%	$11,100	3.18%	$32,500	12.09%
Bars, "Cafetines," Pool Halls, Restaurants and Hostels			$9,020	2.59%	$13,700	5.10%
Cattle	$129,370	35.83%	$128,730	36.93%	$53,740	20.00%
Cattle, Machinery, Dry Goods*	$181,520	50.27%	$136,900	39.28%	$119,750	44.56%
Factories		0.00%	$1,500	0.43%	$1,500	0.56%
Total	$361,090	100%	$348,540	100.00%	$268,720	100.00%

*The category "Cattle Machinery and Dry Goods" includes the assets of the Eastern Sugar Associates Corporation.

Source: AGPR, DH 1940–50. Figures do not include $7,210 of cars and vehicles in 1940 and $27,240 in 1945. The 1950 tax records do not include cars and vehicles.

TABLE 10.9
Vieques: Assessed Value of Land, Improvements to Land,
and Personal Property in 1940, 1945, 1950

Year	Land Value	Land Value (%)	Improve-ment Value	Improve-ment Value (%)	Personal Property Value	Personal Property Value (%)	Total Value
1940	$1,248,512	65%	$294,770	15%	$368,300	19%	$1,911,582
1945	$573,175	49%	$219,721	19%	$375,780	32%	$1,168,676
1950	$328,772	41%	$201,500	25%	$268,720	34%	$798,992

Source: AGPR, DH 1940–1950.

the population was landless. Rural proletarianization and relations of *agrego* were the counterpart of rural landlessness, in a sort of continuum in which it was difficult to differentiate the worker from the *agregado*, as one category blended into the other in the farms and *colonias* of this tropical plantation island. Both *agregados* and workers were a resident labor force on the plantations. Precisely because the class structure was one characteristic of a plantation society, the effects of the expropriations were felt in ways influenced by preexisting social conditions. Landowners received compensation, but the dispossessed majority did not. Because workers lived and worked on the farms of the large landowners, the navy's expropriations signified the simultaneous loss of their homes and their jobs. *Agregados* had certain usufructs and access to the rich, tropical ecology of the island, which they also lost in the process of eviction. Thus the expropriation of the land of the large landowners had a triple effect on the resident labor force: (1) eviction from home; (2) loss of employment; and (3) no access to subsistence crops and the rich, tropical ecology. These three components constitute the whole process commonly referred to simply as "eviction" (*desalojos*), or "expropriations."

The triple-effect evictions took place in the context of a plantation economy that was already facing serious economic difficulties. Viequenses had already started to migrate to neighboring St. Croix in the 1930s in search of employment. The expropriations accentuated the trend toward out-migration. Vieques settled into a role as a reserve of labor in which population growth was stunted due to the constriction on economic development placed by the disappearance of the best lands for agriculture and grazing. Although the conditions of life in the resettlement tracts have not been the subject of any systematic study in scholarly works, it is clear that those who stayed were condemned to squalor. Because no alternative economy was ever established, long-term deterioration of living conditions ensued. For Viequenses, the expropriations of the U.S. Navy were a disaster whose effects continued to be felt over the long term.

NOTES

1. The complete list of owners, their properties, and assessed values can be found at the following internet site: http://www.sscnet.ucla.edu/soc/faculty/ayala/Vieques/ (accessed June 15, 2003).

2. The *Archivo General de Puerto Rico* contains the records of all municipal tax assessments from 1905 until 1955. The assessments in the *Archivo General de Puerto Rico* are organized by *municipio*, in handwritten volumes that measure approximately 15" by 21" and include the following variables: (1) name of the owner (which allows the researcher to determine the gender of the owner); (2) type of property (e.g., farm, urban lot, personal property); (3) location of the property (barrio for farms, street and number for urban lots); (4) area in *cuerdas* (a Puerto Rican *cuerda* is equal to .9712

acres); (5) assessed value of the land; (6) type of improvements to the land; (7) assessed value of improvements; (8) type of personal property (e.g., trucks, cars, cattle); (9) assessed value of personal property. The data was photocopied at the *Archivo General de Puerto Rico* and entered into a computerized database at Lehman College, City University of New York. *Archivo General de Puerto Rico*, Departamento de Hacienda, Registros de Tasación sobre la Propiedad, Vieques, 1940–1950. (Hereafter cited as *AGPR, DH 1940–50*.)

3. The following interviewers participated in the project in Vieques and in Puerto Rico: "Cheo" (no last name in manuscript), Eugenia Acuña, Salvador Beauchamp, "Tuti" Belardo, Viviana Carro, Ana Rosa Cuilan, "Chachi" De Rivera, Pedro Encarnación, Aleida Encarnación, Osvaldo Esquerette, "Ito" Félix, Nydia González, Pablo Hernández, Migda Maldonado, Arturo Morales, Cristina Pérez, Víctor Ruiz, Tita Tirado, Wilfredo Tirado, Diana Tirado, Pablo Torres, Vitalia Velásquez, Soilo Velazques, Abraham Velázquez, and Lisa Wheaton. Hereafter cited as *PCJP (Proyecto Caribeño de Justicia y Paz)* 1979.

4. See the discussion on *agregados* in the section "Expulsion of *Agregados* and Workers."

5. The Eastern Sugar Associates owned both of the lands of what was once the Puerto Real mill in Vieques and the Pasto Viejo mill in Humacao.

6. Barrios are minor civil subdivisions of *municipios*.

7. Interview with Aurelio Tió, by Vivian Carro and Lisa Wheaton, February 1979. Unless otherwise specified, the information presented in this section was provided by Aurelio Tió and obtained from the summary transcript of this interview.

8. Interview and translation to English by Viviana Carro.

9. On the "total" character of plantations, see Best (1968) and Beckford (1970).

10. We use the median because one *agregado* reported "2,000 *cuerdas*," which refers to the extent of the landowner's holding. That extreme value would distort our average if we utilized the mean. Of fifty-three cases, twelve did not report farm size, thirty-one reported less than ten *cuerdas*, six reported between ten and fifty *cuerdas*, and one each reported 300 and 500 *cuerdas*, while two interviewees reported 2,000 *cuerdas*.

11. There were some exceptions. "It also appears that tenants were in some cases made parties in the court actions." Department of the Navy (1979, vol. 1, sect. 2, p. 200).

12. Unless otherwise noted, this section of the chapter is based on the results of the 1979 survey conducted with fifty-three families expropriated or evicted by the navy during the 1940s.

13. The Superior Court of Puerto Rico has a *Sala de Expropiaciones* to deal with private owners who seek further compensation when the government uses its right of eminent domain. The term *expropriation* is not in any way meant to convey a lack of compensation but rather the *compulsory* character of the "sale" to the state.

14. This situation was still prevalent in 1979 at the time of the interviews. As a result of the struggle during that period, the navy began the process of transferring

rights to the Commonwealth of Puerto Rico, which in turn titled some owners, although not all. Some communities are still seeking legal titles. See Giusti-Cordero 1999a.

15. The first round of expropriations lasted from November 1941 until September 1943 (Veaz 1995, 187). According to Pastor Ruiz (1947, 7) "It is estimated that of 33,682 arable *cuerdas*, the base took 22,000." The navy figure is from the Department of the Navy (1979, vol. 1, sect. 2, p. 193).

16. "Puerto Rican migration to an island in such a depressed condition would seem like 'jumping out of the frying pan into the fire.' The answer lies partly in the fact that sugarcane continues to be the main crop of the island, and that cane needs seasonal labor. The Danes formerly brought in workers for the cutting season from the nearby British islands. This practice continued until 1927. The immigration laws of the United States were applied to the Virgin Islands in that year, and the cane growers had to look elsewhere for their labor. They found a situation made-to-order for them in the depressed conditions of the sugar industry on the island of Vieques. Sugar acreage and yield on that island of 51 square miles had been decreasing steadily since 1910, and people were looking for a chance to make a living elsewhere. Agents for the growers recruited sizable groups for transportation to St. Croix. Some of those who went on temporary jobs stayed. The tendency of Puerto Rican migration to St. Croix has been upward since that time" (Senior 1947, 7, 1–2).

17. This calculation does not take into account the assets of the navy. The payroll of the navy to civilians in 1941–1943 was spectacular, but it subsided after that date. The decrease is more extreme than the figures reveal if one considers that houses, particularly the cluster in Isabel Segunda, which were generally not income-generating assets, are included as "improvements" in the figures.

18. In an interview with Ismael Guadalupe (Committee for the Rescue and Development of Vieques), which took place in New York on May 23, 2000, Guadalupe clarified that the proliferation of bars and pubs was not only due to the purchases of the troops. They were small, unstable enterprises in a context of high unemployment.

19. Automobiles were not listed in the tax records of 1950.

20. McCaffrey (1999) is a moving account of the origin and fruition of the movement of the Vieques fishermen, which culminated in massive protests against the navy in 1979. A revised version was published by Rutgers University Press (McCaffrey 2002).

WORKS CITED

Agricultural Experiment Station. University of Puerto Rico. 1943. *Report on the Possibilities of Utilizing Navy Lands in Vieques Island for a Resettlement Project*. Mimeographed report, October 23.

Archivo General de Puerto Rico, Departamento de Hacienda (AGPR, DH), 1940–1950. Registros de Tasación sobre la Propiedad, Vieques.

Associated Press. 2001. "One Who Remained." *New York Newsday*, July 30.

Ayala, César. 1999. *American Sugar Kingdom: The Plantation Economy of the Spanish Caribbean, 1898–1934*. Chapel Hill: University of North Carolina Press.

———. 2001. Interview with Doña Severina Guadalupe, Isabel Segunda, Vieques. April 11.

Beckford, George. 1970. *Persistent Poverty: Underdevelopment in the Plantation Economies of the Third World*. Oxford: Oxford University Press.

Bergad, Laird W. 1983. *Coffee and the Growth of Agrarian Capitalism in Nineteenth-Century Puerto Rico*. Princeton: Princeton University Press.

Best, Lloyd. 1968. "The Mechanism of Plantation Type Societies: Outlines of a Model of Pure Plantation Economy." *Social and Economic Studies* 17:3: 283–326.

Bonnet Benítez, Juan Amédée. 1976. *Vieques en la historia de Puerto Rico*. San Juan: F. Ortiz Nieves.

Department of the Navy. 1979. *Continued Use of the Atlantic Fleet Weapons Training Facility Inner Range (Vieques): Draft Environmental Impact Statement*. N.p. Tippetts-Abbett–McCarthy-Stratton: Ecology and Environment.

El Mundo. 1921. *"La Central Puerto Real está en manos de 'receivers.'"* El Mundo (July 9): 1, 3.

Estades Font, María Eugenia. 1988. *La presencia militar de los Estados Unidos en Puerto Rico, 1898–1918: Intereses estratégicos y dominación colonial*. Río Piedras, Puerto Rico: Huracán.

Fernández y García, Eugenio, ed. 1923. *El libro de Puerto Rico*. San Juan: El Libro Azul.

García Muñiz, Humberto. 1988. *Los Estados Unidos y la militarización del Caribe*. Río Piedras, Puerto Rico: Instituto de Estudios del Caribe, Universidad de Puerto Rico.

———. 1993. U.S. Military Installations in Puerto Rico: Controlling the Caribbean. Pp. 53–65 in *Colonial Dilemma: Critical Perspectives on Contemporary Puerto Rico*, ed. Edgardo Meléndez y Edwin Meléndez. Boston: South End Press.

García Muñiz, Humberto, and Jorge Rodríguez Beruff. 1996. *Security Problems and Policies in the Post–Cold War Caribbean*. New York: St. Martin's Press.

Ghigliotty, Julio. 1999a. *"Reclamo de fincas en Vieques."* El Nuevo Día (August 1): 12.

———. 1999b. Sin esperanza los expropiados. El Nuevo Día, August 1.

Gilmore, A. B. 1930. *The Porto Rico Sugar Manual, including Data on Santo Domingo Mills*. Nueva Orleans: A. B. Gilmore.

Giusti-Cordero, Juan. 1994. *Labor, Ecology, and History in a Caribbean Sugar Plantation Region: Piñones (Loíza), Puerto Rico 1770–1950*. Ph.D. dissertation, State University of New York at Binghamton.

———. 1999a. *Informe histórico preliminar: Asociación Pro-Títulos de Monte Santo et al. vs. Estado Libre Asociado et al.* Civil Núm. KPE 96-0729 (907) Tribunal de Primera Instancia, Sección Superior de San Juan (June 8).

————. 1999b. *"La marina en la mirilla: Una comparación de Vieques con los campos de bombardeo y adiestramiento en los Estados Unidos."* Pp. 133–201 in *Fronteras en conflicto: Guerra contra las drogas, militarización y democracia en el Caribe, Puerto Rico y Vieques*, ed. Humberto García Muñiz and Jorge Rodríguez Beruff. San Juan: Red Caribeña de Geopolítica.

Gonzalez, David. 2001. *"Vieques Voters Want the Navy to Leave Now."* New York Times, July 30, p. 1A.

Harris, W. W. 1980. *Puerto Rico's Fighting 65th Infantry: From San Juan to Chorwan.* San Rafael: Presidio Press.

Hessman, James D. 1979. "Opposed Landings: Vieques, the Navy Comes under 'Constant Bombardment.'" *Sea Power Magazine* (March): 12–16.

Iglesias Pantín, Santiago. 1962. *Luchas emancipadoras.* Vol. 2. San Juan: N.p.

Knoizen, Arthur M. 1980. "Statement of Rear Adm. Arthur M. Knoizen, Commander, U.S. Naval Forces, Caribbean." Pp. 51ff., 329ff. in *Naval Training Activities on the Island of Vieques, Puerto Rico: Hearings before the Panel to Review the Status of the Navy Training Activities on the Island of Vieques of the Committee on Armed Services, House of Representatives, Ninety-Sixth Congress, Second Session, May 28, 29, July 10, 11, September 24, 1980.* Washington, D.C.: U.S. Government Printing Office.

Langhorn, Elizabeth. 1987. *Vieques: History of a Small Island.* Vieques: Vieques Conservation and Historical Trust.

Langley, L. D. 1985. "Roosevelt Roads, Puerto Rico, U.S. Naval Base, 1941–." Pp. 271–75 in *United States Navy and Marine Corps Bases, Overseas*, ed. P. Coletta y J. K. Dauer. Westport, Conn.: Greenwood Press.

McCaffrey, Katherine T. 1999. *Culture, Power and Struggle: Anti-Military Protest in Vieques, Puerto Rico.* Ph.D. dissertation, City University of New York.

————. 2002. *Military Power and Popular Protest: The U.S. Navy in Vieques, Puerto Rico.* New Brunswick, N.J.: Rutgers University Press.

Pastor Ruiz, J. 1947. *Vieques antiguo y moderno.* Yauco, Puerto Rico: Tipografía Rodríguez Lugo.

Picó, Rafael. 1950. *The Geographic Regions of Puerto Rico.* Río Piedras: University of Puerto Rico Press.

Proyecto Caribeño de Justicia y Paz (PCJP). 1979. *Entrevistas a los Expropiados de Vieques.* Vieques, Puerto Rico: Archivo del Fuerte del Conde de Mirasol.

Puerto Rico Reconstruction Administration. 1938. *Census of Puerto Rico: 1935, Population and Agriculture.* Washington, D.C.: U.S. Government Printing Office.

Rabin, Robert. 1994. *Compendio de lecturas sobre la historia de Vieques.* Vieques: Museo Fuerte Conde de Mirasol.

Ramos Mattei, Andrés A. 1981. *"La importación de trabajadores contratados para la industria azucarera puertorriqueña: 1860–1880."* Pp. 125–42 in *Inmigración y clases sociales en el Puerto Rico del siglo xix*, ed. Francisco Scarano. Río Piedras, Puerto Rico: Huracán.

Rodríguez Beruff, Jorge. 1988. *Política militar y dominación: Puerto Rico en el contexto latinoamericano*. Río Piedras, Puerto Rico: Huracán.

Rodríguez Beruff, Jorge, J. Peter Figueroa, and J. Edward Greene, eds. 1991. *Conflict, Peace, and Development in the Caribbean*. New York: St. Martin's Press.

Romero Barceló, Carlos. 1999. *Testimony Before the Committee on Armed Services*, U.S. Senate, October 19, http://www.senate.gov/~armed_services/statemnt/1999/991019cr.pdf. Accessed December 26, 2001.

Senior, Clarence. 1947. *The Puerto Rican Migrant in St. Croix*. Río Piedras: University of Puerto Rico Social Science Research Center.

Tió, Aurelio. 1976. "Prólogo." P. 3 in *Vieques en la historia de Puerto Rico*, ed. Juan Amédée Bonnet Benítez. San Juan: F. Ortiz Nieves.

U.S. Department of Commerce. Bureau of the Census. 1913. *Thirteenth Census of the United States: Volume III, Population 1910, Reports by States, with Statistics for Counties, Cities, and other Civil Divisions: Nebraska–Wyoming, Alaska, Hawaii, and Porto Rico*. Washington, D.C.: U.S. Government Printing Office.

————. 1932. *Fifteenth Census of the United States: 1930. Outlying Territories and Possessions*. Washington, D.C.: U.S. Government Printing Office.

————. 1952. *1950 Population Census Report*. Washington, D.C.: U.S. Government Printing Office.

Veaz, Maribel. 1995. "*Las expropiaciones de la década del cuarenta en Vieques.*" *Revista del Colegio de Abogados de Puerto Rico* 56:2 (April–June): 159–213.

War Department. Office Director, Census of Porto Rico. 1900. *Report on the Census of Porto Rico, 1899*. Washington, D.C.: U.S. Government Printing Office.

ELEVEN

New Dimensions in
Civil Society Mobilization

The Struggle for Peace in Vieques

José Javier Colón Morera and José E. Rivera Santana

A man knocked on the king's door and said, "Give me a boat." The king's house had a lot of doors, but that one was the door for requests. As the king spent all his time seated at the door of gifts (meaning gifts which were brought to him), every time he heard someone at the door for requests, he acted like he couldn't understand, and only when the continuous tapping of the bronze knocker raised to a more than notorious, scandalous tone, impeding the neighbors' peace and quiet (people would start to murmur, "What a king we have, who doesn't answer the door"), he would order his first secretary to go see what the petitioner wanted, as there was no other way to quiet him.
—Saramago, *The Tale of the Unknown Island*

Without monolithic instances, without protagonist parties, from many fronts and with thousands of heroes, with the tranquility that now is the time—and the security that the struggle for democracy and social justice in Vieques still has other stages to come—we continue opening our camps, we multiply our beaches.
—Giusti Cordero, *La Marina*

IN THIS CHAPTER we approach the peak of activity of democratic civil society in a specific sphere of the political, social, economic, and ultimately cultural life of Puerto Rico. We concentrate on the demilitarizing and community development efforts taking place currently in Vieques, as this illustrates how a process of collective maturation is advancing there. Through it, diverse sectors are recognizing the necessity of claiming the fullest exercise of their citizenship for the development of a political agenda and an alternative community cultural and socioeconomic development.

As with other decolonizing demands, the movement for peace in Vieques has been strongly repressed in the past, and its success gives important clues as to how it is possible to defeat aggressive operatives of political intelligence aimed at disarticulating progressive social movements (Comisión de Derechos Civiles 1989). At the same time, it is a paradigmatic social movement of autonomous action, within which has come to be called "civil society," demanding a space of its own action and guided by criteria different from those traditionally outlined by the traditional political leadership (Cotto Morales 2001).

This struggle for demilitarization is a movement of "affirmation of the primacy of self-management, the longing to broaden democracy, and the strategic search to increase the community's power" (Cotto Morales 2001, 23). It is one that has known how to articulate and retain broad support from a coalition of efforts within Puerto Rican democratic civil society, including predominantly its religious, labor, and environmental sectors. It also has transcended the insular framework to project itself into the arena of international civil society. Few Puerto Rican social movements have achieved such an intense and a consistent level of public opinion's general acceptance for a prolonged period of time, as has the matter of Vieques during recent years.[1]

The social movement, in this case, represents a popular effort organized and directed to build a model of alternate social organization to what social life subject to the navy's restrictions represents in Vieques. It postulates goals such as demilitarization, return of the land, decontamination of natural resources, and creation of a model of alternative community development representing very important interests for all of the sectors in conflict (Touraine 1985). It also is a movement of strong symbolic content, because it confirms U.S. military presence as authoritarian and insensitive toward the population and its life conditions.[2] It is part of an increment of what has come to be called, over the last decade, "cultural Puerto Ricanism" (Rivera Ortiz 2001; Benítez Nazario 2001).

At the same time, the Vieques community building effort connects with various international initiatives to protect civil communities lacking protection from the abuses of the military.[3] It is a struggle for the human rights of a community that has seen its social life degraded in a significant way by military institutions insensitive to the consequences of its behavior. This is, precisely, a factor that has prompted broad support within the Latino and African-American communities in the United States.[4]

It is a social movement, in addition, tied to identity claims and which, in a certain way, it strives to recreate in its material as well as symbolic aspects, a sense of cultural belonging gravely affected by the presence of an invasive entity which, in a substantial way, altered communal life (Touraine 1985). This movement seeks a rupture with key elements of the prevailing social structure. In this chapter we scrutinize the different ways in which the Vieques pacifist struggles have had repercussions on the national and international civil society and some evident signs of the effectiveness of its political practices. We also present a brief historical background of the Vieques case, as well as some of the more salient human rights issues that this case raises.

The repression of this demilitarizing initiative has been strongly repressed by federal agencies and the Puerto Rican police. Such events are well documented. In the 1989 Report of the Civil Rights Commission (Comisión de Derechos Civiles 1989), as well as in previous investigations about the repressive work of federal agencies, it is related in detail that the Committee for the Rescue and Development of Vieques and other individuals and groups have been the target of surveillance files and repression (Gautier Mayoral and Blanco Stahl 1997). For years there have been undercover agents in anti-navy organizations actively and systematically dedicated to obstructing their exercise of basic freedoms of expression and association.[5] What is more, the federal court in San Juan has been used as an operative arm of repressive actions.[6]

The direct navy's participation in the persecution of the Vieques peace movement is well documented. Former senator and political analyst Marco Rigau has summarized well the situation: "By the end of the 70s, the fishermen and the people of Vieques, by 1978, blocked military maneuvers in Vieques. There were confrontations for several years. Some Navy officials began to develop an illegal campaign of terrorism, which included the famous bomb placed at the Bar Association in 1980 by Lieutenant Alex de la Zerda."[7]

In this particular case, nevertheless, as we show later, the intelligence forces were not fully able to accomplish their objectives of isolating the pro-peace forces and creating divisions between them. Thus the study of Vieques is significant as a case of vindicating human rights.[8] Additionally, it is necessary to underscore that some of the traditional practices of harassment, such as taking photographs and videotaping anti-navy activities, have taken place from 1999 to the present. Also, a disproportionate number of the Commonwealth's police officials is continuously supervising protesters' public activities in Vieques.

CIVIL SOCIETY

Without making a complex matter more difficult than it really is, it is indispensable to develop a definition, at least normative, of what we are calling "democratic civil society" (Rivera Ortiz 2001). It is, from our perspective, the space in which a citizen's effort breaks with key elements of traditional political participation. Its most promising and lasting signs are dialogue and deliberation as the principal mechanisms to generate agreement for common social action. We exclude from this definition groups within society whose conduct is directed toward promoting political, racial, or cultural intolerance. We are underscoring the need to revitalize civil society through a process of free and open deliberation.

Within the framework of democratic civil society, citizenship exhibits a relative autonomy from the state and traditional political parties and is oriented, above all in its beginnings, by its interest in calling attention to problems marginalized from the main current of public opinion. As we will see later, regular and active public political participation is stimulated in a democratic civil society framework.[9] As we argue here, we agree with Benítez Nazario in his insistence that the space of an autonomous civil society in Puerto Rico is limited and only emerging. But we disagree with the view presented by Nazario, that the Puerto Rican civil society is insipid, due precisely to its limited autonomy. As we explore the Vieques struggle in certain detail, we corroborate an important democratic civic contribution that elaborates political agendas with substantial independence from the state (Benítez Nazario 2001).

The space that constitutes democratic civil society continues to enjoy more pronounced international consequences influencing affairs previously reserved exclusively for the state and traditional political actors (Colón Morera 2001). Héctor Martínez reminds us that in the liberal tradition, the existence of a strong civil society is essential for the existence of an authentic democracy. Using Alexis de Tocqueville as a reference, Martínez explains that the existence of "free associations," similar in important aspects to that which today we call "civil society," promotes democracy in various ways: "First, for having been created in a voluntary way by groups of the society; second, by maintaining independence from the state; third, by fomenting pluralism in the bases of society, making possible the practice of principles of expression, cooperation, equality and freedom in the daily life of individuals; and fourth, serving as a brake on the expansive power of the state" (Martínez 1998, 251–78).

From another perspective, Gaztambide and Colón Morera (2002), students of the concept in the Caribbean context, offer the following on the importance of civil society:

> Since its contemporary coining by Antonio Gramsci, the concept of civil society is counter posed—somewhat ambiguously—to "political society." In his reformulation of the Greek concept of hegemony to explain the actualization of the dictatorship of the bourgeoisie in the democracy of masses, Gramsci coins the concept of political society to designate the space of

power—in and beyond the apparatus of the state—of the socioeconomic and sociopolitical elite. The groups and groupings excluded from this dissimulating and changing space of power, constitute, by way of exclusion, civil society. (Unpublished manuscript.)

Civil society, due to these various uses that emerge from dissimilar philosophical sources, generates confusion in its common use and in its application. Now is not the moment to specify its contours more precisely, but it is clear that the conduct of citizens in democratic civil society is one of relative autonomy from the state and the political class. From our perspective, it has to do principally with sectors subordinated in the social structure that must resort to a political practice based on deliberation and the broadest respect for diversity.

In the case of the democratic civil society we refer to here, this activation is not limited to realizing demands from national governments but rather from multinational or global organizations, as has been the case recently with the World Trade Organization. Regretfully, it is not this form of activation or citizen deliberation that characterizes a good part of Puerto Rico's political conduct. On the contrary, there exists an electoralist political culture.

AN ELECTORALIST POLITICAL CULTURE

In contemporary Puerto Rican political culture, political action is still associated principally with exercising the right to vote every four years (Colón Morera et al. 2000). This is contrary to the U.S. metropolis, and to a lesser extent to other advanced democracies, where nearly 50 percent of the electorate constantly absents itself from presidential elections. In the specific U.S. experience, in municipal elections, participation is even much lower, while in Puerto Rico, over 80 percent of the eligible population votes. While in the United States electoral apathy reigns, in Puerto Rico, on the other hand, we suffer from a certain electoralism, by which citizens associate politics only with voting.

Since the Commonwealth's creation in 1952, only two elections have reflected a percentage of electoral participation lower than 80 percent of eligible voters (Anderson 1998). This high percentage is motivated by the presence of political parties with broad mobilizing capacities.[10] It is important to note, however, that there has been a steady increase in the number of voters that choose among individual candidates and do not follow strict party line voting (Benítez Nazario 2001).

On the island, electoral politics is the main national "sport," and the government occupies a very important space in the creation of jobs and business opportunities.[11] A constant source of political activism is, after all, the very colonial condition of the island.[12] In very few countries in the world is the electorate asked, in a more or less direct way, every four years, if they want to be integrated into another nation or remain autonomous or independent communities. This is precisely the case seen here, where the discussion of the national collective political future is constant and intense.

It must be pointed out, on the other hand, that in the last decade a certain tendency toward reduction of electoral participation of approximately 6 percent has emerged. Such a phenomenon could be associated in part to a substantial increase in indictments and criminal convictions related to corruption cases linked to fraudulent schemes to finance electoral campaigns and for personal enrichment.[13] In the November 2000 general elections, for example, 1,934,278 voters went to the polls, but this number was about 30,000 less than those who voted in 1996, in spite of the fact that voter registration increased. That year, 82.7 percent of voters went to the polls. In 2000, the percent was lower, reaching only 81.7 percent. In the referendum held in Vieques in July 2001 to consult the Vieques electorate about their preferences with regard to the permanence of the navy, a high 80 percent of all eligible voters showed up.

Although the high level of electoral participation is a characteristic of a political culture that has positive elements, in that it reiterates a social interest continued by the peaceful resolution of high-intensity conflicts, such conduct is not free from contradictions and problems, the main one being that for broad sectors of the population, taking part in politics is equivalent to voting. Other possible more quotidian forms of exercising political pressure through citizen deliberation, activation of interest or affinity groups, carrying out lobbying and pickets, protests, and similar activities are underestimated or plainly excluded. An example of relative social inaction is the level of union organization on the island: approximately 10 percent, concentrated mostly in the public sector.

In some ways, parties still monopolize political activity and are protected by a series of privileges in the form of governmental subsidies that cost the public treasury about $20 million annually. It has been calculated that between 1998 and 1999, private donations and public financing of the three political parties that enjoy electoral enfranchisement on the island amounted to $100 million. For this reason, they often act as a wall of contention for independent candidates and newly emerging organizations that question the privileges of such principal groupings. It also explains the often tense, or, in the best of cases, peacefully coexistent, relationship between the political parties and organizations of civil society (Martínez 1998).

TOWARD A PUBLIC, REGULAR, AND ACTIVE PRACTICE: THE VIEQUES CASE

As Howard L. Reiter, student of the U.S. political system, has posited with much clarity, by fomenting exclusive dependence on the vote as a manner of political expression, the elites propitiate a type of participation that, in its essence, is private, intermittent, and passive (Reiter 1987). We agree with Reiter that collective actions with more transformative promise are those that, contrary to the foregoing, are regular, public, and active. This is, precisely, the ambit in which democratic civil society has achieved its major contributions. Fortunately, this dependence on the electoral vote as a principal political expression has begun a very slow but continuous transformation on the island.[14] The Vieques struggle exemplifies such a process. Let us begin with a brief background about it.

Vieques is an island located some 10 kilometers east of Puerto Rico, where the U.S. Navy has carried out military exercises since 1941, when it began to occupy the land through expropriation. Since the island of Puerto Rico (called "Borikén" by its original inhabitants) was colonized by Spain, there were rivalries about the geopolitical control of Vieques. The great European powers continuously argued over the sovereignty of Vieques but never successfully eliminated Spain's control or the gradual development of a Puerto Rican national sentiment among its inhabitants (see the chapter by Sued Badillo in this book). By way of the 1898 invasion and the signing of the Treaty of Paris, this small island came to be, as was the case with the rest of the Puerto Rican archipelago, a possession of the United States (Meléndez 1982).

Before the middle of the twentieth century, the navy occupied approximately two-thirds of Vieques and since then has carried out intense war-related exercises of various types, including amphibious landings, shooting practices, experimenting with new weapons and continuous bombings on specific designated ranges, and submarine activities. Taking part in war games is not limited to U.S. troops. In the past, other countries of the North Atlantic Treaty Organization (NATO) have been invited to use this Caribbean island as a center for training and experimentation in exchange for a rental fee.

The navy planned to continue carrying out military maneuvers for several more years, although President Bush had announced on June 14, 2001, in Gothenburg, Sweden, that the navy would leave Vieques by 2003. The promise made by President Bush, in the face of international public opinion, put the navy in a situation where its most realistic alternative was to find an alternative place to carry out its exercises in the immediate future.

The tragic September 11, 2001, terrorist events were used by some conservative sectors in the U.S. Congress as an excuse to retain the island and remain, using live ammunition there in the military exercises to prepare the troops.[15] The navy argued that military preparations in Vieques were essential in obtaining effective results in Afghanistan.[16] Some U.S. newspapers asked for the continuation of bombings in Vieques.[17] This pressure generated by the navy moved Congress in December 2001 to cancel the celebration of a referendum in Vieques and to question the May 2003 date as the one in which military exercises in Vieques would be finalized. Under new congressional legislation, the ending of military exercises in Vieques is in the hands of the secretary of the navy.

The Vieques peace movement strongly denounced the terrorist attacks against the United States but has also adamantly opposed any attempt to use the war against terrorism as an excuse to maintain Vieques under the oppressive conditions described here.

THE ECOLOGICAL IMPACT

The ecological impact of the war exercises and the effects on the totality of natural resources has been devastating. As a consequence, the population of Vieques suffers a high incidence of illnesses, dramatized by the fact that its residents have 40 percent more probability of dying than the rest of the Puerto Rican population. The 27 percent greater incidence of cancer attracts particular attention (Grupo de Apoyo Técnico y Profesional 2000).

Recent studies evidence a causal relationship between the navy's military activities and the unusual incidence of certain illnesses. An analysis of the hair of twenty-nine persons from Vieques, carried out by Dr. Carmen Colón de Jorge, revealed that many patients have concentrations above a standard deviation of the normal average of aluminum (90%), antimony (69%), cadmium (69%), arsenic (66%), tin (66%), lead (52%), molybdenum (48%), boron (48%), bismuth (41%), mercury (38%), vanadium (38%), manganese (31%), nickel (28%), zinc (21%), cobalt (14%), and barium (14%).

For example, the highest concentrations for some of these elements were from 57 percent above the norm for barium, 182 percent above for mercury, 553 percent above for cadmium, and up to 5,300 percent for antimony. Hair analysis of eighteen other patients in Vieques carried out by Dr. Carmen Ortiz Roque revealed that 44 percent have higher than normal levels of mercury, and some also have abnormal levels of lead, partially confirming Dr. Colón de Jorge's findings. Fecal analysis of seven individuals from Vieques, also carried out by Dr. Colón de Jorge, revealed elevated concentrations of aluminum, cadmium, mercury, and nickel and the presence of uranium, tungsten, thallium, platinum, copper, bismuth, beryllium, arsenic, antimony, and aluminum (Grupo de Apoyo Técnico y Profesional 2000).

Notable among other contaminants and weapons fired or utilized in Vieques by the U.S. armed forces are napalm, Agent Orange, chaff, and depleted uranium bullets.

POVERTY AND MARGINALIZATION

Not all has been direct physical contamination. The navy also implemented a deliberate policy directed toward conserving the "rural" character of this municipality so as not to act upon the training activities it was carrying out.[18] Thus the U.S. armed forces have invaded Vieques in practically every scope of its physical, political, economic, and social space. For example, since 1985, the women of Vieques have to give birth in a hospital leaving the island, as the health center there has no staff trained and certified to operate the birthing room; it only handles emergency cases. In those emergency cases that cannot be treated in Vieques, patients are transferred to Fajardo, a municipality in the eastern part of Puerto Rico. Medical facilities in Vieques are not adequate to treat chronic illnesses, so patients must be taken by sea to Fajardo to receive treatment, with all of the attendant inconveniences and risks.

Limitations on economic activities, imposed by the navy's presence, have generated poverty, marginalization, and poor educational opportunities. The Report of the Special Commission on Vieques, named by the governor of Puerto Rico (Comisión Especial de Vieques 1999), explains that the major impact of the navy, in addition to the environment, has been economic development's stagnation. The military presence has prevented the flourishing of economic activities, including the expansion of maritime and air transportation. As for the principal indicators of the socioeconomic condition of the people of Vieques, the following statistics stand out.[19]

In 1990, per capital income was $2,997, that is, $1,180 (28%) lower than that of Puerto Rico ($4,177). Average family income was $6,486, which compared to $9,988 for Puerto Rico, represents $3,502 less, or 35 percent less. According to the 1990 Population and Housing Census, 73.3 percent of the population was below poverty level, 14.4 percent above that for Puerto Rico.

Prices are 16 percent higher than in Puerto Rico. Vieques residents pay an additional 15 percent for food, 33 percent for construction materials, 22 percent for gasoline, and 4 percent for medicine. The scarce and reduced economic possibilities propel emigration, principally of youth, with their desire to find new economic horizons and jobs that do not exist there.

CITIZEN MOBILIZATION

For the past several decades, various Vieques community organizations, mainly the fishermen, for whom the military presence constitutes a direct obstacle to their subsistence, have demanded the military's elimination and the cessation of bombing that puts at risk the health and life of the civil population.

This has been a very hard, uphill effort. When after a great campaign of civil disobedience in the decade of the 1970s, Puerto Rico achieved the removal of the very same U.S. Navy from the adjacent island of Culebra, the military practices intensified in Vieques. For decades, the elimination of this new intense military activity was never placed as a public policy priority, nor was it an important issue in the domestic public opinion.

At the end of the 1970s and the beginning of the 1980s, pressure intensified to endorse full demilitarization, and solidarity from political sectors of
the island was augmented. In 1978, the fishermen launched out to sea in their
small boats to try to paralyze the maneuvers, while groups of activists set up
civil disobedience camps. Although the matter of Vieques did not receive pri-
mary attention during the electoral campaigns, the activism by the very people of Vieques made their cause somewhat visible.

In the context of the cold war, nevertheless, this attempt was labeled in
many circles as an anti-U.S. campaign. The conservative press at the time,
principally *El Mundo*, justified military abuses as a matter of national security.[20] The leadership of the two main political parties, fearful of creating tensions with their "American neighbor," ignored the question, or, in some cases,
it even tried to impede measures of progressive U.S. congressional representatives who were interested in the problem, as was the case with Representative Ronald Dellums.

Thus a pernicious cycle was established. After incidents of civil disobedience, the situation returned to "normality," with the signing of supposed
accords with the navy for the development of Vieques. Eventually such
"understandings" were then totally ignored, such as the 1983 memorandum
between the navy and the government of Puerto Rico. In this agreement, the
navy committed to actively seek and stimulate the establishment of civil
industries in Vieques. It also provided for joint efforts between agencies of the
government of Puerto Rico and civil groups in search of economic resources,
basic funds, and financial assistance from other departments of the U.S. federal government and committed to achieve full employment on the island
(Grupo de Apoyo Técnico y Profesional 2000).

In any event, resistance in Vieques at the end of the 1970s led to the
arrest of people from Vieques and militant *independentistas* who served jail
sentences for defying injunctions and federal laws. Among them was Angel
Rodríguez Cristóbal, who wound up dead in a federal prison under very suspicious circumstances.[21] At the time, the demilitarizing effort was conceived
as one essentially *independentista*, although organizations such as the
Caribbean Project for Justice and Peace, among others, generated and continue to this day to urge full support for peace among religious sectors within
and outside of Puerto Rico. In that period, the main political parties totally
relegated the issue of Vieques to the back burner.

CIVIL DISOBEDIENCE BREAKS OUT

But all of this was to change drastically. On April 19, 1999, David Sanes, a
resident of Vieques who paid his bills by working as a security guard, died as
a result of a bomb erroneously dropped by a U.S. Navy plane. The accident
occurred while carrying out target practice related to a military campaign by

the United States and various member countries of NATO in Kosovo.[22] This death unleashed a wave of protests, initiating a new, massive, and historical stage of civil disobedience against military activities and the very presence of those armed forces.

One of the ways in which civil disobedience was expressed was through the establishment of permanent camps within the navy's bombing ranges. For almost a year, thirteen camps and hundreds of people challenged federal authority and impeded, with peaceful methods, the military practices of thirty warships, including aircraft carriers and submarines with over 30,000 soldiers and military men. After the massive removal of the camps, carried out by federal marshals and the navy itself in May 2000, acts of civil disobedience have continued and intensified each time the federal government announces its intention to renew bombing. In May 2001, *independentista* leader Rubén Berríos Martínez and the mayor of Vieques, Dámaso Serrano, were arrested. Berríos was given a sentence of four months in jail for these acts.

Between 1999 and 2001, the Vieques community struggle changed in intensity and magnitude, acquiring prominence as a central issue, with coverage by U.S. and international media. Over 1,250 people were arrested for acts of civil disobedience during this period.

CONVERGENCE

The tragic death of David Sanes was a catalyst that provoked what had never before been achieved: a general agreement in favor of the navy's ouster and the adoption of a public policy by the government of Puerto Rico. This new policy "Demand(s) the permanent and immediate cessation and desisting of all Navy military activity in Vieques."[23] In the movement, old and new Vieques leaders converge. Some, like Carlos Zenón and Ismael Guadalupe, are veterans and experienced leaders with several decades of activism. New leaders of the same community united with them, including fisherman Carlos Ventura and environmentalist and historian Robert Rabin. Rabin and Guadalupe are the spokespeople for the Committee for the Rescue and Development of Vieques.

Some of these leaders follow the lines of the fishermen, but new sectors are added to their efforts, such as professors, youth of all ages, women—organized in the Vieques Women's Alliance—professionals, and businesspeople, also directly affected by the problem. This formed the basis for initiating a citizen dialogue in Vieques about strategies to oust the navy in the shortest time possible and to elaborate public policies for the fullest socioeconomic development of said island municipality.

In its new stage, the anti-military effort reflected new levels of broad appeal. The traditional divisions among political parties regarding Puerto Rico's political future were not hidden but took a backseat to the common objective: demilitarizing Vieques in the shortest time possible. This militancy has stayed firm, even after the government of Puerto Rico acceded to the bombing's continuation.[24]

In the process, something else also occurred: a unity of purpose among the hierarchies and the bases of the churches of virtually every denomination. This religious solidarity involved various churches setting up camps of civil disobedience within the restricted zones in 1999, under the assumption that they were fulfilling and following guidelines of "evangelical obedience."[25] For example, when the massive removal of pacifist demonstrators took place in May 2000, eighteen Catholic priests were among those arrested. Seldom has such a process of common action between parishioners of Catholic and Evangelical denominations been seen.

Something similar happened with labor support at the beginning of civil disobedience in Vieques. The Teachers' Federation and the Puerto Rican Workers Central (CPT), for example, set up their own civil disobedience camps. As previously stated, this concurrence led to the creation of a commission named by the governor in 1999, which included the three political parties and some civil society presence.

Within the principal political parties, endorsement to the peace process also was unprecedented. In the PDP, a working team was created in the city of Carolina, led by its mayor, José Aponte, who traveled frequently to Vieques to collaborate with health clinics and other programs. This autonomist sector of the PDP, in addition, participated in the civil disobedience initiatives, with several people being arrested the day the removal took place and then serving prison terms at the Federal Detention Center.

Meanwhile, in the governing NPP, its vice president, Norma Burgos, clearly expressed herself in favor of the navy's immediate departure. She raised substantial support for her position within her party. The case of Senator Burgos is especially consequential, given that this senator from the NPP went into the restricted zones in 1999 and then again in 2001.[26] Her civil and constitutional rights were seriously violated, and she testified about these violations before the U.S. Congress.[27] In spite of the fact that Senator Burgos's active participation has generated strong collisions within the political party to which she belongs, public opinion supporting her appears unchanged. Although very inconsistently, the NPP continued to officially support the end of military practices in Vieques by 2003.

The Puerto Rican Independence Party, for its part, had a notable participation in the anti-navy measures, in that it erected one of the first camps of civil disobedience. Its camp was active for over a year, with the continuous presence of its president, Rubén Berríos Martínez. In 2001, Berríos served a four-month jail sentence for going back, for the third time, to the bombing range. As of the summer of 2001, more than 150 members of this party had been jailed for taking part in various acts of civil disobedience.

But most importantly, in spite of heavy partisan activism, none of the three parties was able to claim exclusively or unilaterally the anti-military demands. The parties were present, an integral part of the process, and the opinions of their leaders were heard with attention, but they did not control it. This was due principally to the fact that the diversity of the forces in motion was so varied, that such party control was impossible. In addition, a short time before, Puerto Rico had lived through an intense process of social struggle known as "the people's strike," as a result of the decision of the annexationist government to sell the telephone company (which had been public property up until then). The strike, initiated by union organizations, evoked the sympathy and support of the broadest sectors of Puerto Rican society, transcending the political parties, although its end result was not very encouraging. This labor dispute partially anticipated what was to occur shortly afterward in Vieques. Another more successful experience of civil society taking place at the time was the broad campaign to liberate pro-independence political prisoners.[28]

NPP GOVERNMENT CHANGES PATH,
BUT THE CONVERGENCE STRENGTHENS

The year 2000 was decisive for the future of Vieques. January began with the unfortunate news that the government of Puerto Rico had retracted its policy of "not one more bomb." Then-Governor Pedro Rosselló opted to abide by the directives of then-President Bill Clinton, which cleared the way for renewed bombing until a referendum could be held in the following years concerning the future of Vieques. The Puerto Rico government's commitment to the directives and the subsequent congressional legislation created the conditions for the removal of dozens of "human shields" on May 4, including the president and vice president of the Independence Party, whose camp had been established one year earlier.

At the same time, it must be recognized, Clinton's accord with the government of Puerto Rico infuriated sectors identified with the navy in the U.S. Congress. In their view, this created a precedent where a civil community could, through voting, alter decisions concerning the national security of the United States. This contradiction became decisive in President Bush's decision of June 2001, recommending the cancellation of the congressional referendum of November 2001 and suggesting unilaterally the cessation of navy military exercises by 2003.[29] Navy spokespeople have admitted that there is too much hostility in Vieques toward the navy's presence, and that the acts of civil disobedience have impeded them from carrying out their exercises effectively.

Once the government of Puerto Rico changed its position and abandoned the understanding achieved during almost one year, some sectors in the leadership of the two principal parties (the NPP and the PDP) were very tentative in their support for the campaign of civil disobedience.[30] There was fear in Vieques that this step would fragment the fragile convergence through a confrontation between the annexationist government and part of the *independentista* leadership, which was at that moment carrying out acts of civil disobedience. Nevertheless, this did not happen, due principally to the call made by the religious sector to continue practicing civil disobedience to interrupt the new scheduled military trainings. In February, this religious leadership, in an ecumenical fashion, convened a huge march demanding peace.[31] The Spanish press described the activity as follows:

> Some 50,000 people came yesterday to the march convened by religious leaders to demand the end of U.S. military practices. . . . A gigantic banner with the message "Peace for Vieques, not one more shot" was carried by Catholic bishops Roberto González and Alvaro Corrada, Episcopal bishop David Alvarez, reverend Wilfredo Estrada of the Biblical Society, reverend Eunice Santana of the Council of Churches, and Francisco Sosa of the Lutheran Church. (EFE News Agency, February 22, 2000)

ELECTIONS OF NOVEMBER 2000 HAVE THEIR IMPACT ON VIEQUES

In the elections of November 2000, 66 percent of the electorate in Vieques endorsed the governmental candidates who rejected the presidential directives and demanded the navy's immediate departure. The new governor of Puerto Rico, Sila María Calderón, committed herself to take steps to alter the presidential directives signed by President Clinton, which authorized the continued use of Vieques for military maneuvers.

The governor also promised to carry out an electoral consultation in Vieques regarding military presence in its territory. This issue was a central one in the electoral campaign and decisive in the victory of Calderón, who won by a comfortable margin of 56,000 votes.

After initiating her mandate, the governor filed a lawsuit in federal court alleging irreparable environmental damage to the Vieques community.[32] In addition, according to her electoral campaign promises, her administration sponsored a vote in Vieques regarding this matter.[33] In its efforts, Puerto Rico has managed to place editorials in important media in the United States, such as the *New York Times* and the *Christian Science Monitor*, favoring the end of military maneuvers.[34] The U.S. secretary of defense is on record saying that the navy should find a substitute for Vieques by 2003, although in the U.S. Congress, opposition to abandoning Vieques still exists.[35]

VIEQUES CIVIL SOCIETY PREPARES ITSELF
FOR A VIEQUES WITHOUT THE NAVY

One of the aspects that have stood out in this endeavor has been the support of an interdisciplinary group of professionals who came together to form the Technical and Professional Vieques Support Group. This initiative responded to calls from community leaders of Vieques interested in receiving advice and assistance in designing the future development of this island municipality. The possibility of finally achieving the return of the lands occupied by the navy presented itself as a probability. Thus the way to manage the Vieques territory, wisely planned, became an imperative. This would allow Viequenses to anticipate a better enjoyment of their natural geography and to arrange for their own criteria when faced with land use proposals that could not be in their best interests.

Additionally, there was an urgency to elaborate a process leading to avoiding practices such as land speculation, which in the past had provoked serious problems for other communities, as was the case on the island of Culebra when the navy was forced to leave. The serious result of bad urban planning, as was the experience in the metropolitan areas of Puerto Rico, was another mistake to avoid.

The participants in this initiative have been sharing with the citizens of Vieques to prepare themselves and constructively collaborate on the development of its demilitarized future. This group includes urban planners, economists, and environmentalists, among others. The initiative proposes, for example, the creation of ecological tourism, land conservation, and the demand for decontamination of the land used for decades for military exercises. Also, the struggle for demilitarization would be of limited use if it did not articulate a plan for sustainable development, so that Vieques not be converted into a platform for a massive and highly contaminating massive tourist model that then marginalizes residents of Vieques in their own land. That would only be substituting one form of social exclusion for another.

Communal activation has begun to bear fruit. When functionaries of the central government held public hearings to discuss the "Plan for the City's Land Management," Vieques residents who attended questioned said plan. The proposal assumed a permanent military presence, but citizens demanded to completely discard this scenario. At the hearings, the people of Vieques "bombarded" officials with questions and criticisms that totally changed the tone, dynamic, and content of the hearings. What could have been limited to a routine and pro forma exercise—as is usual in Puerto Rico—became an exercise in real democracy. Viequenses were, finally, recovering their sense of belonging, their expectation that the government would respond to their interests.

Based on the community's recommendations, the Commonwealth's planning board redefined the land plan, and the last version contemplates no military presence. "The will of the people of Vieques has been fully expressed, and it is that the Navy must leave. As a result of this reality, the plan we will prepare is based on a scenario that the Navy will not be there," said the president of the planning board, José Caballero, to a group of surprised Vieques leaders.[36]

AN EFFORT OF INTERNATIONAL SCALE

This pro-human rights effort in Vieques also has shown a new facet of the struggle of the Puerto Rican democratic civil society, becoming effectively internationalized. A publication of the Comité Pro Rescate y Desarrollo de Vieques (CPRDV) explained this dynamic in the following terms: "The CPRDV shares information and strategies with community organizations in Hawaii, Okinawa, Korea, the Republic of the Philippines, and in the United States affected by military contamination and repression by the U.S. armed forces."[37]

In the United States, efforts have broadened to the point that this committee has participated in multiple conferences and activities to denounce the environmental consequences of the problem. Thus, for example, it managed to make this "the principal topic of an international conference on military contamination," which took place in San Diego, California. Representatives of communities in Japan and Puerto Rico and various U.S. states, including Colorado, New Mexico, Texas, Montana, California, Mississippi, Massachusetts, and Alaska, shared their experiences of struggle against the environmental and health effects from a variety of forms of military contamination: radiation from nuclear aircraft carriers, contamination from military shipyards, problems associated with military exercises, and the warehousing and manufacturing of weapons, among other activities. Respiratory illnesses and high levels of cancer and infant mortality—the same as in Vieques—are present in various sites affected by military contamination.[38]

In the United States, the solidarity with Vieques has been especially relevant in New York, where more than 1 million Puerto Ricans reside. There, Adolfo Carrión Jr. (New York City Council member), Roberto Ramírez (president of the Democratic Party of the Bronx), and José Rivera (state assemblyman) were incarcerated for thirty-seven days.[39] Union leader Dennis Rivera was not left out, also imprisoned as a consequence of his challenging military bombings. Later, Adam Clayton Powell Jr. also was imprisoned for the same reasons.[40]

But this activation has not been limited to Puerto Ricans. A healthy number of individuals and domestic organizations, among them African-American leader Al Sharpton and Jacqueline Jackson, stand out, having also served jail time as a result of their participation in acts of civil disobedience.[41] Environmental leader Robert Kennedy also was an important effort of American solidarity with Puerto Ricans. Kennedy filed a lawsuit in federal courts

challenging the environmental consequences of the navy in Vieques. Frus-
trated with the lack of interest of the federal courts on these important environmental issues, he also was involved in civil disobedience, along with actor
Edward James Olmos.

There is no doubt that the activation of the Puerto Rican community in
the United States has been key to inducing a broad network of support in the
United States and at the international level. Of particular importance is the
enormous potential embodied by the strengthening of relations between the
African-American and Puerto Rican communities in their common struggles.

There also has been a global scale to the efforts developed here. Because
of the Internet, this demand has acquired a dimension that is new to Puerto
Rican progressive social movements on the island. The CPRDV has won
well-deserved international recognition for its efforts. Web sites such as
http://ViequesLibre.com, http://RedBetances.com, and http://CIPDC.org
maintain a constant flow of information accessed from various parts of the
world. This civic effort has been so effective that the navy has been obliged
to create its own "site" on the Internet to promote its case, which has
received considerable attention in the U.S. press.[42] There also have been
many activities on U.S. university campuses regarding the political and social
impact of the case of Vieques.

In the United States, the support lent by Puerto Rican congressional representatives has been decisive.[43] Political support in the United States has
transcended the Puerto Rican and Democratic Party constituency. The governor of New York, George E. Pataki, and the mayor of New York City, Mike
Bloomberg, both Republicans, favored demilitarization, as did the two sena-
tors elected by New York to the U.S. Congress.[44] Various congressional representatives have demonstrated against penalizing Puerto Ricans for their
iron-willed, pro-peace posture.

Delegations of people from Vieques and human rights advocates also
have traveled to Japan and South Korea to international conferences connected to the harmful effects that military bases have on civilian populations.
A delegation also was present during activities of the Japanese Association of
Solidarity with Asia, Africa, and America. The Millennium Forum, which
took place in New York in May 1999, also condemned the effects of excessive militarization on civilian communities. Regretfully, however, these international steps are still unknown to broad sectors of the population in Puerto
Rico as well as in the Caribbean.

In the United States, various strong Latino and African-American organizations such as the League of United Latin American Citizens (LULAC),
the National Association for the Advancement of Colored People
(NAACP), and the Rainbow PUSH Coalition have passed resolutions and
carried out activities in support of demilitarization. Other groups, such as
some Evangelical churches of the United States, also camped out in Vieques

during 1999 and participated in acts of civil disobedience and solidarity. Particularly significant in this sense has been the work to mobilize public opinion within the United States in places where there is a broad Latino and Puerto Rican presence, as in New York City and Chicago. The Committee for the Rescue and Development of Vieques has a permanent representative in Washington who coordinates legal aspects and solidarity from there. In addition, various acts of civil disobedience have been carried out within the United States.

In the United States there also has been a strong level of support from the labor movement. Organizations such as the American Federation of Labor have shown their solidarity.[45] However, this has not impeded U.S. congressional leaders from making statements threatening the Puerto Rican population with cuts in programs and federal economic benefits if the navy is not permitted to train in Vieques.[46]

In June 2001, the United Nations Decolonization Committee reaffirmed its commitment to the full demilitarization of Vieques. The resolution states in pertinent part "to order the immediate halt of its armed forces' military drills and maneuvers on Vieques Island." It calls for the United States to "return the occupied land to the people of Puerto Rico, halt the persecution, incarcerations, arrests, and harassment of peaceful demonstrators, immediately release all persons incarcerated in this connection . . . and decontaminate the impact areas" in the Vieques bombing range.[47]

CONCLUSION

When federal authorities made massive arrests on May 4, 2000, there were those who thought that the current controversy would enter another stage of paralysis. But that has not been the case. The strong message that 68 percent of voters sent in July 2001, asking the navy to stop military maneuvers immediately, is a sign of such strength and determination.

The key appears to be the existence of a civil society for whom "peace for Vieques" is much more than a passing electoral slogan. The citizens' deliberation has put the issue on another level: that of a conscious commitment and solidarity among citizens. It may not seem like a big deal, but in this case, it has made all the difference in the world. The social and political impact of democratic civil society on the struggle for peace in Vieques has been profound and its potential impact far reaching.

Vieques was the principal issue in the 2000 electoral campaign, and the way in which the parties and candidates defined themselves with respect to the navy's departure from the island determined, to a great extent, how the electorate voted.

What is certain is that Vieques is a metaphor for Puerto Rico, mainly because there are many potential Viequenses that exist on the island. Some communities face serious problems of school dropout, racism, unemployment, marginalization, and environmental pollution, and they have not been able to effectively impact the government, the internal political class, or the metropolis. For them, it would be crucial, although by no means easy, to broaden the network of deliberation and action of the democratic civil society to a national, a regional, or an international scale. In this way they could create what some have called "a major social project." The social forces that have generated the struggle against the navy have the potential to provoke a departure in the trends that have characterized up to recent years the political and social conflicts in Puerto Rico.

Never before has a topic with such strong political and ideological repercussions, as in effect Vieques is, generated so much social mobilization. Vieques has become a broad avenue in which the Puerto Rican people begin to understand the strength and power generated by unity and consensus.

Vieques, at the same time, has been a real and concrete experience of articulation and organization of something that is a natural characteristic of society: diversity. It is extremely difficult, and requires a great deal of flexibility, to have all of these "shades" converge into a common social "tapestry." It requires, particularly, a clear understanding of the essential problem posed by a particular social conflict. Historically, one of the deficiencies that political parties have shown is their enormous difficulty to manage and benefit from diversity, including its ideological, gender, and racial manifestations. On this limitation, the democratic civil society's acts demonstrate the shortcomings of the political class. On the other hand, this civil society approach illuminates the need to look for new methods and organizational settings.

It also is extremely important to stress the effectiveness of civil disobedience as an instrument when faced with the clash between two forces, one of which monopolizes the power and the violence with insurmountable military technology. The strength of civil disobedience lies in forcing the adversary, in this instance the navy, a fight in a sphere of action in which it is incapable of winning, since it is totally unprepared for it.

We could say that in Vieques we have seen an equation that combines six factors: (1) clarity of the political goal; (2) unity of purpose; (3) diversity; (4) massiveness and constant support of public opinion; (5) civil disobedience; and (6) internationalization of the claim. These factors, among others already mentioned, have reach ebullition with so much energy that it has mobilized the Puerto Rican diaspora. This, in turn, has added an ingredient that will transcend the particular Vieques issue. Specifically, that the impact of the emerging alliance between Puerto Ricans, Latinos, and African Americans that has resulted from the anti-navy struggle cannot be underestimated. Everything points to the fact that this is one of the most important factors considered by President Bush in Sweden in June 2001, when he announced the withdrawal of the navy in 2003.

At the same time, Vieques has crudely underscored the national conflict that derives from the colonial condition of Puerto Rico, to the extent that Puerto Ricans have joined forces against an institution that has determined, to a large extent, such political relation. The arrogance shown by the navy also has reminded every one of that colonial legacy. The contradiction between nation and metropolis has become more acute.

Vieques has become the scenario in which the power displayed by the metropolis has shown its face as it really is, without native intermediaries diluting its true content. That explains why the political sector that has been more damaged by this conflict has been the one that advances the notion that Puerto Ricans should be continually servile to U.S. government mandates. These ultraconservative sectors have suffered for supporting the Vieques bombing during this crucial period. They are becoming a disarticulated sector that espouses irrational anti-Puerto Rican slogans. It would not be an overstatement to conclude that Vieques has transformed Puerto Rican society and has opened a new window that could facilitate new political scenarios. But the process of changing the electoralist political culture will take time, patience, and a constant civic praxis of social mobilization.

NOTES

1. All of the polls carried out, in Vieques as well as in the rest of Puerto Rico, reflect overwhelming support for the demand that the navy end its military exercises in Vieques. The Catholic Church conducted an opinion poll about this issue, as did the newspaper *El Nuevo Día*, revealing similar results. A high 73 percent of those interviewed had demonstrated against the navy remaining in Vieques. See García Muñiz and Rodríguez Beruff (1999, 106).

2. It is fully justified if we consider the intensity of the military use of Vieques, even when compared to the use of other U.S. training bases in their own territory and abroad. See Giusti Cordero (1999).

3. This preoccupation with the luck of civil communities such as Vieques was well expressed in the Millennium Forum held in New York City in 1999. The declaration signed by hundreds of nongovernmental organizations from all over the world expressed the following:

A much neglected area of human rights violations relates to the activities of the military, not only in situations of conflict, but also in their day to day activities in military bases, training installations, and testing facilities. Prostitution, corruption, and exploitation is often rampant around military bases. Training and testing activities leave killing legacies of depleted uranium and unexploded shells. Degradation of the environment results in destruction of livelihoods. Noise, air, and water pollution disrupt normal schooling activities. Cancer rates in local communities [are] abnormally high. Yet a culture of impunity prevails, justified in the name of defense and national security.

4. Arian Campo-Flores and Michael Isikoff, "On Vieques, No Hispanic Is an Island," *Newsweek* (June 25, 2001): 32–33.

5. See Robert Rabin, *"En Vieques la lucha continua,"* *Claridad*, November 12–18, 1993, p. 8.

6. See, for example, Luis A. Cabán, *"Pescadores de Vieques desacatarán interdicto hasta provocar arrestos,"* *El Mundo*, January 24, 1979, p. 3A.

7. An elaboration of this operative and its consequences can be found in Pérez Viera (2000). For a description of the incidents, see Nilda Rodríguez, *"Pescadores interrumpen maniobras de la Marina en Vieques,"* *El Mundo*, May 18, 1979, p. 3.

8. It should be noted here that the American Association of Jurists, with the support of the Bar Association of Puerto Rico and the Puerto Rican Institute of Foreign Relations, filed a complaint with the Human Rights Commission of the United Nations. Attorney Fermín Arraiza presented the case.

9. See the works of Angel Israel Rivera (1996, 2001), student of the issue in the context of Puerto Rico.

10. This is not the place to stop and consider the many factors that explain this high electoral participation. Suffice it to say that the government of Puerto Rico distributes funds for social programs, for which about 60 percent of the population qualifies. For a more detailed, exhaustive analysis, see Anderson (1998).

11. About 27 percent of the workforce of the country is employed by the government.

12. For a background of the political situation, one can consult Fernández (1992) and Trías Monge (1997). For those interested, there are Spanish versions in both books (Fernández 1995; Trías Monge 1999).

13. In 1999, the island was shocked when governmental functionaries and large political contributors were convicted of defrauding $2.2 million from a not-for-profit institution for the treatment of acquired immunodeficiency syndrome (AIDS) patients. The funds of said institute were regularly rerouted to finance political activities, principally those of the New Progressive Party. See EFE News Agency, *"Culpables todos los acusados por fraude al Instituto del SIDA,"* *El Nuevo Día*, June 14, 1999, p. 36.

14. The Puerto Rican community in the U.S. diaspora, interestingly, seems to be following a different process, in which electoral participation of the 3.4 million Puerto Ricans residing in that country is on the increase, without diminishing activities at the margin of the electoral sphere. Currently there are three Puerto Rican congressional representatives in the U.S. Congress, José Serrano (D-NY), Nydia Velázquez (D-NY), and Luis Gutiérrez (D-Ill), who have effectively collaborated in the process that is now leading to the navy's leaving Vieques. The three have participated in acts of civil disobedience in Vieques and in Washington, and Representative Gutiérrez was incarcerated by federal authorities for interrupting military exercises in April 2001, upon arrest suffering serious violations of his civil rights. Nilka Estrada Resto, *"Luis Gutiérrez pedirá pesquisa congresional,"* *El Nuevo Día*, May 2, 2001, http://www.endi.com (accessed May 3, 2001).

15. Editorial, *"Via Vieques,"* New York Post, November 28, 2001, p. 34.

16. See Richard Sisk, "Marines Honed for Battle on Vieques Range," *New York Daily News*, November 29, 2001, p. 5.

17. Editorial, *"Via Vieques,"* New York Post, November 28, 2001, p. 34.

18. See Benjamín Torres Gotay, *"Conviene el subdesarrollo,"* El Nuevo Día, May 10, 1999, p. 12, citing an internal navy document which states: "Whatever kind of economic development can be fomented in Vieques should not lose sight of the fact that the only thing compatible with Navy activities here—practices with live bombs and munitions—is that the island not lose its 'rural' character. In this document, the Navy says that the population of Vieques should never exceed 10,000, that it has some 9,400 now, and then had 6,000."

19. Mireya Navarro, "Uproar Against Navy War Games Unites Puerto Ricans," *New York Times*, July 10, 1999, p. 8.

20. See, for example, *"Impropia actitud en Vieques,"* El Mundo, May 17, 1979, p. 29.

21. Rafael Anglada López, *"Asesinato rodeado de interrogantes,"* Claridad, November 16–22, 1979, pp. 2–3.

22. Associated Press, "Civilian Killed in U.S. Navy Exercise," *Los Angeles Times*, April 21, 1999, p. 12.

23. For the Puerto Rican government's official position on this matter, see *Informe de la Comisión Especial de Vieques para Estudiar la Situación Existente en la Isla Municipio con Relación a las Actividades de la Marina de Estados Unidos*, June 7, 1999. On the unity of purpose achieved with respect to Vieques, see the Associated Press article, "Politicians Demand Navy Stop Bombing Puerto Rican Island," April 21, 1999.

24. For an excellent description of the dynamic of struggle in the Vieques process, see John Marino, "Emboldened Protesters Digging in on Vieques Civilians Control Gate, Decry Clinton Decision," *Washington Post*, December 9, 1999, p. A03.

25. The Evangelical Council of Puerto Rico was one of the religious institutions that endorsed civil disobedience in Vieques.

26. Luis Penchi, *"Defiende Vizcarrondo a Burgos,"* El Nuevo Día, December 28, 1999.

27. See Leonor Mulero, *"Desgarradores testimonios contra el Navy,"* El Nuevo Día, June 6, 2001, p. 14. The Puerto Rican House of Representatives decided to begin its own investigation into these events. See Magdalys Rodríguez, *"A sondear la violación de los derechos civiles,"* El Nuevo Día, May 8, 2001, p. 32. A New York Times columnist editorialized against the navy's abuses. See Bob Herbert, "Treated like Trash," *New York Times*, June 14, 2001, p. 33.

28. See John M. Broder, "12 Puerto Ricans in Prison Accept Offer of Clemency," *New York Times*, September 8, 1999, p. 1A.

29. David E. Sanger and Christopher Marquis, "U.S. Said to Plan Halt to Exercises in Vieques," *New York Times*, June 14, 2001, p. 1A.

30. In the PDP important sectors support civil disobedience. The NPP, at one point, recognized the utility of civil disobedience as a last resort. See EFE News Agency, *"Apoya el PNP la desobediencia civil,"* October 18, 1999. The report states: "The Directorate of the New Progressive Party (NPP) agreed today to support civil disobedience as a last recourse to stop the U.S. Navy's exercises with live munitions on the island municipality of Vieques."

31. In its February 22, 2000 edition, *El País Digital* reported as a news headline that *"Puerto Rico se moviliza contra EEUU"* ["Puerto Rico Mobilizes against the U.S."].

32. David Stout, "Judge Refuses to Block Bombing on Puerto Rican Island," *New York Times*, April 27, 2001, p. 10A.

33. Associated Press, "Puerto Rico Sues Navy Over Bombing," April 24, 2001.

34. See the editorials, "Untimely Exercises on Vieques," *New York Times*, April 28, 2001, p. 14, and "The Navy Should Ship Out," *Christian Science Monitor*, June 11, 1999, p. 10.

35. Mulero, Leonor, *"Rumsfeld se compromete a buscar otro lugar para las prácticas,"* *El Nuevo Día*, June 22, 2001, p. 22.

36. See Benjamín Torres Gotay, *"No cuenta con la Marina el plan territorial viequense,"* *El Nuevo Día*, September 15, 2000, p. 8.

37. Press Release, Committee for the Rescue and Development of Vieques, October 10, 2000.

38. Press Release, Committee for the Rescue and Development of Vieques, November 15, 2000.

39. Andy Newman, "Three Vieques Protesters Emerge from Prison," *New York Times*, June 30, 2001, p. 1B.

40. Juanita Colombani, *"Preso por desobediencia Adam Clayton Powell,"* *El Nuevo Día*, June 30, 2001, p. 22.

41. Nilka Estrada Resto, *"En 'el hoyo' Jackson por negarse a un registro,"* *El Nuevo Día*, June 22, 2001, p. 26.

42. See, for example: Paul Richter, "Battle over Bombing Range in Puerto Rico Spreads to Campaign," *Los Angeles Times*, September 21, 1999, p. 14; Michael Remez, "Clinton's Offer Bought Time, But Not a Solution," *Hartford Courant*, December 8, 1999. As for the way in which the U.S. press is treating the environmental problem, see, for example, Juan Tamayo, "Puerto Rican Islanders Sue Navy over Its Bombing Range, Cancer Rate Is Claimed To Be Military's Fault," *Miami Herald*, December 12, 1999, p. 3A; Christopher M. Lehman, "Selling Out Vieques," *Washington Times*, December 17, 1999, p. 19A. For an editorial opinion favorable to the Vieques cause on the part of people in the United States, see Mary McGregory, "The Navy Way on Vieques," *Washington Post*, April 26, 2001, p. 3A.

43. See note 14.

44. Pataki has criticized some of his colleagues in the Republican Party who have repudiated the Vieques struggle in racist terms. See Leonor Mulero, *"Pataki critica el odio racial de James Hansen,"* *El Nuevo Día*, June 20, 2001, p. 22.

45. See *People's Weekly World*, "AFL-CIO Opposes U.S. Navy in Vieques," October 20, 1999, http://www.pww.org/past-weeks-1999/U.S.%20Navy%20in%20Vieques. htm (accessed December 26, 2001). The paper reports: "Nothing better illustrates the progressive changes in the direction of the labor movement than the passage of a resolution against the U.S. Navy's bombing of the Vieques Island in Puerto Rico by last week's AFL-CIO convention."

46. Leonor Mulero, *"Amenaza Lott con afectar a la isla,"* *El Nuevo Día*, October 30, 1999, p. 8.

47. Edith Lederer, "U.N. Approves Vieques Resolution," Associated Press, June 22, 2001.

WORKS CITED

Anderson, Robert W. 1998. *"Las elecciones y política."* Pp. 13–58 in *Política Electoral en Puerto Rico*, ed. Robert W. Anderson. Río Piedras, Puerto Rico: Editorial Plaza Mayor.

Benítez Nazario, Jorge. 2001. *Reflexiones en torno a la cultura política de los puertorriqueños*. San Juan: Instituto de Cultura Puertorriqueña.

Berríos Martínez, Rubén. 1999. "Bombs Away from Puerto Rico." *Washington Post*, November 1, p. A27.

Colón Morera, José Javier. 2001. *"La sociedad civil internacional: Los hechos y las palabras."* *Diálogo* (January): 21.

Colón Morera, José Javier, Ángel Israel Rivera Ortíz, Marielis Rivera, and Jorge Benítez Nazario. 2000. *El proceso electoral de Puerto Rico*. San Juan: Editorial Santillana.

Comisión de Derechos Civiles (CDC). 1989. *Informe sobre discrimen y persecución por razones políticas: La práctica gubernamental de mantener listas, ficheros y expedientes de ciudadanos por razón de su ideología política*, 1989-CDC-028. San Juan: CDC.

Comisión Especial de Vieques. 1999. *Informe de la Comisión Especial de Vieques para Estudiar la Situación Existente en la Isla Municipio con Relación a las Actividades de la Marina de Estados Unidos*, June 7, 1999.

Coss, Luis F. 1996. *La nación en la orilla: Respuesta a los posmodernos pesimistas*. San Juan: Editorial Punto de Encuentro.

Cotto Morales, Liliana. 2001. *"Paz para Vieques: Identidad colectiva de proyecto."* *Diálogo* (May): 23.

Fernández, Ronald. 1992. *The Disenchanted Island: Puerto Rico and the United States in the Twentieth Century*. New York: Praeger.

———. 1996. *La Isla Desencantada*. San Juan: Editorial Cultural.

García Muñiz, Humberto, and Jorge Rodríguez Beruff, eds. 1999. *Fronteras en conflicto: Guerra contra las drogas, militarización y democracia en el Caribe, Puerto Rico y Vieques*. San Juan: Red Caribeña de Geopolítica.

Gautier Mayoral, Carmen, and Teresa Blanco Stahl. 1997 [1979]. "COINTELPRO en Puerto Rico. Documentos secretos del FBI, 1960–1971." Pp. 255–97 in *Las carpetas: Persecución política y derechos civiles en Puerto Rico (ensayos y documentos)*, eds. Ramón Bosque-Pérez and José Javier Colón Morera. Río Piedras, Puerto Rico: Centro para la Investigación y Promoción de los Derechos Civiles (CIPDC).

Gaztambide, Antonio, and José Javier Colón Morera. 2002. *Sociedad civil internacional en el Caribe, Apuntes sobre una investigación en curso, en Sociedad Civil y Cultura en el Caribe, en Sociedad y cultura en el Caribe.*

Giusti Cordero, Juan A. 1999. *"La Marina en la mirilla: Una comparación de Vieques con los campos de bombardeo y adiestramiento en los Estados Unidos."* Pp. 133–201 in *Fronteras en Conflicto*, ed. Humberto García Muñiz and Jorge Rodríguez Beruff. San Juan: Red de Geopolítica.

Grupo de Apoyo Técnico y Profesional (GATP). 2000. *Guías para el Desarrollo Sustentable de Vieques.* San Juan: GATP.

Kearns, Rick. 1999. "U.S. Navy Tests Create Health Risks in Vieques." *Hispanic Magazine* (September): 12.

Lederer, Edith M. 2001. "U.N. Approves Vieques Resolution." Associated Press, June 22.

Marino, John. 1999. "Emboldened Protesters Digging in on Vieques Civilians Control Gate, Decry Clinton Decision," *Washington Post*, December 9, p. A03.

Martínez, Héctor. 1998. *"Sociedad civil y partidos políticos."* Pp. 251–78 in *Política Electoral en Puerto Rico*, ed. Robert W. Anderson. Río Piedras, Puerto Rico: Editorial Plaza Mayor.

Meléndez, Arturo. 1982. *La batalla de Vieques.* San Juan: COPE-CECOPE.

Morris, Nancy. 1995. *Puerto Rico, Culture, Politics, and Identity.* Westport, Conn.: Praeger.

Pérez Viera, Edgardo. 2000. *El juicio de la historia.* San Juan: Editorial Cultural.

Reiter, Howard L. 1987. *Parties and Elections in Corporate America.* New York: St. Martin's Press.

Rivera, Angel Israel, Ana Irma Seijo, and Jaime W. Colón. 1991. *"La Cultura política y la Estabilidad del Sistema de Partidos."* *Caribbean Studies* 24: 3–4.

Rivera Ortiz, Angel Israel. 1996. *Puerto Rico: Ficción y mitología en sus alternativas de status.* San Juan: Ediciones Nueva Aurora.

———. 2001. *Poder social versus poder electoral: En la autodeterminación nacional de Puerto Rico, Tomo 1, Los dilemas del tranque.* San Juan: Ediciones Nueva Aurora.

Saramago, Jose. c1999. *The Tale of the Unknown Island.* New York: Harcourt Brace.

Touraine, Alain. 1985. "An Introduction to the Study of Social Movements." *Social Research* 52:4: 749.

Trías Monge, José. 1997. *Puerto Rico: The Trials of the Oldest Colony of the World*. New Haven, Conn.: Yale University Press.

————. 1999. *Puerto Rico: Las penas de la colonia más antigua del mundo*. San Juan: Editorial de la Universidad de Puerto Rico.

World Commission on Environment and Development. 1990. *Our Common Future*. Oxford and New York: Oxford University Press.

Further Reading

Acosta, Ivonne. 1987. *La Mordaza: Puerto Rico 1948–1957*. Río Piedras, Puerto Rico: Editorial Edil.

Acosta-Belén, Edna, ed. 1986. *The Puerto Rican Woman: Perspectives on Culture, History, and Society*. 2d. ed. Westport, Conn.: Praeger.

Acosta-Belén, Edna, et al. 2000. *Adiós, Borinquen Querida: The Puerto Rican Diaspora, Its History, and Contributions*. Albany: Center for Latino, Latin American, and Caribbean Studies (CELAC).

Barreto, Amílcar Antonio. 2002. *Vieques, the Navy, and Puerto Rican Politics*. Gainesville: University Press of Florida.

Benítez Nazario, Jorge. 2001. *Reflexiones en torno a la cultura política de los puertorriqueños: Entre consideraciones teóricas y la evidencia empírica*. San Juan: Instituto de Cultura Puertorriqueña.

Berman Santana, Déborah. 1996. *Kicking off the Bootstraps: Environment, Development, and Community Power in Puerto Rico*. Tucson: University of Arizona Press.

Berríos Martínez, Rubén. 1997. "Puerto Rico's Decolonization." *Foreign Affairs* 76:6: 100.

Bosque-Pérez, Ramón, and José Javier Colón Morera. 1997. *Las carpetas: Persecución política y derechos civiles en Puerto Rico*. Río Piedras, Puerto Rico: Centro para la Investigación y Promoción de los Derechos Civiles (CIPDC).

Burnett, Christina Duffy, and Burke Marshall. 2001. *Foreign in a Domestic Sense: Puerto Rico, American Expansion, and the Constitution*. Durham, N.C.: Duke University Press.

Cabán, Pedro A. 1999. *Constructing a Colonial People: Puerto Rico and the United States, 1898–1932*. Boulder, Colo.: Westview Press.

Colón Morera, José Javier, Rafael Albarrán, and Angel Israel Rivera. 1993. "The United States Congress and the Puerto Rican Political Status Question: A Report from the Field." *Caribbean Studies* 26:3–4: 363–91.

Comisión de Derechos Civiles. 1989. *Informe sobre discrimen y persecución por razones políticas: La práctica gubernamental de mantener listas, ficheros y expedientes de ciudadanos por razón de su ideología política.* San Juan: Comisión de Derechos Civiles.

———. 1998. *¿Somos racistas?: Cómo podemos combatir el racismo.* San Juan: Comisión de Derechos Civiles.

Cruz, José E. 1998. *Identity and Power: Puerto Rican Politics and the Challenge of Ethnicity.* Philadelphia: Temple University Press.

Dietz, James L. 1986. *Economic History of Puerto Rico. Institutional Change and Capitalist Development.* Princeton: Princeton University Press.

Estades Font, María E. 1988. *La presencia militar de Estados Unidos en Puerto Rico 1898–1918: Intereses estratégicos y dominación colonial.* Río Piedras, Puerto Rico: Ediciones Huracán.

Fernández, Ronald. 1996. *The Disenchanted Island: Puerto Rico and the United States in the Twentieth Century.* 2d. ed. Westport, Conn.: Praeger.

García Muñiz, Humberto, and Jorge Rodríguez Beruff. 1999. *Fronteras en conflicto: Guerra contra las drogas, militarización y democracia en el Caribe, Puerto Rico y Vieques.* San Juan: Red Caribeña de Geopolítica.

Gautier Mayoral, Carmen. 1983. "Notes on the Repression Practiced by U.S. Intelligence Agencies in Puerto Rico." *Revista Jurídica de la Universidad de Puerto Rico* 52:3: 431–50.

Helfeld, David M. 1964. "Discrimination for Political Beliefs and Associations." *Revista del Colegio de Abogados de Puerto Rico* 25:1: 5–276.

Informe de la Comisión Especial de Vieques para Estudiar la Situación Existente en la Isla Municipio con Relación a las Actividades de la Marina de Estados Unidos, June 7, 1999.

López, Adalberto, ed. 1980. *The Puerto Ricans: Their History, Culture, and Society.* Cambridge, Mass.: Schenkman.

Maldonado-Denis, Manuel. 1972. *Puerto Rico: A Socio-Historic Interpretation.* Translated by Elena Vialo. New York: Vintage Books.

Matos Rodríguez, Félix V., and Linda C. Delgado, eds. 1998. *Puerto Rican Women's History: New Perspectives.* Armonk, N.Y.: M. E. Sharpe.

McCaffrey, Katherine T. 2002. *Military Power and Popular Protest: The U.S. Navy in Vieques, Puerto Rico.* New Brunswick, N.J.: Rutgers University Press.

Meléndez, Edgardo. 2000. *Puerto Rican Government and Politics: A Comprehensive Bibliography.* Boulder, Colo.: Lynne Rienner.

Meléndez, Edwin, and Edgardo Meléndez. 1993. *Colonial Dilemma: Critical Perspectives on Contemporary Puerto Rico.* Cambridge, Mass.: South End Press.

Merrill-Ramírez, Marie A. 1990. *The Other Side of Colonialism: COINTELPRO Activities in Puerto Rico in the 1960s.* Ph.D. dissertation. University of Texas, Austin.

Morris, Nancy. 1995. *Puerto Rico: Culture, Politics, and Identity.* Westport, Conn.: Praeger.

Muñoz Vázquez, Marya, and Idsa Alegría Ortega. 1999. *Discrimen por razón de raza en los sistemas de seguridad y justicia en Puerto Rico*. San Juan: Comisión de Derechos Civiles.

Murillo, Mario. 2001. *Islands of Resistance: Puerto Rico, Vieques, and U.S. Policy*. New York: Seven Stories Press.

Nina, Daniel. 2001. *"Fragmentos de nación, modernidad y racismo: Nueva visita al problema de la esclavitud."* Revista del Colegio de Abogados de Puerto Rico 62:2: 48–65.

Pantojas-García, Emilio. 1990. *Development Strategies As Ideology: Puerto Rico's Export-Led Industrialization Experience*. Boulder and London: Lynne Rienner. Río Piedras: Editorial de la Universidad de Puerto Rico.

Paralitici, José (Che). 2003. *Sentencia impuesta: Cien años de encarcelamientos por la independencia de Puerto Rico*. San Juan: Ediciones Puerto.

Pérez y González, María E. 2000. *Puerto Ricans in the United States*. Westport, Conn.: Greenwood Press.

Ramos, Aarón G., and Angel Israel Rivera Ortiz. 2001. *Islands at the Crossroads: Politics in the Non-Independent Caribbean*. Boulder, Colo.: Lynne Rienner.

Rivera-Batiz, Francisco, and Carlos E. Santiago. 1996. *Island Paradox: Puerto Rico in the 1990s*. New York: Russell Sage Foundation.

Rivera Ramos, Efrén. 2001. *The Legal Construction of Identity: The Judicial and Social Legacy of American Colonialism in Puerto Rico*. Washington, D.C.: American Psychological Association.

Romany, Celina. 2001. *Race, Ethnicity, Gender, and Human Rights in the Americas: A New Paradigm for Activism*. Washington, D.C.: American University Press.

Sánchez Korrol, Virginia E. 1994. *From Colonia to Community: The History of Puerto Ricans in New York*. Berkeley: University of California Press.

Scarano, Francisco A. 2002. *Puerto Rico: Cinco siglos de historia*. 2d. ed. México: McGraw-Hill Interamericana.

Seijo Bruno, Miñi. 1989. *La insurrección nacionalista en Puerto Rico, 1950*. Río Piedras, Puerto Rico: Editorial Edil.

Silén, Juan Angel. 1971. *We, the Puerto Rican People: A Story of Oppression and Resistance*. New York: Monthly Review Press.

Silvestrini, Blanca G. 1989. *"Contemporary Puerto Rico: A Society of Contrasts."* Pp. 147–67 in *The Modern Caribbean*, ed. F. W. Knight and C. A. Palmer. Chapel Hill: University of North Carolina Press.

Suárez, Manuel. 1987. *Requiem on Cerro Maravilla: The Police Murders in Puerto Rico and the U.S. Government Coverup*. Maplewood, N.J.: Waterfront Press.

Sued Badillo, Jalil. 2000. *La pena de muerte en Puerto Rico: Retrospectiva histórica para una reflexión contemporánea*. Santo Domingo, Dominican Republic: Editora Centenario.

Torres, Andrés, and José E. Velázquez, eds. 1998. *The Puerto Rican Movement: Voices from the Diaspora*. Philadelphia: Temple University Press.

Trías Monge, José. 1997. *Puerto Rico: The Trials of the Oldest Colony of the World*. New Haven and London: Yale University Press.

Zavala, Iris, and Rafael Rodríguez, eds. 1980. *The Intellectual Roots of Independence: An Anthology of Puerto Rican Political Essays*. New York: Monthly Review Press.

Contributors

IVONNE ACOSTA-LESPIER is a history professor and president of the history section of the *Ateneo Puertorriqueño* (Puerto Rican Athenaeum). She is the author of *La Mordaza: Puerto Rico 1948–1957* (1987), *La palabra como delito: Los discursos por los que condenaron a Pedro Albizu Campos, 1948–1950* (1993), *Santa Juana y Mano Manca: Auge y decadencia del azúcar en el valle del Turabo en el siglo XX* (1995), and numerous articles on nineteenth- and twentieth-century Puerto Rican history. She has a B.A. from Manhattanville College of New York, an M.A. from the University of Puerto Rico, and a doctoral degree from Nova University in Florida. *La Mordaza* was originally submitted as her thesis for a master of arts degree, with a specialization in Puerto Rican studies at *Centro de Estudios Avanzados de Puerto Rico y el Caribe*.

CÉSAR J. AYALA is an associate professor of sociology in the Department of Sociology at the University of California, Los Angeles (UCLA). He previously taught in the Department of Latin American and Puerto Rican Studies at Lehman College, City University of New York (1988–2002) and the Ph.D. program in sociology at City University of New York Graduate Center. He is a graduate of Princeton University (B.A.) and the State University of New York at Binghamton (Ph.D.). He is the author of *American Sugar Kingdom: The Plantation Economy of the Spanish Caribbean, 1898–1934* (1999). His specialty is the sociology of development and industrialization in Latin America and the Caribbean. He also has written about migration from Puerto Rico to the United States. He is currently co-authoring a book with Laird W. Bergad, entitled *Land Tenure and Social Structure in Puerto Rico, 1894–1934*.

JORGE BENÍTEZ-NAZARIO is a professor in the Political Science Department, University of Puerto Rico (UPR), Río Piedras. He obtained his B.A. there and continued his graduate studies at the University of Wisconsin, Madison, majoring in political culture, contemporary political thought, and Latin

American political parties. He obtained his Ph.D. there in political science in 1989. He has published many professional articles on the Puerto Rican political culture, public policies regarding education and social welfare in Puerto Rico, and the ethics of political research, areas in which he concentrates his research efforts. He also is co-director for Puerto Rico for the project on comparative political culture, "World Study on Values." He is the author of *Reflexiones en torno a la cultura política de los puertorriqueños* (2001).

Ramón Bosque-Pérez is a researcher at the Center for Puerto Rican Studies, Hunter College of the City University of New York. He has concentrated his recent research efforts in the area of political persecution and human rights in the Puerto Rican context, including the analysis of formerly secret documents released by the Police of Puerto Rico, the Federal Bureau of Investigation, and other agencies. He is the co-author of *Las carpetas: Persecución política y derechos civiles en Puerto Rico* (1997), which was awarded an honorable mention by the Puerto Rico Chapter of PEN International Writers Association. Previously he co-edited *Puerto Ricans and Higher Education Policies* (1994) and was one of the associate editors of the *Centro Journal* (1993–1995). He has taught courses on contemporary Puerto Rico and the history of Puerto Rico at the John Jay College of Criminal Justice and the Borough of Manhattan Community College. He obtained a B.A. in social sciences from the University of Puerto Rico and an M.A. in sociology from the University of Michigan, Ann Arbor, where he also completed the coursework in the doctoral program.

Viviana Carro-Figueroa is an associate rural sociologist and a researcher at the University of Puerto Rico Agricultural Experiment Station. She has an M.A. from the University of London, where she majored in Latin American history and rural sociology and has pursued doctoral studies in development sociology at Cornell University. She received the Rural Policy Award from the Woodrow Wilson National Fellowship Foundation (1988) and the USDA Hispanic Serving Institutions Fellows Award (1998), both to conduct research on agricultural, food, and rural policy issues in Puerto Rico. She collaborated from 1979 to 1981 on the Caribbean Project for Justice and Peace and coordinated the component on militarism of the project. More recently, she has been part of *Grupo de Apoyo Técnico y Profesional para el Desarrollo Sustentable de Vieques*, a nongovernmental organization working with the *Comité Pro Rescate y Desarrollo de Vieques* in the design of sustainable socioeconomic development proposals for a Vieques without the navy.

José Javier Colón Morera is a professor and former chair of the Political Science Department, University of Puerto Rico, Río Piedras. He teaches courses on political systems, civil rights, political relations between Puerto

Rico and the United States, and public opinion and propaganda, among others. He obtained his Ph.D. in political science at the University of Boston (1992). He holds a B.A. and a Juris Doctor from the University of Puerto Rico and has been licensed to practice law since 1983. He is the co-author of *Las carpetas: Persecución política y derechos civiles en Puerto Rico* (1997, honorable mention, Puerto Rico Chapter of PEN International Writers Association), *El Congreso de Estados Unidos y el Status Político de Puerto Rico: Buscando Respuestas* (1995), and *Historia y Geografía de Puerto Rico, Serie Norma de Estudios Sociales* (1994). He has published numerous professional articles on the political relations between Puerto Rico and the United States and on civil rights, areas in which he concentrates his current research efforts.

María E. Estades-Font received her Ph.D. in Latin American studies from the *Universidad Nacional Autónoma de México*. She is a professor in the History Department, University of Puerto Rico, Río Piedras, where she teaches undergraduate and graduate courses on contemporary Puerto Rican history. She is the author of *La presencia militar de Estados Unidos en Puerto Rico, 1898–1918: Intereses estratégicos y dominación colonial* (1988), as well as several articles published in Puerto Rican and foreign journals on the historical aspects of U.S. policy toward Puerto Rico. She is currently working on a book about the Lake Mohonk Conferences of Friends of the Indian and Other Dependent Peoples.

Alberto L. Márquez is an attorney with a private practice in San Germán, Puerto Rico. He has focused his political work and research in the areas of political education, international relations, and the analysis of the processes and mechanisms of neocolonial repression and domination. He obtained a Juris Doctor from the University of Puerto Rico in 1962. He has published many articles in journals and newspapers, in and out of Puerto Rico, such as *La Escalera, Tricontinental*, and *Claridad*. His writings analyze the political processes between Puerto Rico and the United States and other historical subjects such as the Vietnam War, the struggles of the Palestinians, and political and military tactics and strategies. He is currently working on a collection of literary stories related to Hormigueros, his hometown, parting from the oral history of several generations of the town's inhabitants.

José (Ché) Paralitici is an associate professor at the *Universidad de América*, Bayamón, where he teaches political science and social sciences courses. He holds a doctoral degree from the *Universidad de Valladolid* in Spain and is the author of *No quiero mi cuerpo pa' tambor: El servicio militar obligatorio en Puerto Rico* (1998) and of *Sentencia impuesta: Cien años de encarcelamientos por la independencia de Puerto Rico* (2003). He was the editor of the journal *América* and a member of the editorial committee of the journal *Cultura* of the Program for

Cultural Centers of the Institute of Puerto Rican Culture. He has published mainly on the subject of militarism in Puerto Rico and the history of the Lares township and its historical *Grito de Lares* in local and foreign journals and newspapers such as *América, Surcos Lareños, Pensamiento Crítico,* and *Claridad.* He is the spokesperson for *Todo Puerto Rico con Vieques,* a civil society organization that supports the Vieques demilitarization effort.

José E. Rivera Santana is an environmental planner at *Estudios Técnicos* in San Juan, Puerto Rico, and teaches courses in urban planning at the *Universidad Metropolitana* in San Juan. He obtained his B.A. in 1985 and his M.A. in environmental planning in 1994 from the University of Puerto Rico, where he was an activist and a student leader in the late 1970s and early 1980s, involved in human rights issues since that time. He has done extensive community advocacy in Vieques and is actively involved in the articulation of community strategies to create an equitable, environmentally friendly and sound socioeconomic future for Vieques. He published *Así fué: Crónicas de un desobediente civil por la paz de Vieques,* a testimonial of his activism in the Vieques peace movement, in 2001.

José E. Serrano, Congressman (D-NY), was born in Mayagüez, Puerto Rico, on October 24, 1943. When he was seven years old, his family moved to the South Bronx, where he attended public schools and completed courses at Lehman College, City University of New York. Serrano has been in Congress for seven terms and is the most senior member of the three members of Congress of Puerto Rican origin. Before being elected to the U.S. Congress, Serrano had a distinguished sixteen-year career (1974–1990) in the New York State Assembly. During his time in Congress, Serrano has cosponsored a number of major bills, including the Civil Rights Act, the Family and Medical Leave Act, the Higher Education Act, the Brady Gun Control Bill, and the César Chávez Workplace Fairness Act. In 1992, he was appointed to the prestigious Appropriations Committee, responsible for approving the expenditure of federal funds and for applying fiscal discipline to the federal budget process. Currently Serrano serves as the Ranking Democrat on the Appropriations Subcommittee on Commerce, Justice, State, and the Judiciary. In March 2000, he obtained a commitment from the Federal Bureau of Investigation to begin the release of thousands of secret documents compiled by that agency on Puerto Rican organizations and individuals.

Jalil Sued-Badillo is a professor and chair of the Interdisciplinary Social Studies Department, University of Puerto Rico, Río Piedras. He is the author of several anthropological and history books and numerous articles and chapters published in Puerto Rico and abroad. His books include: *La pena de muerte en Puerto Rico: Retrospectiva histórica para una reflexión contemporánea*

(2000); *Puerto Rico negro* (1988, co-author); *Cristóbal Colón y la esclavitud del indio en las Antillas* (1983); *La mujer indígena y su sociedad* (1983); *Bibliografía antropológica del Caribe* (1979); *Los caribes, realidad o fábula: Ensayo de rectificación histórica* (1978); and *Bibliografía antropológica para el estudio de los pueblos indígenas en El Caribe* (1977). His doctoral thesis, *Economía minera en Puerto Rico durante la primera mitad el Siglo XVI*, for the *Universidad de Sevilla* is being revised for publication. He is the editor of the first volume of *Historia del Caribe*, sponsored by the United Nations Educational, Scientific, and Cultural Organization (UNESCO).

JAN SUSLER is an attorney and associate of the People's Law Office in Chicago. She has been involved in the legal efforts to obtain the release of Puerto Rican political prisoners and has visited almost all of the institutions where they have been placed to investigate prison conditions. She has written extensively on the subject and made personal appearances in different forums on behalf of the political prisoners' claim for human rights. She is the author of the book *Palomas voladoras por cielos de libertad* (1995). Her essays have been included in *The Puerto Rican Movement: Voices from the Diaspora* (1998) and *Las carpetas: Persecución política y derechos civiles en Puerto Rico* (1997) and in journals such as the *Yale Journal of Law and Liberation*, the *International Review of Contemporary Law*, *Social Justice*, and *Humanity and Society*. Her legal practice focuses on the defense of citizens' civil rights and suits for damages due to inappropriate police conduct.

Index

Made in the USA
San Bernardino, CA
28 August 2014